# THE PATTERN OF
# IMPERIALISM

# THE
# PATTERN
## OF
# IMPERIALISM

A STUDY IN THE THEORIES
OF POWER *by E. M. Winslow*

## OCTAGON BOOKS

A DIVISION OF FARRAR, STRAUS AND GIROUX

New York   1972

*Reprinted 1972*
*by special arrangement with Columbia University Press*

OCTAGON BOOKS
A DIVISION OF FARRAR, STRAUS & GIROUX, INC.
19 Union Square West
New York, N. Y. 10003

LIBRARY OF CONGRESS CATALOG CARD NUMBER: 78-159238

ISBN 0-374-98685-1

Printed in U.S.A. by
NOBLE OFFSET PRINTERS, INC.
New York, N.Y. 10003

To B. M. W.

# PREFACE

THE theories of economic imperialism which have developed in the literature of radicalism during the past fifty years belong to a realm of speculation which has been left almost exclusively to socialists and other critics of capitalism. The great bulk of the original writings dealing with and advocating the idea that economic motives, especially as they operate under capitalism, lead to imperialism and war, is the work of German and Austrian Marxists. So great has been their influence that much of what today passes as political economy is the product of the tireless efforts of the "theoreticians" of this group, and in particular their views on "economic imperialism" have made a great impression on present-day popular economic-political thinking. Whatever the pattern of imperialism actually is, the established pattern of thought regarding this phenomenon of power comes predominately from these sources.

Some of the theories of economic imperialism are the fruit of serious scholarship and represent a high order of analysis. The critic can always find flaws in the various theoretical treatments, and the severest criticism of socialistic studies on this subject has come from socialists themselves. Consequently there is by no means a unanimity of theoretical treatment and understanding of this problem among the professed followers of Marx. Indeed, the fundamental ideological differences which divide socialists and communists, evolutionary and revolutionary Marxists, and the orthodox and the revisionist schools of thought are tied up with, if not directly dependent upon, differences of opinion regarding the precise relation of capitalism to imperialism and war. Yet all hold in common the assumption that the basic cause of these and other undesirable political phenomena is somehow economic in nature.

In presenting the main points of this endless controversy I have sought to avoid adding still another round of detailed criticism. My purpose has been to question the basic assumption of all such theories—that economic forces constitute the effective causes of imperialism and war. The conclusion that the causes of this sort of phenomenon are noneconomic still leaves much room for disagreement over the meaning of "noneconomic" as well as for differences of opinion regarding the meaning of "economic." Thus, there is every prospect that the controversy will continue, but at least there is some hope of placing it on a level different from that which has so long intrigued those who, taking economic causation for granted, have expended their analytical zeal on the mechanics of the economic system.

This whole field of thought has been greatly neglected by economists of the classical-orthodox tradition. The term "economic imperialism," like the term "capitalism," is not of their devising, and the critical ideas implied in such terms are foreign to this tradition. Economists, therefore, cannot be criticized for failure to put content into these terms. Rather, their failure to examine the implications of "economic" in the various theories of economic imperialism in order to discover what meaning, if any, such a term can have or in what sense, if any, capitalism can be held responsible for causing imperialism and war, has permitted these ideas to intrude themselves almost unchallenged into the popular thought of our time. In the developmental period of the science of economics economists were highly conscious of the implications and importance of "political economy." Later generations of those who carried on the classical tradition became more and more preoccupied with the theories of value and distribution and tended to lose interest in the broader aspects of the relation between economics and politics. Recent concern with monetary, banking, and fiscal problems has done much to revive this interest, because in these fields the contact, and very often the conflict, between the state and economic life comes into sharp focus.

My interest in the field began in France in 1918–19 when, as an uprooted undergraduate, I came into close contact with much speculation on what had caused the war. The greatest impression on my mind was made by a German prisoner of war who seemed as versed in economic jargon as I was innocent of it. He was an ardent Social Democrat, and what impressed me was his utter lack of resentment against the French, who had held him prisoner for four sodden years, and his complete hatred of something he called "Kapitalismus," which had held him prisoner all his life and furthermore, he said, had caused the war. This view of history seemed reasonable then, and it is regrettable, in a way, that so simple an idea has to be examined, haggled over, and very largely thrown upon the scrap heap of wrong ideas that have influenced the very course of history.

The second World War, which was so plainly caused by the first and by all the same old political ineptitude which contributed to causing both, has made many people more cautious than they formerly were of writing the whole business off in terms of economic motives and the mechanics of capitalism. Many socialists who once followed this line of reasoning will now admit that their formula was wrong and that it should be abandoned. This does not mean that they love capitalism more; it is only one of the signs that people are beginning to look for the causes of conflict elsewhere than in the market place and to see that one of the first victims of war is the market place. Little by little the idea may take hold that the solution of this condition is not to be found in changing the economic system, but in changing the pattern of political thinking and behavior which brings about conflict and war and destroys the economic system along with the material and human bases which make possible any decent economic and social order. The vast ruins of Europe today and the poverty and degradation of great masses of people are testimonials, not of man's failure to make economic sense out of his world, but of his failure to match a high order of economic rationality with comparable gumption in his political relationships. The upward struggle for freedom as it expresses itself in the so-called "black market" is again expressing itself in the economic sphere, but there are as yet few signs that the people of the Western World will this time emerge triumphant from the far worse political blackness that surrounds them.

As one hopeful sign in the world, I have not hesitated in the closing chapter to point to Gandhi's movement in India. Here, it seems to me, is political wisdom of a high order, far more advanced and hopeful and far more in accord with the principles of economic and political freedom than exists elsewhere. But I am under no illusion that men of the Western World, despite their hard-headedness in economic matters, will soon become as hardheaded politically as the humble little man who today stands as the symbol of political maturity.

I wish to express my sincere appreciation for the encouragement of those who were kind enough to take a critical look at the manuscript in its more advanced stages. Each from his own angle of interest in problems of this sort made valuable suggestions, and all, I believe, agreed with my general purpose of trying to put the theory of imperialism and war on a level of discussion which moves away from the pitfalls of the economic interpretation. Without in the least wanting to imply that they agree with the way I have tried to do this or with some of my conclusions and points of view, I wish particularly to thank Eugene Altschul, Richard W. Nelson, Carl J. Ratzlaff, Lloyd L. Shaulis, Jacob Viner, and William G. Welk for their contributions of time and thought. To Columbia University Press, and especially to Miss Ida M. Lynn, whose editorial work on the manuscript was handicapped by the distance over which we were obliged to communicate, goes my deepest gratitude. In the conventional language of prefaces, the author claims all errors, weaknesses, and any failure to heed the advice of others as his own responsibility.

In a study of this sort it is often more economical and pointed to reproduce the words of other writers, and in a few cases I have availed myself of this privilege to an extent which calls for special acknowledgment. I wish particularly to thank the publishers for permission to quote from the following works: *War and Its Causes,* by L. L. Bernard, copyright 1944 by Henry Holt and Company, Inc.; *General Theory of Employment, Interest and Money,* by J. M. Keynes, copyright 1936 by Harcourt, Brace and Company, Inc.; *History of Militarism,* by Alfred Vagts, by permission of W. W. Norton and Company, Inc.; copyright 1937 by the publishers.

E. M. Winslow

*Darmstadt, Germany*
*May 3, 1947*

# CONTENTS

# I ·

# IMPERIALISM VERSUS
# NATIONALISM

THE story of imperialism and militarism constitutes the history of power as it has been exercised by one group over another, by the strong over the weak and the free over the slave, in that one-sided and un-mutual relationship which makes up the great bulk of the human chronicle as it has come down to us in the form of recorded history—that great record of events, as someone has remarked, which never should have happened.

We shall use the terms "imperialism" and "militarism" repeatedly, and it may as well be said first as last that they are coeval terms, representing the same general pattern of thought and behavior in the ordering of human relationships. It makes little difference whether we speak of "militarism and war," or "imperialism and war." A nation that is militaristic is likely to want to give its militarism an aggressive outlet, which can only mean an attitude of belligerency and an act of hostility towards some other nation. Imperialism is only a more concrete term for the same behavior; it suggests not only ability and willingness to use military power, but also the territory on and against which such power must be employed. It is not a synonym for colonialism—many colonies have been established by people innocent of imperialistic aggression, in places empty of other people against whom aggression needed to be used in order to make the settlement a success. Even where the intruders fought the natives, as so often—but not always—happened in the colonization of the Americas, the conflict was rarely waged primarily as an expedition of military or naval power. William Penn and his colonists demonstrated that it was possible to deal amicably with the Indians and to share a vast territory with them without conflict. Other colonists apparently had no desire to try such a "holy experiment," but followed the ancient practice of treating the Indians as inferior beings with no rights.

On the whole, and in the detail-obliterating perspective of history, we have come to regard all this colonial activity and conflict as colonialism rather than as imperialism. The latter term quite properly suggests something more organized, more military, more self-consciously aggressive, bent on objectives above and beyond the mere occupation of virgin territory in which conflict was incidental, or even unnecessary, and subordinate to the desire of Europeans to find a new place to live. We readily associate imperialism with what the Romans did in Gaul and elsewhere and what Napoleon, Hitler, and Mussolini were up to; with British policies in India, French and Dutch policies in Africa, Asia, and the Pacific, and Japanese policies in China. And we must not be too modest—we Americans are accused, and we accuse ourselves, of following imperialistic policies in Latin America, in the Caribbean, in the Philippines, and in other parts of the world too numerous to mention. Soviet Russia, despite the protests of Marxists that communism is incapable of following an imperialistic policy, appears to the more imaginative to be no less imperialistic than the so-called capitalist powers, which the critics of capitalism have long regarded as the only groups capable of committing the sin of imperialism.

We shall try to deal with the problem of imperialism, not as historians usually deal with it in describing the expansion and conflicts of the human race, but from the point of view of "theory." The theory involved is not hard to grasp, but there are so many different theories, or hypotheses, or explanations and interpretations of this phenomenon in history that it has taken a sizable book in which to set forth the most important of a considerable number of widely divergent views on the subject.

The theory of imperialism in some form or other has long been almost a monopoly of the radicals—socialists, communists, Marxists, or other critics of capitalism who ascribe modern imperialism to the workings of the private enterprise economy. Therefore, we shall try to understand their point of view. It is important to understand it, because these writers and professional "theoreticians" have had great influence on professional and popular thought in their own ranks and have, indeed, added to their ranks by the very appeal of their ideas; they have also influenced the thinking of people, directly or indirectly, who have no notion of joining the ranks of radicalism. But there are other theories, hypotheses, explanations, and interpretations of imperialism, which have not had their origin in radical or Marxian thought, which must be taken into account in any study as broad as this investigation of the theories of imperialism. These range from almost-socialistic theories, to a complete denial of the view that capitalism or any economic system can be a cause of imperialism, accompanied by the affirmation, based on various premises and reasonings, that the causes must be looked for in behavior patterns which are far older than capitalism.

One of the common assumptions of those who undertake to interpret history is that nationalism, or the spirit of the modern nation-state, reflects on the political side what capitalism reflects in the economic sphere, and that nationalism and capitalism combine to produce "economic imperialism." While the chief concern of this study is to examine various forms of the idea that economic motives and capitalistic processes influence or actually determine international relations, especially as these relations take the form of imperialistic activity, it is necessary to say something about the place of nationalism in this scheme of things. Although nationalism, or at least the existence of nation-states, is clearly antecedent to the existence of internationalism, it cannot be assumed that the existence of nation-states is also a prior condition of that other form of relations which we call imperialism.

It is only comparatively recently that history has been told in terms of nationalism and internationalism; in terms, that is, of conflict as well as peaceful intercourse between nations, with emphasis sometimes on international trade, international co-operation, and international peace, and again on economic nationalism, international rivalries, and international war. But it is important to make clear at the beginning that the imperialism with which we are about to deal is not an extension or expansion of nationalism. It is much older than nationalism as modern man understands the latter term, and yet it is not a predecessor in the ancestral sense. Nationalism as we know it did not emerge until the eighteenth century, when the French Revolution brought its first real manifestation. It developed simultaneously with democracy and industrialism, and the phenomenon which marked all three movements was the overthrow of absolute monarchic forms of government by the ideas and realities of popular sovereignty.[1] As a process of integrating masses of people into a common political form recognizable as "their" government and nation, nationalism nevertheless presupposed the existence of a highly centralized form of government and a clearly demarked territory, both of which were inherited from the monarchic system. They constitute the minimum requirements of its material basis. From here on the essence of nationalism is largely a matter of the emotions.

To all this, imperialism is entirely foreign; it is not a product of popular mass revolt against absolutism such as produced democracy, industrialism, and nationalism, but the opposite. There is meaning and significance in asking, "What nationality are you?" but none in asking, "What imperiality are you?" Consciousness of belonging to an empire, even one as relatively innocuous as the British Empire has become, is completely subordinate to the consciousness of belonging to a nationality. No modern ruler or popular government can literally or straight-facedly refer to "my" empire, although convention still permits the phrase. Absolute monarchs and emperors of the premodern period not only could do this, but they could do so without offense to their subjects. Nationalism in the modern sense was not in the consciousness of either ruler or ruled. The ruler looked first to his own realm, and became an imperialist, as a rule, when he looked covetously beyond it to the realms of other absolute rulers. His subjects looked to their own localities and had little or no interest in what lay beyond. Their vision was much narrower than that of their ruler, and conservative where his was generally aggressive. They were the stuff of which nationalism eventually was made, but in the meantime they were merely the stuff by which empires were made. Their localities contained no "foreigners"; by usage they were separately identified from other localities by having little or no admixture from the outside. Likewise, the modern nation contains no foreigners, except as a transient phenomenon. But empires always contain "foreigners"—people alien to the mother or ruling country. And these foreigners are universally regarded, consciously or unconsciously,

[1] Kohn, *The Idea of Nationalism*, chap. i.

either as objects of charity and solicitude (the white man's burden, the recipients of a civilizing mission, etc.), or as slaves, never quite as equals. This is clearly a much more ancient attitude than that expressed in nationalism, or nationality.

No—nationalism does not necessarily lead to imperialism; it may be the road to internationalism. On the other hand, imperialism never leads to interimperialism. Nationalism has within it the same feeling as has democracy, that of mutuality, but imperialism is an exclusive concept. Wherever the spirit of exclusiveness creeps into a nation, as it well may, it is a sign that that nation is losing the attributes of nationalism, internationalism, and democracy and is setting forth on the ancient business of telling "foreigners" what to do and what not to do, which is the path of empire.

The fact that modern nationalism was so largely a reflection of the revolt of the masses against absolutism in government undoubtedly goes a long way to explain why there never has been any popular animosity towards nationalism. It is just as natural that there should have been a popular revolt against imperialism and militarism, which are integral parts of absolutism. To be sure, many people have been as severe in their criticism of nationalism as of imperialism and at times have even appeared to regard them as almost synonymous, or at least merely as different stages in the same process, with nationalism paving the way to imperialism. But nation-building and empire-building by no means involve the same set of attitudes; in fact, they involve attitudes which are essentially opposed to each other, and which find their opposite expressions in popular rather than scholarly reactions.

Our ultimate task is to trace the history of ideas regarding imperialism, and at that we are concerned mostly with very modern ideas; but as background it is important to get some impressions, incomplete and scattered though they may be, of both those trains of thought mentioned above—common attitudes and the beginnings of reasoning about the whys and wherefores of mankind's great cross, imperialism and war.

Probably the greater part of the popular reaction to the kind of power that is represented by such symbols as imperialism and militarism has been emotional, favorable or unfavorable according to whether the person concerned was on the giving or the receiving end of the process or in the favored or exploited class. In neither case can we expect to find much objectivity in the language of those expressing their reactions. But as we approach modern times, an element of greater objectivity begins to appear, and it is at this point that men begin to look for causes and even for remedies.

No explanation has been more widespread than that based on the view that human selfishness and cupidity, translated into the "economic cause" and refined again into a whole complex of "economic causes," which finally become subsumed under "capitalism," constitute the source of imperialism and war. This is a modern development of thought, but its beginnings can be detected wherever men have spoken of those desires which express themselves in terms of property and gain. In the Western World, with whose ideas on this question we are alone concerned, the story begins with Greece and Rome.

# II ·

# THE BEGINNINGS OF
# CONTROVERSY

THE modern anti-imperialist movement came earliest and has been strongest in those countries where the professions of democracy, liberty, and free enterprise were most advanced and in which, at the same time, the old policies of expansion and conquest were still strong enough to dominate the field of foreign relations. The conflict was essentially between the ancient world and the modern, between absolutism and freedom, yet staged entirely in what we are pleased to call "modern times." The anti-imperialists could see in their opponents, the imperialists, a species of contemporary ancestor and in imperialism itself an anachronism, or an atavistic throw-back to a primitive form of human behavior.

If Great Britain was the greatest practitioner of this anachronism in the modern world, that country likewise harbored some of the most vocal anti-imperialists; and these in turn stirred up some eloquent defenders of empire, both bombastic and enlightened. Wherever imperialism has been put on the defensive and made self-conscious by the attacks upon it, its defenders have not always gone untouched by the spirit of liberalism, as is shown by a certain degree of apology for an institution which appears to have outlived its ancient reasons for existence. Anti-imperialism was at first primarily a political movement, infused with moral and economic arguments against the building and holding of empire. It was a political movement in the sense that the anti-imperialists were trying to change policy, and the economic arguments used against the old policy were of a practical and empirical nature rather than hypothetical. Their reasoning was of the sort which says "empire does not pay," rather than the more recent type of argument, which tries to show that imperialism is an inevitable expression of capitalism. As a political movement, anti-imperialism attained its classic expression in Britain, just as the art of imperialism reached its classic form in ancient Rome.

## THE UNSELFCONSCIOUSNESS OF CLASSIC IMPERIALISM

Classic imperialism has fired the ambition of every empire-builder since Caesar's time and has roused the imagination of historians without number. It was militarism in its ablest, most glamorous, and least inhibited form. It was the epitome of absolute power. And it was carried on apparently with no more sense of social guilt on the part of its leaders than might be found in the maraudings of a pack of wolves. For imperialism in its classic form was totally lacking in self-consciousness, and it needed no economic *raison-d'être* or any apologists to spin economic reasons for the kind of activity which it represented.

To Caesar and his kind it was a natural, interesting, exciting, and usually profitable adventure. It was part of the great universal process of making war or having war made upon you. It involved territory and resources and man-power. But who can believe that these alone made imperialism necessary? They made it possible, but what role could they have played in the field of economic motive and economic necessity, compared with the motive and necessity of fighting and expanding or being fought against and made the victims of expansion? The choice was not between starving for lack of territory and resources and going forth to find greener pastures— at least, not in classic times—but between exercising power yourself and having it exercised against you.

Philosophers and poets might dress the whole matter up in elegant language, might even suggest motives that sound as modern as the white man's burden. Virgil, for example, said let the Greeks make statues, learn astronomy, and practice the nobler arts, but the imperial arts belong to Rome.

> Let others better mold the running mass
> Of metals, and inform the breathing brass,
> And soften into flesh a marble face;
> Plead better at the bar; describe the skies,
> And when the stars descend, and when they rise.
> But, Rome, 'tis thine alone, with awful sway,

> To rule mankind, and make the world obey,
> Disposing peace and war thy own majestic way;
> To tame the proud, the fetter'd slave to free:
> These are imperial arts, and worthy thee.[1]

Rome, like other states, had stumbled into empire through a series of specific accidents, or incidents, which led the Romans unwittingly from one conquest to another.[2] They learned early that the more they had, the more they had to have to hold what they had. The Greeks had also known that logically a thoroughgoing imperial policy demands the establishment of a universal empire, but it was left to the Romans to impress the idea of universality upon the term "empire" and to establish as an essential part of this concept the relation of inferior to superior.[3] The Roman feeling for *imperium* [4] thus constituted that feeling for universal power which became the classic pattern for the Western World. It meant absolute power over life and death; and, despite some rather unnecessary modern refinements of technique and practice, it still means that today. To those in positions of superiority *imperium* has always been the ultimate form of power—power for the sake of power, power as an end. To those on the receiving end it has always meant catastrophe in the bitter form of having to accept the shame and degradation of being inferior, with all the physical and spiritual suffering which only the slave can know from experience. And this pattern of universal power contains one element which, above all others, is the essence of modern power politics—the logic that imperialism as a movement can never stop until one nation has conquered the entire world.

Despite the basic identity of the pattern and logic of modern imperialism with that of the ancient world, there is in modern man an element which was almost totally lacking among the Greeks, the Romans, or any other ancient imperial nation. This is the self-conscious, rationalized, and "so-sorry" attitude of modern conquer-

---

[1] *The Aeneid*, Book vi (Dryden's translation) in *The Poetical Works of John Dryden* (Cambridge Edition), p. 609.

[2] Frank, *Roman Imperialism*, p. 93. Frank regards the Punic War as epoch-making because in it Rome acquired its first tribute-paying dependency, accepted an "alien principle," and "set out on the devious road of imperialism."

[3] Ferguson, *Greek Imperialism*, pp. 2, 4, 5.

[4] Glover, *Democracy in the Ancient World*, p. 169; Frank, *Roman Imperialism*, p. 120.

ing nations towards their victims. Some historians have become so impressed by this difference that they conclude, as one writer puts it, that "We English have no word to express the concentrated and absolute power originally connoted by this memorable term." [5] This is a very enlightening statement. It is true not only of the English but also of all modern empire-building nations, precisely because the concentrated nature of Roman *imperium* has been diluted with a modern ethic which condemns it, while its absolute nature has been challenged by a sense of relativity and the consequent realization that power itself is relative. And yet part—the really essential part—of the full force and meaning of *imperium* still remains, and the process differs in degree rather than in kind. It still entails the use of naked power and the concept of superior and inferior peoples.

Why is it that modern imperial nations are more godlike than the ancients in that they first smile on those whom they are about to destroy? The answer is that they are self-conscious and need to rationalize simply because they operate in a world that regards imperialism and conquest as wrong. The mental conflict created by the existence side by side of religious idealism and the exercise of naked power prompts one half of the mind to be at least decent enough to throw a cloak over power's nakedness and call it the white man's burden, or civilizing mission, a war of liberation, or whatever suits the occasion.

No doubt it is an advance over the ways of the ancients to clothe the mailed fist in a silk glove, because it means that the wrongdoer is at least somewhat "under conviction" of his deeds. But it is still inexcusable behavior in view of the fact that modern man has the advantage of two thousand years of certain holy teachings and in addition can carry on his "international relations," if he really wants to, through the great modern complex mechanism of production and trade. To the ancient these reasons for better behavior were lacking—he had neither very much religious tolerance served up to him either by precept or priest nor any highly developed mechanism for engaging in economic activity on a basis of mu-

---

[5] Heitland, *The Roman Republic*, I, 41. Similar views are to be found in Fowler, *The City-State of the Greeks and Romans*, p. 75; Grundy, *History of the Greek and Roman World*, pp. 115–16; and Kat Angelino, *Colonial Policy*. See especially Vol. I, chap. vi, "Empire Building in the Ancient World."

tuality. Therefore he had to be violent in his expansion if he was to expand at all. And for this he needed no *apologia* and no silk glove. He was at least honest and straightforward in his business of *imperium*.

## EARLY MODERN VIEWS ON "WARS, CONQUESTS, AND COLONIES"

It is a long leap from the almost complete absence of apology for or opposition to imperialism in Roman times to the modern self-conscious reaction to war and conquest. The basic logic and principles of imperialism may have changed very little throughout the centuries, but the judgment of modern man is unique. The growth of the idea of democrary and freedom, producing its own type of political movement, came into sharp conflict with the type of political philosophy represented by the concept of absolute power found in imperialism.

It is not surprising that the rise of democratic and liberal ideas in an imperial country such as England would produce a strong reaction towards the undemocratic and illiberal elements of colonial policy. Out of this opposition to imperialism, or colonialism, there developed, first, a type of criticism which simply regarded contemporary colonial policy as incompatible with newer and more liberal professions and institutions. While this opposition often took the form of an attack on mercantilism, or "the mercantile system," it was always part of the more general attack on absolute power in all its manifestations. In England, where this issue was first sharply drawn, it became a conflict between the imperialist (or tory, or mercantilist, or protectionist) and the anti-imperialist (or democrat, or liberal, or free trader). Rarely was there any deep-seated philosophizing about the "causes" of imperialism by those who opposed it or anything more than a practical defense of imperialism by those who defended it. Much later—and largely, too, from sources outside Britain—there occurred the second stage in the controversy over imperialism, the period in which people began to talk about the phenomenon in terms of economic necessity, surplus goods seeking foreign markets, and other hypotheses which sought to take the issue out of the realm of political or moral debate and put it on a level where it became essential to intelligent discussion to base both the pros and the cons of imperialism on a kind of logic which had its roots in material and economic realities.[6]

We are first concerned with what might be called the empirical approach to this question, which developed into a debate on a "commonsense" level, regarding the advantages and disadvantages of maintaining colonies. It is largely the old familiar story of the controversy over mercantilism.

The early English mercantilists, who were also characteristically defenders of the colonial system, looked upon foreign trade and the acquisition of territory from a commercial point of view which identified the interests of a relatively small class—their own class, of course—with those of the entire nation. To them colonies were the property of the mother country—plantations to be exploited to the fullest extent, while prevented from becoming economic rivals of the colonizing power. Thomas Mun, for example, very strongly preached this view, as is well known; [7] and James Harrington, usually regarded as a utopian with very advanced democratic and even socialistic principles (he favored the breaking up of estates and the redistribution of lands), nevertheless entertained such ideas as this: "If the empire of a commonwealth be an occasion to ask whether it be lawful for a commonwealth to aspire to the empire of the world, it is to ask whether it is lawful for it to do its duty, or to put the world into a better condition than it was before." [8] Postlethwayt stated it clearly: "It is a law founded on the very nature of colonies," he said, "that they ought to have no other culture or arts wherein to rival the arts and culture of the parent country." [9]

Such sentiments as these characterized the farthest reach of imperialist thought in seventeenth-century England. Back of these ideas, and dating practically from the discovery of America, was the

[6] In Chapter IV, we shall again discuss early ideas about imperialism and war, but in a context in which the emphasis is directly on causes and remedies. The present chapter, on the other hand, is concerned with early discussions of the advantages and disadvantages of colonies which brought out the political conflict between the mercantilists and the anti-mercantilists. While this is to some extent an artificial separation of ideas and often more sharply drawn than was apparent to contemporary thought, it nevertheless brings out the important distinction between the discussions which moved on a political level and those which were carried on with a view to providing a philosophical or theoretical basis for understanding the phenomena of expansion and conflict.

[7] Mun, *Discourse of Trade* and *England's Treasure by Foreign Trade.*

[8] Harrington, *Oceana* (Morley's Universal Library edition), p. 241.

[9] Postlethwayt, *Britain's Commercial Interest Explained and Improved,* I, 153.

common view that the new world could produce literally anything and produce it cheaper than it could be produced in England or any other European country. Colonies not only produced gold and silver, but in a broader sense they were regarded as "gold mines." Out of this grew the familiar mercantilist doctrine that colonies were valuable as a means of redressing England's unfavorable balance of trade in Europe and that such valuable assets should be controlled, monopolized (by navigation laws, etc.), and defended; out of the idea of defense grew the movement for a powerful navy. England was well on the way to prove that the more she had the more she had to have to hold what she had.

Eventually it became obvious to some that this was also the road to constantly recurring war, but before this highly moralistic idea was much used, the anti-imperialists were content to meet the mercantilists on their own level of discussion. On this level the arguments of the anti-mercantilists against colonies seem puerile—that everybody would go to the colonies and leave England depopulated; that the colonies would wax strong and break away sooner or later; that in the meantime they were certain to compete with the mother country; and that England was "biting off more than it could chew." In the seventeenth century it was still too early for anyone to make much headway against the balance-of-trade assumptions of the mercantilists.

What the controversy over colonies and war lacked as long as it was kept on a shilling-and-pence level was the high moral tone of the reformer, the insight of the philosopher. Montesquieu, more than any other writer of his day (1689–1755), added this tone when he declared that trade and commerce are naturally peaceful and represent a great advance over the old method of acquisition by war and conquest. He sounded the gulf of difference between these methods when he wrote that "Commerce is the cure for the most destructive prejudices . . . wherever we find agreeable manners, there commerce flourishes . . . wherever there is commerce, there we meet with agreeable manners." [10] Furthermore, "Peace is the natural effect of trade. Two nations who traffic with each other become reciprocally dependent; for if one has an interest in buying, the other has an interest in selling; and thus their union is founded

---

[10] Montesquieu, *The Spirit of the Laws* (tr. by Thomas Nugent; rev. by J. V. Prichard), Vol. I, Book XX, chap. i.

on their mutual necessities." [11] "The spirit of trade produces in the mind of man a certain sense of exact justice, opposite, on the one hand, to robbery, and on the other to those moral virtues which forbid our always adhering rigidly to the rules of private interest, and suffer us to neglect this to the advantage of others. The total privation of trade, on the contrary, produces robbery." [12] Montesquieu then pays his respect to the English, who have always made their political interests give way to those of commerce, while other nations have made the interests of commerce yield to those of politics. The English, he says, "know better than any other people upon earth how to value, at the same time, these three great advantages—religion, commerce, and liberty." [13]

Another early source of strength to liberalistic views on the colonial question was Francis Bacon. A contemporary of Thomas Mun, and therefore in the midst of the most vocal and most narrow mercantilist period, Bacon did not fully escape the influence of mercantilist views. Nevertheless, he had an extremely wide grasp of social problems. Much better than most of his contemporaries, Bacon could see the difference between good and bad colonial policies, both from the viewpoint of the mother country and that of the colonies. In his essay "Of Plantations," [14] in which he discusses his preferences in things colonial, Bacon observes that "new plantations" (colonies) are the children of former kingdoms; that they ought to be established in " 'pure soil'; that is, where people are not displanted to the end to plant in others; for else it is rather an extirpation than a plantation." He disapproved of purely treasure-grabbing colonial expeditions, and points out that ". . . the principal thing that hath been the destruction of most plantations, hath been the base and hasty drawing of profit in the first years." Nor did he approve of using colonies as dumping grounds for "the scum of people and wicked condemned men." Rather, the colonists ought to be "gardeners, ploughmen, labourers, smiths, carpenters, joiners, fishermen, fowlers, with some few apothecaries, surgeons, cooks, and bakers." Finally, he wanted the mother country to give encouragement to these good people in the early stages of their set-

---

[11] *Ibid.*, chap. ii.       [12] *Ibid.*, chap. ii.       [13] *Ibid.*, chap. vii.
[14] *The Works of Francis Bacon, with a Life of the Author,* by Basil Montagu, I, 41–42.

tlement by relieving them of customs duties, and by permitting them, "except where there be some special cause of caution," to sell their produce where they could get the most for it.

The title of Bacon's essay "Of Empire" [15] seems to the modern mind more appropriate than "plantations" for a discussion of colonies and imperialism, but to Bacon it meant something else: the relation of a ruler to other monarchs. He is here concerned with the dangers that confront kings in dealing with their "neighbours." There is one thing they always have to watch for, says Bacon, "which is, that princes do keep due sentinel, that none of their neighbours do overgrow so (by increase of territory, by embracing of trade, by approaches, or the like) as they become more able to annoy them than they were."

War and the threat of war had always greatly occupied men's minds, but by the eighteenth century this preoccupation was beginning to bear more positive fruit than mere dread and a fatalistic acceptance of the evil. People were starting to seek causes and to propose remedies. To most writers of the liberal tradition, however, the test of their liberalism was to be found in their advocacy of freedom for colonies rather than in speculation regarding such a far-off event as a parliament of nations. As they saw it, the block to peace lay simply in the threat of revolt by colonial peoples and the constant menace of war among the colonial powers over their possessions. Removal of this single bone of contention, therefore, appealed to them as the obvious solution. They also generally assumed that the reduction or abolition of navies and such restraints to trade as the Navigation Laws would be part of the same program. While such a general reformation in international policy would require common agreement by treaties, it did not occur to most men that any more machinery of international government was needed; the idea of a world parliament lingered on only in the minds of the more idealistic few. Nor did it seem reasonable, apparently, to the latter to think that "independence" and treaty relations were enough. Actually, one program was about as realistic as the other: given the will and high moral character among statesmen to solve the war problem it would have made little difference whether they started with the ideal of colonial freedom and disarma-

15 *Ibid.*, I, 26–28.

ment or with the ideal of common purpose in an international federation.

Penn's proposal in 1693 to put an end to increasing "my dominion by the acquisition of my neighbours' countries" [16] by creating a parliament of nations was the most notable proposal for what might be called the "wholesale" method of reform. Himself a great colonist, Penn was certainly not opposed to colonies, however much he was opposed to the way in which they were usually administered. Good colonies and good mother countries would both have a place in this good man's scheme for world government. No doubt a century later Penn would greatly have regretted (as many of his Quaker followers did) the Revolution, which was to weaken rather than strengthen the cause of unity and world government.

Josiah Tucker, an eighteenth-century clergyman and economist, was one of the most vociferous early advocates of colonial independence. He favored freedom for the American colonies years before the revolt broke out in open warfare. Tucker summed up his position in the succinct statement that "war, conquests and colonies are our present system, and mine is just the opposite." [17] Since, he believed, it is the nature of colonies to seek independence, his own system of co-equal nations united in mutual trading relations was premised on the realization of this independence. This, indeed, was "just the opposite" of the prevailing system of navigation acts, trading monopolies, jealousies, recriminations, and constant warfare which marked the colonial period.

Tucker appears also to have been the first economist to criticize the colonial system and its attendant regulations because of their deleterious effect on domestic policy and politics, resulting in the growth of tyranny. [18] This point was made much of at a later period

[16] See below, p. 72.

[17] See Clark, *Josiah Tucker, Economist*, p. 64. The quotation is from a letter written by Tucker in 1761.

[18] Knorr, *British Colonial Theories, 1570–1850*, p. 125. Those interested in further accounts of the anti-imperialist movement in Great Britain will find a wealth of material in the following sources: Schuyler, "The Climax of Anti-Imperialism in England," *Political Science Quarterly*, XXXVI (Dec., 1921), 537–60; Schuyler, "The Rise of Anti-Imperialism in England," *Political Science Quarterly*, XXXVII (Sept., 1922), 440–71; Mullett, "English Imperial Thinking, 1764–1783," *Political Science Quarterly*, XLV (Dec., 1930), 548–79; Wagner, "British Economists and the Empire," *Political Science Quarterly*, XLVI (June, 1931), 248–76, and XLVII (March, 1932), 57–74.

by Joseph Priestley and Richard Price [19] and was not overlooked by Adam Smith. Arthur Young, in 1780, summed up a large body of contemporary thought by saying that the colonies were founded by the commercial system, were reared on commercial profits, monopolized by commercial avarice, while "commercial ignorance now wars to recover the possession of what is not intrinsically worth the powder and ball that are shot away in the quarrel." [20]

James Anderson, also writing during the American Revolution, thought that countries with colonies were always in danger of being embroiled in wars. A lone figure, apologizing for his lack of access to libraries, Anderson was a man with a commonsense message which he was burning to place before the public.[21] All past history he regarded as little else than a vicious circle of conquests by weak or wicked princes to enlarge their domains, followed by revolutions by their victims which in turn brought ruin on the conquerors. "The only states in which the felicity of the people has been considerable, and of long duration," he says, "have been those whose want of power precluded any idea of conquest." [22] And further: ". . . extended empire must ever prove pernicious. But it is not on this account alone that our connection with the American settlements is to be dreaded. The temptation it affords for frequent wars, is a source of still greater mischiefs to a free, commercial, and manufacturing state." [23] Such ideas were becoming increasingly common; the vicious circle and how to break it was always at the center of the speculations of thoughtful men.[24]

With Jeremy Bentham and his followers the anti-imperialist movement of the late eighteenth and early nineteenth centuries in England reached its most eloquent climax. Still concerned with political rather than economic aspects of the problem, these writers are more in line with the tradition of Tucker and Anderson than

19 Knorr, *British Colonial Theories*, pp. 195 ff.

20 Young, *Tour in Ireland*, p. xiii.

21 He was not unacquainted with Adam Smith's *Wealth of Nations*, however.

22 Anderson, *The Interest of Great-Britain with Regard to Her American Colonies, Considered*, pp. 32–33.

23 *Ibid.*, p. 102; *see also* p. 105: The "extent of empire in every case, affords numberless temptations to enlarge in war; and an empire extended like the British empire in America, is peculiarly liable to this defect."

24 Looking back over this period forty years after Anderson wrote, John Nicholls stated that "every acquisition renders it more necessary for us to extend our conquests."—Nicholls, *Recollections and Reflections*, I, 247.

with that of Adam Smith. Indeed, Bentham himself admits that "Two original writers have gone before me in this line, Dean Tucker and Dr. Anderson. The object of the first was to persuade the world of the inutility of war . . . the object of the second to show the inutility of the colonies." [25]

Scattered throughout his vast works are to be found Bentham's own statements exposing the "inutility" of war and colonies. In a piece addressed to the National Convention of France, 1793, entitled "Emancipate your Colonies!" Bentham argued that consistency demanded that the French permit their colonies, like themselves, to choose their own government.[26] But the emancipation of colonies constituted only part of his program of reform. In his "plan for an universal and perpetual peace" Bentham proposed both the reduction and fixation of armaments and the emancipation of colonies. Neither of these proposals, he adds, would be complete without the other. His scheme also included the abolition of military and trade alliances and of all regulations for the augmentation or maintenance of naval forces, "such as the Navigation Act, bounties on the Greenland trade, and other trades regarded as nurseries for seamen." [27] But Bentham was not to be put off with the argument that no nation dared to take the first step. "Whatsoever nation should get the start of the other in making the proposal to reduce and fix the amount of its armed force," he says, "would crown itself with everlasting honour. The risk would be nothing—the gain certain. This gain would be, the giving an incontrovertible demonstration of its own disposition to peace, and of the opposite disposition in the other nation in case of its rejecting the proposal." [28]

Somehow the vicious circle had to be broken, and Bentham was convinced that this never could be done until the supporters of the navy ceased to regard navigation "as an end, rather than as a means: or if as a means, as a means with reference to colonies." "Here again," he continues, "comes in the ancient and favourite circle: a

[25] *The Works of Jeremy Bentham*, ed. by John Bowring, Vol. II, Essay IV, "A Plan for an Universal and Perpetual Peace," p. 546.

[26] *Works*, IV, 408.

[27] *Works*, Vol. II, Essay IV, "A Plan for an Universal and Perpetual Peace," p. 546.

[28] *Ibid.*, p. 551.

circle by which in defiance of logic and mathematics, political conduct is squared, and wars generated. What are colonies good for?—
for nursing so vast a navy. What is so vast a navy good for?—
for keeping and conquering colonies." [29]

Back of this political sort of appeal lay some firm convictions regarding the causes of war. "War is mischief upon the largest scale,"
says Bentham,[30] but he refused the easy generalization which would
identify it with wickedness in general or with the cruelty and the
selfish nature of man. War, he says, has other causes, which are not
common to the quarrels of individuals, such as "the war-admiring
turn of histories . . . the prejudices of men [and] . . . the notion
of natural rivalry and repugnancy of interests." When a person is a
party to a dispute about property, he goes to law; "when a state
has sustained what it looks upon as an injury, in respect of property,
from another state—there being no common superior ready chosen
for them—it must either submit to the injury, or get the other state
to join in the appointment of a common judge, or go to war." [31]

There were many who shared Bentham's views and tied them in,
on the economic side, with the ideas of Adam Smith. James Mill
continued the tradition when he declared that "colonies are a
grand source of wars," and that they "multiply exceedingly the
causes and pretext of war." [32] And he connected with this thought
the view that military preparedness reflects the ease with which
men are governed by fears and that such government is bad. The
constant agitation for defense, he thought, degrades the minds of
the people with poverty and slavery, while big navies, especially
the policy of using the colonies as a nursery for the navy, is the
worst expression of this reactionary attitude.[33]

Thus, James Mill's contribution to the question of colonialism
and war was emotional rather than analytical, but he succeeded
nevertheless in reflecting a growing body of public opinion. He
did, however, echo Adam Smith when he declared that "the mother

29 *Works*, Vol. IV, "Panopticon *versus* New South Wales," p. 209.

30 *Works*, Vol. II, Essay III, "Of War, Considered in Respect of Its Causes and
Consequences," p. 544.

31 *Ibid.*

32 James Mill, *Essays*, reprinted from the Supplement to the *Encyclopaedia
Britannica*, pp. 32–33.

33 *Ibid.*, pp. 28–29.

country, in compelling the colony to sell goods cheaper to her than she might sell them to other countries, merely imposes upon her a tribute; not direct, indeed, but none the less real because it is disguised." [34]

## ADAM SMITH ON THE "MEAN AND MALIGNANT EXPEDIENTS OF THE MERCANTILE SYSTEM" AND THE "FOLLY AND INJUSTICE" IN ESTABLISHING COLONIES

Although some of the writers whose views were considered in the previous section were contemporaries, or even followers, of Adam Smith, they represent a line of thought regarding colonies which was still very largely on the political and moral level, without much professional economic content. It might even be maintained that Adam Smith's contribution was mainly of this sort, but at least Smith had injected into the great controversy over colonies an element of logical and mature economic reasoning which marked the beginning of a new approach to problems of this nature.

Economics as a separate discipline and Adam Smith's *Wealth of Nations,* which inaugurated it, came at the most critical stage of the old colonial system. It is not too much to say that the very excesses of this system were the chief inspiration for the appearance of the new science, for they challenged men like Smith to attack the crude thought and theory, as well as the crude practices, which characterized the whole sorry colonial episode. In turn, the doctrines of political economy helped to undermine the colonial system and the mercantilist philosophy which accompanied and supported it. From this stemmed the anti-colonial movement in the nineteenth century and the theories of imperialism in the twentieth. Centering on a new theory of international trade to replace mercantilism, classical economics became the bastion for the argument that free trade was the only decent policy between nations and that colonies, as emerging nations, should become participants in the free-trade system. There would be no room for "closed doors" and exclusive trade monopolies under this scheme, and no excuse for imperialistic wars.

Smith's contribution to this train of thought consisted for the

[34] James Mill, *Elements of Political Economy* (3d ed.), p. 213.

most part in arguing the case against international trade barriers and the system of colonial monopolies and in advocating freedom of trade and an enlightened colonial policy. This was important because it played a great role in creating the anti-mercantilist views which were to become the anti-imperialist views of the nineteenth century. In the correlative field of ideas, which deals with motives for colonialism and finally turns into highly sophisticated theories of imperialism, Smith's influence on later thought is less apparent. Although he considered the question of motives, his discussion belongs more to the realm of commonsense observations regarding the obvious, and it laid virtually no groundwork for the later theories that economic motives, working through the capitalist mechanism, make imperialism a necessary adjunct to capitalist enterprise. Yet, in other parts of his work Smith launched into a discussion of profits which started a controversy regarding the running down of the capitalist system and the relation of this decline to imperialistic activity. But Smith himself envisaged no such connection.

In arguing the case against the "mercantile system" and in defense of the economic internationalism which was its opposite, Smith had a telling analogy and basis in the division of labor. To him the colonial system was part of the price system; the binding element between a colony and its mother country was the trade and commerce which flowed back and forth by virtue of the division of labor, the price mechanism, and the desire for profits. An empire, in his opinion, needed no other cement. Furthermore, this system, which had replaced the age of violence, was pacific. "What all the violence of the feudal institutions could never have effected, the silent and insensible operation of foreign commerce and manufacturers gradually brought about." [35]

Smith, in contrast with later and more doctrinaire anti-imperialists, was not opposed to the possession of colonies. He was against only the mercantile ("imperialistic") policy which regarded colonies as the special monopoly of the mother country, to be exploited as huge plantations and their occupants treated as little better than slaves. To Europe as a whole, regardless of whether a particular

[35] *Wealth of Nations* (Cannan's edition), I, 386. *See also* Innis, "The Penetrative Powers of the Price System," *The Canadian Journal of Economics and Political Science,* IV (August, 1938), 299–319.

country possessed colonies, the colonies of the New World had brought great advantages, first by benefiting the possessors, and then, indirectly, by increasing the trade of all countries which carried on commerce with the colonial powers. The iniquity of the existing system, therefore, was not that it brought no benefits to Europe, but that it prevented those benefits from becoming greater and more widespread than they were. Furthermore, by trying to monopolize the trade of their colonies, Great Britain and other colonial powers were put to an expense of administration, defense, and so forth, which was greater than the gain, so that the possession of colonies had proved a liability. They were an asset to Europe as a whole, and the colonial powers shared in the general gains to trade flowing from Europe's overseas commerce despite, not because of, all attempts to reap an exclusive advantage.[36]

This was a great piece of economic reasoning—so nearly the final word, as well as the first, on this question that little has been added since. Smith did not go so far as Tucker in expressly voicing the fear that tyranny would spring up in England as a result of exercising it on the colonies; in fact, despite his condemnation of the mercantile system and the colonial policy that went with it, Smith repeatedly praised the relative liberality with which Great Britain treated its colonies. Nevertheless, he regarded it as a bad system. Britain's trade prohibitions and restrictions, even though never very harmful, he called "a manifest violation of the most sacred rights of mankind." [37] And so involved in and dependent upon this system had England become that Smith was almost at a loss to know how it could ever be relaxed. "Such are the unfortunate effects," he says, "of all the regulations of the mercantile system! They not only introduce very dangerous disorders into the state of the body politic, but disorders which it is often difficult to remedy, without occasioning, for a time at least, still greater disorders." [38] Monopoly of the colony trade upsets the "natural balance" [39] of industry at home, and the high profits which it makes possible divert capital from the improvement of the land, destroy the parsimony of the merchant class, and prevent the accumulation of capital. Worse, the merchant class, in abandoning the "sober vir-

[36] *Wealth of Nations,* I, 91–140.    [37] *Ibid.*, p. 83.
[38] *Ibid.*, pp. 106–7.    [39] *Ibid.*, p. 105.

tue" of parsimony for "expensive luxury," [40] worsens the manners and habits of the workers. "It is thus," he says, "that the single advantage which the monopoly procures to a single order of men, is in many different ways hurtful to the general interest of the country." [41] And elsewhere: "The monopoly of the colony trade, therefore, like all the other mean and malignant expedients of the mercantile system, depresses the industry of all other countries, but chiefly that of the colonies, without in the least increasing, but on the contrary diminishing, that of the country in whose favour it is established." [42]

One writer has called Smith a "liberal imperialist" with a "cosmopolitan vision" [43]—an imperialist in the sense that he wanted to see the British Empire endure, a liberal in that he wanted it to adopt and foster free trade. It may even appear that Smith was an imperialist in one sense, since he opposed political independence for the colonies, because he very plainly went no further than to propose "some moderate and gradual relaxation of the laws" [44] restricting colonial trade, while warning against opening the colony trade all at once to all nations, lest it "not only occasion some transitory inconveniency, but a great permanent loss to the greater part of those whose industry or capital is at present engaged in it." [45] But he had no specific recommendations as to how trade might be freed from its restrictions; this and kindred details he was willing to leave "to the wisdom of future statesmen and legislators to determine." [46]

Beyond his proposition to relax the restrictions on trade Smith did not go. Complete freedom for the colonies he regarded as politically out of the question. "To propose," he says, "that Great Britain should voluntarily give up all authority over her colonies . . . would be to propose such a measure as never was, and never will be adopted, by any nation in the world. . . . The most visionary enthusiast would scarce be capable of proposing such a measure, with any serious hopes at least of its ever being adopted." [47]

Empire, in other words, is a matter of pride, prestige, and emo-

[40] *Wealth of Nations*, II, 113    [41] *Ibid.*, p. 114.    [42] *Ibid.*, p. 111.
[43] C. R. Fay, *Great Britain from Adam Smith to the Present Day*, p. 3. Cf. Knorr, *British Colonial Theory*, p. 190.
[44] *Wealth of Nations*, II, 106.    [45] *Ibid.*    [46] *Ibid.*, p. 107.
[47] *Ibid.*, p. 116.

tions; but Smith still hoped that a more rational economic policy for the colonies might be adopted by "future statesmen and legislators" once they could be made to see the problem of the wealth of nations in the light of pounds, shillings, and pence.

In fact—looking at the motives for colonization—Smith was of the opinion that the greed for gold and quick profit, which he clearly regards as possessing no imperative quality, had in modern times come to be a stronger incentive than among the ancients. In contrast with Greek and Roman colonies, which were established either from "irresistible necessity"—inability of the people to expand farther at home—or from "clear and evident utility," [48] the European colonies in America were established for no such impelling reasons. They arose "from no necessity," [49] and their utility was not appreciated at the time and therefore could not have been a motive. "Every Spaniard who sailed to America expected to find an Eldorado," says Smith,[50] and the hope of quick fortune continued to be the sole motive for exploration or conquest. "Human avidity" and the passion for gold generally overrode "the judgment of sober reason and experience concerning such projects," [51] and the "first adventurers . . . who attempted to make settlements in America, were animated by the like chimerical views." [52]

Despite his sharp criticism of his own countrymen, Smith still could give them credit for being the best colonial administrators of the whole period after the discovery of the New World; but even the English were motivated by the same mercantile spirit as were other nations, and they followed much the same ruthless policy towards the natives. Therefore Smith could sum up the whole episode in these words:

Folly and injustice seem to have been the principles which presided over and directed the first project of establishing those colonies; the folly of hunting after gold and silver mines, and the injustice of coveting the possession of a country whose harmless natives, far from having ever injured the people of Europe, had received the first adventurers with every mark of kindness and hospitality.[53]

The greed for quick fortune could never, in Smith's opinion, be a rational basis for colonies, since it was not a basis for colonial

48 *Ibid.*, p. 60.      49 *Ibid.*      50 *Ibid.*, p. 66.

51 *Ibid.*, p. 65.      52 *Ibid.*, p. 66.      53 *Ibid.*, p. 90.

trade on a continuing basis. It was sheer exploitation. The greed for profit, to Smith's way of thinking, had none of the character of absolute necessity and inevitability which modern critics of capitalism associate with the profit motive in imperialism. Smith reserved the idea of "irresistible necessity" for the phenomenon of surplus populations being forced to seek new homes.

The more Smith thought about colonial follies and injustices and about the selfishness of merchants and manufacturers in general, the more disheartened he became. He was sure that economic laws, if allowed to operate freely, would prove to be the cure for human misdeeds, and his only source of optimism was the thought that in time rational behavior might prevail. But for the time being there was little ground for optimism.

Commerce, [he says] which ought naturally to be, among nations, as among individuals, a bond of union and friendship, has become the most fertile source of discord and animosity. The capricious ambition of kings and ministers has not, during the present and the preceding century, been more fatal to the repose of Europe, than the impertinent jealousy of merchants and manufacturers.[54]

There was completely lacking, in Smith's reasoning, any economic factor or law (as distinct from the human element) which made it necessary for a country to go outside the confines of its own industrial system to prevent its decline into poverty and bankruptcy. Removing the restrictions on trade, while keeping an eye on would-be monopolists, would, in Smith's opinion, make possible a perfect economic system, in which selfish interests would work for the common good and the wealth of nations would flourish as never before. Capital would accumulate without hindrance, the international division of labor would guarantee its being put to the best possible use, while competition would bring about a constant readjustment of supply and demand. Smith never questioned that consumption would keep pace with the accumulation of capital and production or that any serious disequilibrium was possible. He thought that one effect of competition for capital might be to reduce the rate of profit, but to him this presaged no downfall of the system. Since he envisaged neither overproduction nor underconsumption, there was nothing in the prospective new system to be

54 *Wealth of Nations,* I, 457.

pessimistic about. All Adam Smith's pessimism was reserved for the mercantile system. Laissez faire, in the sense of permitting a maximum of free enterprise and free trade and a minimum of governmental interference, was to be the remedy for mercantilism, just as, a century later, socialism was to be put forward as the remedy for the natural tendencies and excesses of the very capitalism on which Adam Smith had bestowed his blessing.

## THE NEW DEFENDERS OF EMPIRE

It would be a mistake, of course, to imagine that the defense of the Empire in the period overshadowed by Adam Smith became so weak as to deserve no notice. On the defensive as they were, there were influential voices on the side of the old British policy long before the strong revival of interest in empire which came towards the end of the nineteenth century. Those who earlier stood out against the tradition of such men as Penn, Tucker, Anderson, Bentham, and Smith, opposed nearly everything that these men regarded as enlightened, or at most they insisted upon discovering a middle ground between extreme liberalism and extreme conservatism. In general they placed the attributes of power above those of welfare, yet they were becoming conscious of the need for identifying the interests of power and welfare. Although opposed to the views of Smith, the liberal ideas which Smith represented had the effect, nevertheless, of stimulating the challengers to a somewhat higher level of debate than had prevailed in the old simple days of mercantilist ascendency. They were generally opposed to reducing or abolishing navies, at least their own navies; they were against the emancipation of colonies—their colonies; they saw good in the Navigation Acts and other restrictions on trade—when such measures were designed to help their interests: and in their kind of world there was no place for a parliament of nations. Being rarely in the position of feeling obliged to present new and striking arguments for their case, they left little that stands out today as forceful or cogent reasoning; much of their argument seems puerile. They had no theories of war, or were inarticulate on the subject if they did have any ideas, and they left no body of thought on which a theory of imperialism might be based.

Henry Brougham came most conspicuously to the fore among the representatives of this group. While he professed to appreciate Adam Smith's attack on the mercantile system, he could not bring himself, as Bentham did, to see no good in colonies, and he could see no connection between colonies and war. He even thought that "the wars which a state carries on in the colonies or remote dominions, are attended with important advantages to the contiguous territories." [55]

Out of an evident desire to be fair, he adopted a conciliatory course, of which the following statement is typical.

While the Mercantile theory favoured the establishment of colonies by every possible means, and viewed them as a certain mine of wealth; that of the OEconomists considered them as a drain to the resources, and a diversion to the force of the mother country. Statesmen of the former school (as almost all statesmen have been), encouraged them, as the scene of rich and secure monopoly: The converts of the latter doctrine (whose influence on public affairs has unfortunately been very slender), disapproved both of the colonies, and of the colonial monopoly.

Between these two opinions, Dr. Smith has adopted a middle course. He loudly condemns the monopoly; and labours, with his usual force of reasoning and illustration, to prove, that it has been alike detrimental to the colonies, and to the parent state. But he admits, that a distinction ought carefully to be drawn between the trade of the colonies and the monopoly of that trade: The former, he allows to be, in every case, beneficial; the latter, he maintains, must always be hurtful, even upon the principles of the Mercantile system.

I think it must strike every one, who attentively examines the very elaborate Treatise of this celebrated writer upon the subject of Colonies, that his views have been biased by the events and the temper of the times in which he drew up that part of his Inquiry. His illustrations are chiefly drawn from the state of North America; his arguments are frequently deduced from those partial illustrations; and the general texture of his reasonings by no means presents to us that bold and consistent aspect which is, for the most part, a characteristic feature of his work. Had it been composed at a more favourable moment, we should certainly have met with an explicit reprobation of all colonies, and colonial policy —instead of a censure, confined to the abuses of power, and the mo-- nopoly of the colonial trade; unless, indeed, a farther examination of the subject, in its various relations, political as well as oeconomical, had led him to relax somewhat of his severity against this employment of the national capital and force; and then we might have found him likewise abating somewhat of his condemnation of the exclusive policy itself. It will afterwards appear, from an examination of Dr. Smith's reasonings,

[55] Brougham, *An Inquiry into the Colonial Policy of the European Powers,* I, 129.

that they do not apply to the monopoly alone; but that the trade itself, in every form in which it can be imagined to exist, is liable, in a very great degree, to the animadversions which he has confined to the monopoly. On the other hand, it will probably be found that the monopoly is much more harmless than has been supposed; and that the trade itself, when rightly considered, is, in every respect, advantageous to the mother country.[56]

Herman Merivale was another influential writer of the early nineteenth century. Writing in the 1840's in defense of Britain's overseas dominions, Merivale tried to mix his belief in empire with economics by holding that such outlets were necessary for Britain in order to offset the tendency for capital to accumulate and for the rate of profit to decline.[57] Here was the germ for a theory of capitalist imperialism, but Merivale was not the man to draw such a conclusion. He was a forerunner, rather, of later writers and historians—Buckle, Dilke, Seeley, and others—who were to defend the Empire in the late Victorian era, when Britain was casting off the old idea that colonies were like ripe fruit, destined to drop from the tree. The old anti-colonial tradition and economic liberalism were left largely in the hands of a few economists, who traced their intellectual heritage back to Adam Smith. Alongside this group arose a new school of thought in economics, which jumped the classical track and pioneered ideas from which sprang a theory of capitalist imperialism.

The time between Brougham and Merivale and the end of the nineteenth century was one in which Britain seemed to be going two ways at once—on the one hand, in the direction of closer ties with the existing Empire and the acquisition of more colonial possessions, and on the other, towards a colonial policy which at times seemed so liberal that it could end only in the complete separation and independence of the colonies. This confusion of direction was further complicated by the fact that there were both "Liberal" and "Tory" imperialists working for the interests of the Empire. The Liberals characteristically wanted free trade, not only between different parts of the Empire but also between the Empire countries and the rest of the world, while the Tories wanted free trade within the Empire, but protection around the Empire. The choice thus

[56] *Ibid.*, pp. 7–9.          [57] Merivale, *Lectures on Colonization and Colonies.*

appeared to be between universal free trade and imperial preference.

To complicate matters still further, these sentiments were reflected in the colonies, especially in those which were later to constitute Canada, Australia, and New Zealand. The colonial Liberals wanted what the Liberals of Great Britain wanted—free trade everywhere. What the colonial Conservatives wanted was, first of all, freedom to adopt protective tariffs of their own; as a secondary measure, which constituted their concession to imperial unity, they were willing to fit their tariff systems into the scheme of imperial preference. But the granting of preference, once the right to have their own tariffs was recognized, had to remain a one-sided affair. So long as Britain insisted upon remaining a free-trade country, a tariff wall around the Empire was out of the question, but there was nothing to prevent the colonies—or the new dominions—from granting preference on British goods if they so desired; in fact, they did so despite Britain's inability, because of her free trade policy, to reciprocate.

Although the lack of a protective policy for Britain placed both the British and the colonial Conservatives at a disadvantage, it was the Liberals who were really in a dilemma. Among the Liberals in the British Parliament there was a strong feeling around the middle of the century that "the principle of self-government [for the colonies] was even more important than the principle of free trade." [58] This meant that they would rather give up the principle of liberal imperialism than to use force to retain colonies that wanted freedom to adopt protectionism. Above all, they had no use for Tory imperialism as a British policy, no matter how much their own policy might have the natural consequences of permitting the development of Tory imperialism, or "economic nationalism," in the colonies. The issue was squarely whether the colonies should be forced by illiberal and imperialistic methods to remain free trade in a free-trade empire or allowed freedom to become as illiberal and protectionist as they might wish.

In the end the British colonies which acquired dominion status turned out to be among the most highly protectionist countries

[58] Allin, *Australasian Preferential Tariffs and Imperial Free Trade*, pp. 205–6.

in the world and, from the point of view of liberal sentiment in England, the most hopelessly illiberal. Far from being willing or able to do anything to stem the tide of protectionism in the dominions, the United Kingdom finally—in 1932—abandoned its own free-trade policy and joined with the rest of the Empire in a system of imperial tariff preference. Even before the coming of the new commercial policy, Britain's policy towards the self-governing dominions had changed so radically from the old idea of "possessions" to partnership that there actually was some ironic significance in the reminder that "after all, one of the most important parts of the British Empire is Great Britain itself." [59]

From the point of view of the mother country, imperialism had weakened, in the sense that England as an imperialist power had long since given up the idea of dictating policy to its own "possessions." Indeed, it had never been the policy of Liberals in England to do otherwise. Liberalism and free trade were clearly incompatible with the old conception of imperialism. Yet from the point of view of the Empire as a whole, "empire" acquired a new meaning in the conception of a commonwealth of nations. In terms commonly used to express such ideas, "economic nationalism" had become blended with "economic imperialism" to form a British commonwealth which is neither liberal in the old economic sense nor imperialistic in the old political sense.[60]

But that contradiction in terms "liberal imperialism" was no match for the forces of nationalism which beset the Empire from within, and it was never intended to meet the challenging forces of rising and rival empires which were threatening it from without. The British Empire—or Commonwealth of Nations—presented to the world a united front, not for offense, but for self-protection. In a world of power politics, where resources and markets are the stakes of diplomacy, liberal or free-trade imperialism is obviously not a weapon; it is not even imperialism as the twentieth century understands the term.

The foregoing brief condensation of a great deal of British history needs next to be supplemented by what, in the meantime, was happening on the intellectual front to change the direction of

[59] Knowles, *The Economic Development of the British Overseas Empire,* p. xi.
[60] Allin, *op. cit.,* p. 227.

British attitudes towards imperial policy. Politically, the issue was squarely drawn between Little Englanders and imperialists, between Liberals and Tories, between free traders and protectionists, and between welfare and power. To use a sports term, the ball now went to the defenders of the Empire, and the Little Englanders, Liberals, and free traders were again on the defensive. The conditions under which the new debate took place were, furthermore, much more complex—if no less tense—than those which prevailed when Adam Smith and his followers had taken the offensive against mercantilism and the whole colonial policy of the earlier period. It became more difficult to distinguish between political and economic thought and between the influence of economists and that of historians; but it was chiefly from a group of eminent historians that the new interest in and defense of the Empire emanated.

Students and political leaders alike were being awakened to new forces and new sources of power, and they were especially impressed by the fruits of the English industrial revolution and the growth of trade and commerce. To economic and political liberals this great advance appeared to be the fruit of free trade, and they were so convinced that at last the age of reason and peace had arrived that they had virtually no interest in colonies and certainly no interest in imposing the will of Britain on its overseas possessions. Looking abroad, they could find very little interest in colonies on the part of any nation. In Germany, Bismarck professed no interest in colonies, preferring continental hegemony; France was only mildly interested; while the United States had turned its back on Europe and the world for the more interesting and profitable business of exploiting its own continental empire.

Meanwhile, Marx talked of colonialism as if it were a thing of the past, Mill was championing the intellectual battle of economic liberalism, Cobden and Bright were extending the field of free trade (even Napoleon the Third was a convert to this liberal doctrine), and the historians were recording that the way to peace had at last been found. Wars of religion and wars of race, wars of commerce and territorial conquest, were happily gone forever; nationalistic wars such as those waged between Germany, on the one hand, and Denmark, Austria, and France, on the other, were at least localized and short. To Marx they signalized the great opportunity for the socialist counterrevolution, while to nearly everyone else, apparently, they were merely to be regarded as unfortunate reminders that the goal of reason and peace, after all, was still long and difficult.

All this, far from being an economic interpretation of imperialism and war, was an economic interpretation of peace and freedom. And it called for no special formula, except, perhaps, the formula that general enlightenment had taught men that commerce is superior to war and conquest as a means of increasing the wealth of nations and the general welfare. It was a peculiar combination of the teachings of Christianity (whose founder two thousand years earlier had also optimistically declared that the Kingdom of Heaven is at hand) and the "enlightened self-interest" of Adam Smith.

Buckle, in 1857, at the height of free-trade sentiment, had believed that the growth of commerce and industry was fast making international war impossible.[61] The historian Lecky shared these views in 1865;[62] but thirty years later he had come to believe, as a result of the wars of the period, that the trading and commercial spirit was the chief impulse towards territorial aggrandizement, because the system of large-scale manufacturing industry and high tariffs made it necessary for great manufacturing countries to secure exclusive markets by incorporating new territories within their dominions.[63]

It was partly on this note of despair and partly on a certain new note of optimism that the revival of interest in the British Empire developed. If the old system did not work, in the sense of converting the whole world to the ways of peace, and if a tightening of the bonds of the Empire held out some hope of correcting the situation and redressing the growing unbalance of power in Europe, then the logic seemed to be on the side of the imperialists.

The historian Seeley was one of the most influential in directing attention to a more hopeful outlook for the British Empire. Seeley rejected both the old bombastic school which clamored for empire

---

[61] Buckle, *History of Civilization in England,* I, 193, 198, 209. Salz, "Die Zukunft des Imperialismus," *Weltwirtschaftliches Archiv,* XXXII (October, 1930), 317–48, refers (pp. 318–23) to the contributions of Buckle and Lecky to an understanding of the connection between economics and war.

[62] Lecky, *History of the Rise and Influence of the Spirit of Rationalism in Europe,* II, 383 ff.

[63] Lecky, *Democracy and Liberty,* I, 307–8.

on purely jingoistic grounds, and the Little Englanders who had regarded colonies as ripening fruit, destined to drop from the tree. Between these extremes he found a new and much more concrete element of cohesion in the simple fact that the developments in transportation and communication had made it easy and therefore possible for Britain to keep in touch with and maintain her interest in the distant parts of her crumbling Empire. To him this was the sort of realism which could turn the old conception of colonies as conquered territories or possessions into a new kind of colonial system.[64]

Seeley was aware of the danger from the "precarious and artificial" power of a state which goes beyond the limits of its own nationality,[65] and in this respect he shared the stay-at-home views of the Little Englanders.[66] Yet the spirit of self-conscious imperialism in Britain can be traced to his famous lectures on *The Expansion of England*.[67]

Among Seeley's contemporaries two other names stand out because of a similar impetus which their writings gave to the new interest and pride in the Empire: Sir Charles Dilke, who published his *Greater Britain* in 1870, and J. A. Froude, whose *Oceana* appeared in 1885. Langer [68] remarks that Seeley and these two men were more concerned with the Empire as it was than with its expansion. It may also be added that this has characterized the writings of most of the great names among English historians—an inclination to say much about the Empire as a going concern and relatively little (compared with German and American historians) about the dynamics and "causes" of empire building.

A source of considerable strength to the defenders of British imperialism undoubtedly comes from the fact that an old and well-established empire can be justified with relative ease, simply because it behaves less imperialistically and arouses less opposition than does one which is in the making. In Great Britain there is almost as little disposition to question the institution of imperialism as there is to criticize the Crown itself. This fact probably goes a long

---

[64] Seeley, *The Expansion of England*. See especially Lectures III, IV, VI, and VIII.
[65] *Ibid.*, p. 46.
[66] Gooch, "Imperialism," in his *The Heart of the Empire*, pp. 331, 346.
[67] Trevelyan, *British History in the Nineteenth Century, 1782–1901*, p. 410.
[68] Langer, *The Diplomacy of Imperialism, 1890–1902*, I, 71.

way towards explaining why the English, "who really have more to boast of in this respect than anybody else, talk least about it." [69] Although Hobson and a few other Englishmen became absorbed in the theory of imperialism (characteristically, chiefly in the theory and practice of British imperialism) and have made a great to-do about it, most British scholars have taken very little interest in the subject. This was left to the Germans, where empire was still a dream of ambitious men and the fear of imperialism became the special obsession of the followers of Marx. Not in the seat of an empire which had arrived did the theory of imperialism find the most fertile ground for debate, but in a country where the imperialism of other peoples, especially that of the British, excited admiration, envy, and fear. Much better suited to the British temperament than fine-spun theories are various bemused observations about the Empire, such as the toast "Here's to the British Empire on which the sun never sets—and wages never rise" or Lord Byron's doggerel

> The world is a bundle of hay,
> Mankind are the asses who pull,
> Each tugs it a different way,—
> And the greatest of all is John Bull! [70]

The long-ingrained British habit of taking the Empire for granted, the feeling of security in a nation that had reached the imperial saturation point, English empiricism and the Englishman's disinclination to philosophize—these explanations can be marshaled to account for the English lack of interest in creating abstruse theories about what appeared to them an entirely natural British institution. Even the word "imperialism" is not often found in the vocabulary of British historians or in the indexes of their books, although concrete terms such as "imperial unity," "imperial federation," "imperial preference," and "imperial defense," are not lacking. Empire has its cult, but the stanchest defender of empire shrinks from being called an imperialist, just as military men dislike to be called militarists. Such terms find ready currency only in the vocabulary of "radicals." The British Commonwealth of Nations is regarded by some as a fitting substitute for the old im-

---

[69] Sumner, *The Conquest of the United States by Spain*, p. 8.
[70] *Letters and Journals of Lord Byron: with Notices of His Life*, by Thomas Moore, II, 494. These lines appeared for years on the front page of Horatio Bottomley's paper, *John Bull*.

perial idea of superior and inferior, but even too fulsome praise of the Commonwealth [71] is likely to meet somewhere the rejoinder that its devotees confuse it with the Kingdom of Heaven.

So much criticism and ridicule have been heaped upon the transparent euphemism of "shouldering the white man's burden" as justification for imperialism that only an outright Tory can nowadays spring to the defense of such a shibboleth. There are some apologists who talk in this way, but their tone is usually gentle rather than bombastic. It is still relevant, as some see it, to point out that the white man does have something to offer less favored races, that he does have (or at least has assumed) a civilizing mission, and that the recipients of such favors have not always resented them, and by certain objective tests have been decidedly benefited.[72]

[71] As, for example, by Curtis, in *The Commonwealth of Nations*. See especially the last page of the book—a most ecstatic peroration.

[72] Space will not permit an extended survey of the attitude of English historians towards the use of the term "imperialism," but an examination of their works will convince the reader that they are generally very reluctant to use it, that a few use it but to praise, and others because it is not easily avoided, because of its increasing usage. G. P. Gooch illustrates the "reluctant" school. In discussing "The Scramble for Africa" (*History of Modern Europe, 1878–1919*, chap. iii), he confines his account to the role of individuals and diplomatic wranglings where many other historians have found no end of opportunities for illustrating the workings of "economic imperialism." J. Holland Rose (*The Development of the European Nations, 1870–1921*, p. 541) regards the spread of British influence as often due to the influence of individuals such as Cecil Rhodes, playing a lone hand, rather than to any combination of the state and leading personalities, as in the case of France and Germany. J. A. Cramb, in his *The Origins and Destiny of Imperial Britain*, is a thorough believer in imperialism, at least that of Britain, which he regards as unique in conception and in practice. It unites, he says, the modern concept of Empire and Freedom, whereas all other forms, at least before the eighteenth century, were molded on the Roman pattern, which was completely lacking in freedom. Like the state itself, it must be judged, not on the material basis of whether it "pays," but as the epitome of human co-operation (pp. 5, 12, 15). Egerton (*British Colonial Policy in the XXth Century*, pp. viii, ix) regrets that the words "empire" and "imperialism" are so charged with prejudicial meaning as to blind certain people to its real benefits. Ramsay Muir (*The Expansion of Europe*, p. 1) finds the terms useful because they so aptly describe the influence of European civilization upon the world; at the same time he regrets the necessity of using them when they imply "purely military dominion" and only the worst aspects of a process that contains much good.

The factor of sheer imitation is often emphasized to help explain the rise of imperialism outside of the British Empire and to account for the revival of interest in empire in Great Britain after her imitators had made the process highly competitive and the spirit increasingly contagious; as, for example, in Howard Robinson, *The Development of the British Empire*, pp. 288 ff.

There are various good accounts of the attitude of English historians towards British imperialism. Two of these, by American authors, may be mentioned as particularly helpful: Langer, *The Diplomacy of Imperialism, 1890–1902*, Vol. I, chap. iii; and Strauss, *Joseph Chamberlain and the Theory of Imperialism*.

# III ·

# THE HISTORIANS
# AND IMPERIALISM

THE history of the New World is peculiarly rich in lessons of
imperialism and in the reactions which the experience of discovery, settlement, and expansion have created. And in this history
the United States has played a central role. This country had the
unique experience of throwing off the imperial yoke and launch-
ing forth as a great modern nation. But as it grew and expanded, the
United States showed unmistakable signs of flexing its own imperial brawn, and this in turn precipitated some of the sharpest
anti-imperialist sentiment ever developed in any country. In this
atmosphere of action and reaction certain ideas and theories were
bound to develop, and it was also a fertile ground in which to plant
the seeds of the economic interpretation.

The overland territorial expansion of the United States, especially that associated with the Mexican War and the acquisition of
Texas, has usually appeared more imperialistic to Europeans and
Latin Americans than to even the most radical citizens of this country. Americans have always been more or less shocked to hear their
country called an empire or have regarded terms such as "the
American Empire" with the mild amusement aroused by such fancy
names as Empire State, Empire Grill, and Empire Laundry. If
this country were small (like most empire countries), our overseas possessions might seem more grandiose as well as more
necessary, but it is difficult for the citizens of a large country to get
very enthusiastic over an "empire" that seems no more important
as an appendage than a tail appears on an elephant. Nevertheless,
the acquisition of our territories, continental as well as insular, and
especially the method of acquisition and the jingoism that ac-

companied most of it has caused no little amount of uneasiness on the part of those who have seen dangerous portents for democracy in following the path of empire.

## ANTI-IMPERIALISM IN THE UNITED STATES

Not until well after the Civil War do we find the word "imperialism" coming into general use as a new and derogatory term for aggrandizement. One of the earliest American articles, apparently, to include the expression appeared in 1879. A. H. Thompson, of Topeka, Kansas, severely criticized the British for suppressing the Zulus, drawing the moral that big nations ought to protect and care for the weaker ones rather than suppress them. But more interesting is the fact that the author felt obliged to explain what was meant by imperialism. The following statement from the London *Times,* quoted by Thompson, indicates the novelty of a term which was still so unusual as to call for quotation marks. The *Times,* he says,

states that Lord Beaconsfield "is avowedly devoted to what is now well known as 'Imperialism,' that is to say, to a system under which the people are to submit to a course of secret policy directed to objects of conquest and aggrandizement few of them would approve," and the actions and policy of the Tory Premier and his tools, his "Jingoism" and his "Jingos," are roundly censured.[1]

Another attack on imperialism—this time American imperialism —appeared in 1892 under the intriguing title *Imperialism in America; Its Rise and Progress,* by Mrs. Sarah E. V. Emery.

There is no feature of history more sad [says the author], no phase of human nature more dismal, than that innate desire in man's heart to rule over his fellow men. This ambition has been the curse of the world. Its slain are legion. But the battle field is not its only place of carnage. . . . The spirit of imperialism that has arisen in America has not sprung spontaneous from our soil, but has been nursed and fostered through the strategic ministrations of despotic Europe.[2]

It soon turns out, however, that Mrs. Emery was concerned with the growth of despotic power in the United States rather than with territorial aggrandizement, the "money-power" and Wall Street

[1] A. H. Thompson, "British Imperialism and the Autonomous Rights of Races," *Kansas City Review of Science and Industry,* III (1879), 229.

[2] Emery, *Imperialism in America,* pp. 5–7.

being the new enemies of the masses, foreboding terrible disaster
for America.

Mrs. Emery was particularly alarmed by the fact that powerful
interests could have started a movement in 1868 to make Grant the
Emperor of this country, even before he was elected President. She
mentions the anonymous publication *The Imperialist,* which appeared early in 1868, as the mouthpiece for the movement. It
carried an imperial crown as its figurehead, with the motto "The
empire is peace, let us have peace." Democracy was denounced because it means "lawlessness, corruption, insecurity to person and
property, robbery of the public creditors [i. e., the holders of government bonds issued to finance the Civil War], and civil war"
while "the empire means law, order, security, public faith and
peace." [3]

Sumner's *Conquest of the United States by Spain* stands as a
classic indictment of the new imperialism which, in the opinion of
an old-fashioned liberal of 1899, was invading the sacred portals
of American Democracy.

Spain [says Sumner] was the first, for a long time the greatest, of the
modern imperialistic states. The United States, by its historical origin,
its traditions and its principles, is the chief representative of the revolt
and reaction against that kind of a state. I intend to show that, by the
line of action now proposed to us, which we call expansion and imperialism, we are throwing away some of the most important elements of the
American symbol, and are adopting some of the most important elements of the Spanish symbol. We have beaten Spain in a military conflict, but we are submitting to be conquered by her on the field of ideas
and policies. Expansionism and imperialism are nothing but the old
philosophies of national prosperity which have brought Spain to where
she now is. [4]

The man who spoke these lines was too good an economist
and sociologist to be fooled by the facile interpretation of this behavior as "economic."

War, expansion, and imperialism [he continues] are questions of statesmanship and of nothing else. I disregard all other aspects of them,

[3] *Ibid.,* pp. 75–76.
[4] Sumner, *The Conquest of the United States by Spain,* p. 3. Sumner was address-
ing the Phi Beta Kappa fraternity at Yale. For his pains in exposing the dangers of
imperialism to American Democracy, Sumner "was ridiculed where he was not
written down as crazy."—Villard, *Fighting Years,* p. 137.

all extraneous elements which have been intermingled with them.[5] . . .

Everywhere you go on the Continent of Europe at this hour you see the conflict between militarism and industrialism. You see the expansion of industrial power pushed forward by the energy, hope, and thrift of men, and you see the development arrested, diverted, crippled, and defeated by measures which are dictated by military considerations. . . . It is militarism which is eating up all the products of science and art, defeating the energy of the population, and wasting its savings. It is militarism which forbids the people to give their attention to the problems of their own welfare, and to give their strength to the education and comfort of their children. It is militarism which is combating the grand efforts of science and art to ameliorate the struggle for existence. . . . What will hasten the day when our present advantages will wear out, and when we shall come down to the conditions of the older and densely populated nations? The answer is: war, debt, taxation, diplomacy, a grand governmental system, pomp, glory, a big army and navy, lavish expenditures, political jobbery,—in a word, imperialism.[6]

Had the interpreters of history taken the cue that the conflict is between "militarism and industrialism," they could not have filled the pages of books during the next generation with the thesis that industrialism (capitalism) either causes or uses militarism and imperialism; had they seen the situation as Sumner saw it, they would have used their energies in making it clear that militarism and imperialism use or "eat up" all the products of science and art, diverting them from welfare to the age-old purposes of the quest for power.[7]

But the tide of the economic interpretation and the fashion of "blaming it on the economic system" was in full swing, and it was

[5] *The Conquest of the United States by Spain*, p. 4.

[6] *Ibid.*, pp. 23, 24, 25.

[7] The Anti-Imperialist League was organized in 1898 in Boston for the specific purpose of opposing ratification of the treaty whereby Spain ceded the Philippines to the United States. After this failed, the League devoted its energies "to ameliorating the conditions and making reparation for the wrongs caused by the colossal blunder or crime involved in the efforts to subdue and retain under the United States sovereignty a people who had substantially won their independence from the Spanish power."—Winslow, *The Anti-Imperialist League*. During 1899–1900 the league issued a publication, *The Anti-Imperialist*, under the editorship of Edward Atkinson, a prominent Boston liberal. At its height the league claimed 150,000 members, including Benjamin Harrison, Grover Cleveland, Charles W. Eliot, F. W. Taussig, and many other prominent persons. Most of them probably agreed with Senator Hoare's prediction that the fall of the Republic would date from the seizure of the Philippines. Without doubt it was the most energetic and the most highly concentrated group that ever opposed imperialism in this country.

an unusual historian who escaped at least some of the influence of this doctrine.

## TYPES OF HISTORICAL TREATMENT

Historians are truly among the architects of the universe. The chroniclers of history, in the process of trying to explain events and to find causal relations, and the special philosophers of history, who spin theories first and apply them to historical events afterwards, are creators of patterns of thought which, along with real events, pure fables, and political myths, constitute the historical memories on which subsequent history is so largely based.

One of the most influential philosophies of history, grown to maturity and great power during the past hundred years, is the economic interpretation of history. We shall say more about it in later chapters, but for our present purpose—to show how the idea has been used by historians—it is sufficient to state its broad outlines. It is from the economic interpretation of history that ideas such as economic imperialism and the economic causes of war have developed. For the historian's purpose the refinements of the theory are not necessary. All he wants is some formula that sounds reasonable in order to be an interpreter, not a mere chronicler, of history; in fact, if the economic interpretation appeals to him, he requires not much more than his own commonsense observation, unimpeded by the trained economist's critical attitude towards the more deeply hidden pitfalls and fallacies of the economic interpretation. For what can be more obvious to the interpreter in search of a formula than that nations are rivals for territory, markets, and spheres of influence and will fight to gain them or to hold them?

Slightly less difficult to grasp than these surface phenomena is the idea that modern industrialism, or capitalism, produces more goods and capital than can be used within the confines of its homeland and perforce must seek outlets abroad. Back of this outward thrust, supplying the motive, is the constant search for profits by private capitalists. The commonsense conclusion, to those who go no farther than this, is obvious: the very nature of the economic system and the motives on which it grows are responsible, in large part, if not entirely (depending on how far the interpreter feels like pushing the influence of the economic factor at the expense of such factors as prestige, adventure, and glory), for those great international rivalries that lead to imperialism and war. The interpreter who has gone no farther can hardly escape an equally simple conclusion regarding the remedy: change, or at least reform, the economic system; let production henceforth be for use, not for profit; force industry to pay higher wages at home so the national population which creates a surplus of wealth will have sufficient purchasing power to absorb the surplus, thus preventing it from being channeled abroad, where it can only cause trouble; confine foreign trade to the barest essentials required from abroad; and—above all—do not lend abroad or make investments in foreign countries, backward or otherwise.

For ordinary practical purposes these general ideas are enough for the historian in the role of economic interpreter. He need not be concerned with the question of whether imperialism is an "economic necessity" or an "economic policy." The first view, strongly defended by one school, simply means that neither capitalists nor the state, which itself is regarded as a capitalistic institution for the protection of property, can escape the pressure of the economic forces of overproduction, underconsumption, or declining profits, and has to expand or die. The second view goes no farther than to say that capitalism does not have to expand outwardly, that although it could exist as a self-contained system, it follows imperialistic financial and other policies because that is what politicians desire, regardless of the cost or whether it makes economic sense, inasmuch as it fits in with the motives of the capitalists, who invest and trade abroad for the sake of profits.

The historian does not ordinarily make distinctions of this sort. Rather, he makes use of some simple concatenation of events which seems to explain the circumstances. For example, merchants and bankers penetrate into backward areas in search of profits, get into trouble or feel uneasy about the security of their investments or concessions, and finally appeal to their governments for diplomatic or even military intervention. To this it may be added that merchants and capitalists are more or less "forced" abroad by the lure of greater economic opportunity and that the state has no choice but to follow suit; but such assertions are rare in historical works. Sometimes, however, the interpreter keeps adding factors and ends up by making it appear that every economic act is imperialistic, from selling goods to lending money (either private or public) for building railways, developing mines, or for any other ordinary commercial purpose. Territory may not be involved at all, or even sovereignty, in many of the imperialistic processes envisaged by some writers. Historians have generally found it easy to believe that "economic" motives are purely one-sided expressions of human selfishness and that economic competition, or the clash of economic motives, is exclusive and nonreciprocal. It is much more difficult to grasp the kind of argument that denies this point of view and difficult not to regard it as a kind of sophism that makes the lesser seem the greater good. But, worse still, what is there left to discuss if one must give up the economic interpretation of history?

The economic interpretation of imperialism and war has one great advantage over other interpretations, and thereon doubtless depends its great popularity: it gives people something concrete and apparently simple to talk about.[8] Whatever the causes of war may be, one of the major causes of the economic interpretation is the ease with which it can be invoked. It appeals to the logical and scientific mind in an age that places great store on economic values and science. It deals with concrete factors and material forces which people feel they can understand. Above all, it carries an air of sophistication which can be imparted with great educational facility. By an easy transference to personal motives and experiences, it enables the man in the street to see the world as himself writ large.

[8] Geopolitics as a theory of imperialism and war had become a close rival by the time of the second World War, but it shows no present promise of ever becoming as popularly accepted as the economic interpretation. At most it can hardly be regarded as a substitute for the economic interpretation. Rather, it is the economic interpretation, with some political overtones, as worked out by geographers who were impressed most by space and spatial relations. They have taken over what is generally regarded as the province of the political scientist and economist, and without much insight into the realities either of economics or politics they have made these entirely subsidiary to geographic conglomerations and "heartlands." Furthermore, it has been characteristic of students of geopolitics to make their "science" a tool of a particular state or group of peoples. In some respects this repeats the tendency of some of the advocates of the economic interpretation to make it appear that certain groups called "capitalists," or "capitalist nations," have constituted the economic "heartland" of the world and the center of world conflict. One approach is probably about as fictitious as the other.

To the social scientist and the historian it came as a boon, lifting historical explanation, at last, from its naïve dependence on the wrath of God and the ambition of kings to the greed of man. A poet might say:

> But war's a game, which, were their subjects wise,
> Kings would not play at.[9]

But modern man must talk in terms of "social forces."

The Boer and Spanish-American wars produced a host of anti-imperialists and anti-imperialist literature, but it was not until about the time of the first World War that the economic interpretation of imperialism began to bulk large in the history books.[10] American students took the idea largely second-hand from the Germans, with a substantial amount of help from Hobson,[11] but they never succeeded in becoming as excited as the Germans or as passive as the English over either the subject of empire building or the ideology of imperialism. There have been waves of anti-imperialism in this country, but they never resulted in any elaborate or original theory of expansion; always they have sprung from a deep and almost instinctive feeling that imperialism spells the doom of liberalism and democracy. "Yankee imperialism" has been viewed as a sinister force not only by Latin Americans who have had it practiced on them, but also by those Americans who have had to stand by and watch certain special interests practice it. There has developed no indigenous theory of this Yankee imperialism. With the exception of a few writers who regard our foreign relations as considerably less sinister than those of Britain, France, Germany, Russia, or Japan and doubt that the same word should be used in comparing our policies with theirs, most writers simply treat the imperialism of all nations as of the same general order. Economic imperialism, it is assumed, characterizes all such relations, regardless of where they are found, by whom practiced, or by whom experienced.

[9] Cowper, "The Winter Morning Walk," in *The Task*, Book V, p. 153.

[10] Not in all of them, for some historians are content to remain chroniclers, letting the facts speak for themselves, and there are a few who studiously avoid the economic interpretation while stressing other causal factors. But by and large the present-day writers of historical works and textbooks interpret modern wars in terms of imperialism, and imperialism in terms of economic forces.

[11] Hobson's views are discussed in Chapter V, below.

The new generation of historians had not only much more important events to chronicle and interpret than ever before but also more refined tools of analysis. While the more dramatic events transpired mostly in Europe and Asia, the historians who were to make the greatest use of the economic interpretation of these events were mostly Americans. In addition they had the less dramatic "Yankee imperialism" of their own hemisphere to record and assess. A few examples from works by American students of imperialism and international relations will indicate their general method of approach.

For instance, there is among specialists some difference of opinion concerning the part economics played in the origins of the first World War. Probably the great majority regard "economic imperialism" as powerful enough to justify its inclusion as one of the great causes; to some it was the one determining factor. Thus, Turner believes not only that imperialism is inevitable but also that it is chiefly economic,[12] and Schmitt states [13] that "this so-called imperialism has been bitterly condemned, but it was an ineluctable necessity of modern industrialism"—both statements having reference to the origins of the war. Barnes concludes [14] that nationalism, capitalism, imperialism, and militarism all contributed to international anarchy and "conspired" to make the first World War possible.

Fay is somewhat more cautious. He believes that economic imperialism (examples of which are railway concessions and protective tariffs) is usually exaggerated as a cause of the World War; it was not economic jealousy between Great Britain and Germany that made the conflict inevitable, but "prestige, boundaries, armies and navies, the Balance of Power, and possible shiftings in the system of alliances." [15] Occasionally an author frankly states that he does not know where to place most of the blame, holding, for example, that "it is still open to debate whether late nineteenth-century imperialism should be regarded as an economic movement using political weapons, or as a political movement using economic

[12] Turner, *Europe since 1789*, p. 528.
[13] Schmitt, *The Coming of the War, 1914*, I, 5.
[14] Barnes, *World Politics in Modern Civilization*, p. 4.
[15] Fay, *The Origins of the World War*, I, 46.

weapons." [16] It is not a very great step from this position to one of complete dissent from the economic interpretation of imperialism.[17]

The temptation is almost irresistible, once the term "economic imperialism" has been fastened onto contemporary events, to extend its application backwards into the far reaches of history. In addition to ancient imperialism, the historian finds both the "old" and the "new" imperialism of modern times; the "commercial imperialism" of the era between the discovery of America and the Industrial Revolution—the age which saw the rise of mercantilism and ended not only with the rise of industrialism but with the American Revolution as well; the period of "industrial imperialism," which had hardly begun before it slackened under the counter movement of laissez faire and free trade, the latter representing a "twilight zone" [18] (approximately 1763 to 1870) between the old imperialism of the sixteenth, seventeenth, and eighteenth centuries and the period of revival, which began about 1870 and by the end of the century had developed into so-called "financial imperialism."

Within each historic epoch some writers find special types of imperialism at work. The War of 1812 between England and the United States, according to one American economic historian, was an expression of "military imperialism," and the general period is referred to as one of "agricultural imperialism." Following this came "overseas imperialism," which characterized the policy of the United States soon after the Civil War, culminating in the war with Spain in 1898.[19] Another historian, while certain that the same economic factors are at work in modern imperialism as operated under mercantilism (the need for colonies as outlets for population and manufactured goods and as sources of raw materials), nevertheless raises a fundamental question when he says that "no divining rod could accurately reveal the hidden forces that moved the pioneer, the industrialist, the railroad builder, and the working-

---

[16] Carr, *The Twenty Years' Crisis, 1919–1939,* p. 147.

[17] See below, pp. 60–64.

[18] Cf. Clough and Cole, *Economic History of Europe,* p. 617.

[19] Humphrey, *An Economic History of the United States,* especially pp. 172, 174, 315, 419, 425, 436.

man. A belief in God, earth hunger, love of progress, the search for profit, a mere biological restlessness, a dim craving for a better or a fuller life—which was it?" [20]

Imperialism is not only seen as characterizing broad historic eras, but also as a process which goes through several fairly well-defined stages or steps in any given instance of its shortrun development. Thus, Harry Elmer Barnes regards the process as passing through three phases, once the accumulation of large surplus capital makes the search for an outlet inevitable:

1. Merchants and bankers recognize the opportunities for pecuniary gain in certain relatively backward political and economic areas. 2. Their penetration is followed by appeals to the foreign offices of their respective states. 3. These requests lead immediately to military intervention and the political administration of such areas.[21]

The accuracy of this stereotyped pattern of imperialism was really put to the test by the authors of numerous case studies carried on under the direction of Barnes. Professor Jenks, author of *Our Cuban Colony,* found that American imperialism in Cuba has not conformed "to the pattern of political behavior laid down by the evolutionary school of political science," which somewhat naïvely "has charted the course of the imperialist process in a series of well-defined stages." [22] In a study of Santo Domingo, in the same series, Professor Knight was impressed by the lack of similarity between the European type of imperialism which gave some credence to the idea of well-defined stages and the American type of activity in the western hemisphere. He speaks of the innumerable allusions in Santo Domingo to "Yankee Imperialism" and the "Yankee peril," and to widely circulated works by outsiders which refer to the country as a "protectorate," a "virtual protectorate," an "actual protectorate," a "financial protectorate," and a victim of economic imperialism.

[20] Kirkland, *A History of American Economic Life,* p. 711. Cf. also Faulkner, *American Economic History,* pp. 650–52; Bogart, *Economic History of the American People,* pp. 758–59, 783, in which the "need" for markets, raw materials, and opportunities for investment is used to explain the United States' entry into new paths of imperialism; and Flügel and Faulkner, *Readings in the Economic and Social History of the United States.*

[21] Found in Barnes' introduction to a number of "Studies in American Imperialism," of which he was editor. The first of these studies was Jenks, *Our Cuban Colony.*

[22] Jenks, *op. cit.,* pp. 3–4.

All of these terms [he says] can be misleading if carelessly applied to the territorial expansion of the United States or the business of Americans abroad. One writer after another has borrowed a terminology which grew up around the penetration of Africa and Asia by rival European States, and have artificially forced the American experience into the same mould.[23]

The author of *The Bankers in Bolivia*,[24] however, is frankly a strong believer in the general views of Hobson and other developers of the evolutionary school of thought with respect to the imperialist process. She found in Bolivia the "stuff of which spheres of influence, protectorates, economic imperialism in short are made," [25] and declares that economic nationalism, which has become the guiding principle of American foreign policy, will sooner or later express itself in "dollar diplomacy" in Bolivia.[26]

Even more decidedly leftist was an earlier study in American Imperialism (which was not in the Barnes series), the well-known book on *Dollar Diplomacy*, by Scott Nearing and Joseph Freeman. These authors proclaim their belief in economic determinism and in the thesis that imperialism is an inescapable phase of capitalist development; there is no line of demarcation between the economics of penetration and the politics of intervention.[27] They are thoroughly Marxian in their point of view and pay their respects to the theories of Hobson, Woolf, Hilferding, and Lenin. In a later book Nearing "follows the Marxian method," which takes him considerably beyond Hobson, who "stressed the economic aspect of imperialism," to the views of Lenin, who "added the development aspect—placing imperialism in its historic setting." [28]

No writer has employed the term "imperialism" more forcefully or with a more varied and universal application than Professor Parker T. Moon, whose *Imperialism and World Politics* has become almost a classic among the histories dealing with the long line of events preceding the first World War. Moon draws heavily on the ideas found in Hobson's *Imperialism*, which he calls "the classic indictment of imperialist doctrines and practices." [29] To

[23] Melvin M. Knight, *The Americans in Santo Domingo*, p. 161.
[24] Margaret Alexander Marsh; also in the series edited by Barnes.
[25] *Ibid.*, p. 3.      [26] *Ibid.*, pp. 126, 133.
[27] Nearing and Freeman, *Dollar Diplomacy*, pp. xiii–xv.
[28] Nearing, *The Twilight of Empire*, p. 15.
[29] Moon, *Imperialism and World Politics*, p. 475n.

Moon, as to Hobson, the causes of imperialism are inherent in surplus manufactures and surplus capital, the latter having become dominant in twentieth-century imperialism. These surpluses, he says, were "an inevitable result of the economic laws governing capitalist production." [30]

Similar views are held by the English publicist H. N. Brailsford, who also pays tribute to Hobson, whose *Imperialism* is described as "one of the most notable contributions of our time to the scientific study of contemporary politics." [31] But there are other theorists besides Hobson to whom the student of imperialism may turn for guidance, although most of them are themselves disciples of Hobson or developed views similar to his. One of these is Leonard Woolf, whose *Economic Imperialism* (1920) is often cited as a source of doctrinal support.[32] Woolf gives even more emphasis to the economic factor (as compared with non-economic motives) than did Hobson, and calls "economic imperialism" the logical application of capitalism to internationalism,[33] while at the same time rejecting the "fatalistic view of history" as a delusion.[34] Thus the theory of economic imperialism spreads, but directly or indirectly nearly all the doctrines go back to Hobson as the starting point, and as each new voice becomes authoritative new names are added to the list of the theorists of imperialism.[35]

Most students of American imperialism present a vigorous indictment of the way in which the American government and American business interests have treated the people and the resources of the areas into which penetration has been made and of the governments of the penetrated areas for allowing their countries and their people to be shamelessly exploited. Jenks believes that American

[30] *Ibid.*, pp. 30–31.

[31] Brailsford, *The War of Steel and Gold*, p. 74.

[32] As, for example, by Herbert F. Fraser, who, in his *Foreign Trade and World Politics*, p. 105, says of Woolf that he is "the foremost British student of the subject and I have been greatly influenced by his writings."

[33] Woolf, *Economic Imperialism*, p. 101.

[34] *Ibid.*, p. 9. In an introduction to Woolf, *International Government*, p. xiii, Bernard Shaw adds his own support with the observation that "the wise man looks for the cause of war not in Nietzsche's gospel of the Will to Power, or Lord Roberts's far blunter gospel of the British Will to Conquer, but in the custom house."

[35] Nowhere have I found a more striking similarity to Hobson's views than in Nathaniel Peffer, "Peace or War," in Joseph Barnes, ed., *Empire in the East*, pp. 297–318.

imperialism in Cuba was manifest in the "empire of American business," and yet it was not this element of the imperialist process which wanted war; the war-mongers were mostly politicians.[36] The causes of the Spanish-American War, in short, were not economic; they arose out of the spirit of journalistic and practical jingoism, heightened by the infectious spirit of competitive imperialism in other parts of the world.

In a similar vein Knight declares that "the real 'Yankee peril' in the Dominican Republic is the process of economically North-Americanizing the western hemisphere."[37] The menace consists of "the unpremeditated effects of our commercial efficiency, backed by highly organized and generally well-intentioned government services, which are nevertheless often blind to the consequences of what they promote. Whether or not this is 'economic imperialism,' it is none the less dangerous for being largely unconscious."[38]

In Central America the United Fruit Company, according to another study in the Barnes series, "throttled competitors, dominated governments, manacled railroads, ruined planters, choked co-operatives, domineered over workers, fought organized labor, and exploited consumers. Such usage of power by a corporation of a strongly industrialized nation in relatively weak foreign countries constitutes a variety of economic imperialism."[39] The United Fruit Company is "'a State within a State.' It is more than that: it is an empire superimposed upon numerous American states and controlling many phases of inter-American relations."[40] While the United States government has not used its public power to support this powerful corporation—apparently because the "Banana Empire" has been strong enough to do as it pleases without such support—neither has it used its power to check this sort of private

[36] Jenks, *Our Cuban Colony*, pp. 6, 53–55.

[37] *The Americans in Santo Domingo*, p. 176.

[38] *Ibid.*, p. 165. In a textbook on European economic history, of which Barnes and Knight were joint authors with Felix Flügel, is found this brief discussion of imperialism: "Where the flow of the people toward the resources, and vice versa, is arbitrarily interfered with by political means, the process is often called 'economic imperialism.' Economics is only the aim and the tool, however. Imperialism is really political, and is always associated with the *citizenship* of the people who move, the *nationality* of the capital invested, and the *political frontiers* crossed by the goods involved."—Knight, Barnes, and Flügel, *Economic History of Europe*, p. 745.

[39] Kepner and Soothill, *The Banana Empire*, p. 336.     [40] *Ibid.*, p. 255.

imperialism, nor, for that matter, have the governments of the countries in which the corporation operates.[41]

These case studies of imperialism [42] are indeed powerful indictments. There is no gainsaying that real evils exist in situations of the sort described, but for the most part they are evils which can be matched where no "international relations" exist, in "strongly industrialized" nations, and in those in a less-advanced stage of industrial development—in short, wherever monopoly power has been allowed to go uncurbed towards the ultimate goal of creating "a State within a State." Private monopoly, left unchecked, goes far beyond purely economic means to gain its ends, and the means it uses are identical in nature with those of imperialism.

Given the causes of imperialism, or at least its important factors, and given the indictment, what do these writers think should be done to correct old evils and to prevent new ones from arising? It is largely the old problem of what to do with colonies. Knight, for one, came to his answer, not in his study of Santo Domingo, but in a later study of Morocco, which furnishes an example of "open door imperialism." The open-door policy as applied to colonies means, of course, that the colonies are kept open to the free trade of the world, but Professor Knight's point is that these doors have not really been open, but latched on the inside (hence the phrase, "open door imperialism"). "The permanent unlatching of these doors," says Knight, "assumes either the growth of free trade outside or permanent irresponsibility inside." [43] He reviews three possible alternatives to old-fashioned imperialism: (1) political redistribution of colonial territories—which the "haves" have rejected because it would "merely whet appetites and subject native populations to the confusion of successive national systems and languages"; [44] (2) international mandates—which would require "a more adequate international authority than any existing at present"; and (3) permitting colonies to remain in present hands "but denaturing the military, commercial, and political causes of

41 *Ibid.,* pp. 356–60.
42 Others appearing in the same series under the editorship of Barnes are: Rippy *The Capitalists and Colombia;* and Bailey W. Diffie and Justine Whitfield Diffie, *Porto Rico.*
43 Melvin M. Knight, *Morocco as a French Economic Venture,* p. 241.
44 *Ibid.,* p. 240.

strife" [45]—which seems unlikely under the present tendencies towards national self-containment.

In view of the barriers in the way of these alternatives, Knight sees little hope for improvement, unless it be in the mandate type of solution or in the mutual and friendly termination of such relations, such as has occurred between the United States and the Philippines. But unless public order is maintained in these freed areas and conventional economic and social relations maintained, he believes that no area "will be let alone in a world shrunken by cheap transport." [46]

If free trade and open doors are out of the question, and if mandates will not work, the other alternative that suggests itself (perhaps more forcibly to most people who write on imperialism than any other solution) is "socialism." Back of this proposal is the conviction, as Barnes sees it, that "Nationalism, Capitalism, Imperialism, and Militarism" [47] all contribute to the international anarchy that leads to war, and the further conviction that the League of Nations and the mandate system have proved unable to stop the old struggle over raw materials, markets, and capital investments, which, as Barnes said in 1930, still "goes merrily on," conspiring to bring about another World War.[48] Although Barnes was critical of the single-track dogma of the socialistically inclined regarding the causes of imperialism, he was, nevertheless highly favorable to the socialist remedy. Socialism might not cause imperialism to disappear immediately, he says, but "if we could have a world-wide socialist revolution which successfully carried into immediate execution upon an international scale the transition from an acquisitive economy based upon private profit, to one founded on the objective of production for social service, then, indeed, imperialism might disappear rapidly." [49]

This is very general language, but, omitting the details and the usual polemics, it gives the substance of the socialist position, which

[45] *Ibid.*, p. 240.  [46] *Ibid.*, p. 242.

[47] This is part of the subtitle to Barnes, *World Politics in Modern Civilization* (see above, p. 46n).

[48] *Ibid.*; cf. pp. 104, 189–90, 287, 525.

[49] This is to be found in Barnes' introduction to Jenks, *Our Cuban Colony* (p. xii), and appears in the introduction to the earlier "Studies in American Imperialism" (e. g., by Knight, or Marsh), but is dropped from the later Studies (e. g., by Kepner and Soothill).

is a sweeping condemnation of capitalism and all its works. Those who think that the remedial measures are to be found in correcting certain evils of capitalism without destroying it as a system are usually somewhat more specific in their recommendations. They are likely to propose curbs or embargoes on foreign investment or the curbing of saving (by the payment of higher wages and lower profits) so that automatically there will be less for foreign investment. Moon echoes Hobson when he suggests that what will curb the temptation to resort to imperialism is "more wages and more spending, and less profits and less investing. . . . As it becomes more difficult to export surplus capital, the remedy is to spend the surplus." [50] Culbertson would like to see "the abandonment by nations of all aggressive economic measures, such as monopolies of essential raw materials and economic penetration of foreign countries by loans or investments." [51]

The idea seems to be that lending abroad inevitably leads to bad relations and trouble, while lending or using the same money internally promotes domestic harmony and avoids international disharmony. This feeling is doubtless justified, especially where money is loaned abroad primarily or even largely for political (including military and strategic) purposes and under conditions which are preferential and discriminatory, as when the lender (especially the lending nation or government) seeks exclusive rights of some sort as a condition for making the loan. But this simply means that the motive and purpose behind the transfer of money and the specific uses to which it is put, not the mere fact of lending and borrowing, are the causes of trouble. Obviously, if loans are for "imperialistic" purposes they are likely to cause imperialistic difficulties and had better be kept at home or used abroad without political ties and commitments. Money used internally with sinister intent can also lead to trouble.

[50] Moon, *Imperialism and World Politics*, p. 540.

[51] Culbertson, *International Economic Policies*, p. 426. See also, by the same author, "Raw Materials and Foodstuffs in the Commercial Policies of Nations," *Annals of the American Academy of Political and Social Science*, CXII (March, 1924), 1–145. In this study the author takes the position that wars result largely from economic causes (p. 5), and his discussion of "economic imperialism" (pp. 5–6) is in the same vein. Although he believes the roots of modern imperialism are to be found in the tendency of capitalism to produce more goods than can be sold at a profit, and of capitalists constantly to seek new markets, Culbertson is careful to add that such statements "are not made in condemnation of capitalism." (p. 5)

## WEIGHING IMPERIALISM IN THE BALANCE

It is sometimes assumed that if it can be shown that imperialism does not pay, a vital blow has been struck at the roots of the institution, providing that imperialists or would-be imperialists would seriously study the findings.

A century and a half of economic theory and studies has shown conclusively that mercantilism and protectionism are wrong methods of increasing the wealth of nations, but such warnings by economists have had utterly disappointing results so far as their effect on policy is concerned. It looks as if statistics rather than mere theorizing could supply an answer to such a question as, "How much does the tariff cost the people of a nation in a given period?" Economists know that it is impossible to give a statistical answer to questions of this kind, because it is impossible to segregate the effect of tariffs on prices from other effects. No attempt would ever be made by an economist, therefore, to draw up a "balance sheet of protectionism."

Drawing up balance sheets of imperialism is a less difficult proposition, because it is possible to balance a country's exports to its colonies against its imports and to find, or fairly accurately calculate, the cost of administration, so that expense and income can be reduced to a matter of dollars and cents. The results may not be very satisfactory or conclusive from a broad economic point of view, because, as in the case of tariffs, there are a number of questions which cannot be answered statistically, but so far as it goes, drawing up balance sheets of imperialism is a salutary exercise.

It is almost a foregone conclusion that such studies will show that "imperialism does not pay," as does Grover Clark's ambitious *The Balance Sheets of Imperialism* (1936).[52] Knight's study of Morocco is also an attempt to appraise a special case of colonialism in "accounting terms." He reaches the conclusion that the French colonial empire, judged by trade alone, has been "an expensive national luxury during the depression period," and, although better trade conditions are optimistically hoped for once

[52] See also Grover Clark, *A Place in the Sun,* which was intended as a companion volume to the compilation of statistics in his *The Balance Sheets of Imperialism.*

the national investment is salvaged, Knight thinks such an outcome unlikely, since more than a century of French colonial ventures in Algeria have never paid for the investment. He also points out that "colonies may contain business ventures of French citizens without being business ventures of the French nation." [53]

In an earlier study of the French Empire, Constant Southworth also comes to the conclusion that it has been a losing venture economically. Without anywhere using the term "economic imperialism" (he speaks only of "colonialism"), and with very little philosophizing, beyond the observation that it may perhaps be futile to try to evaluate colonization in the light of cold business calculations, because such a process "is like describing a beautiful woman in terms of statistics," [54] the author gets down at once to a concrete economic analysis in terms of costs and profits. He concludes that the French colonies have been an unprofitable venture for France from an economic point of view and that this situation will likely continue for many years. He also suggests that the same could be said for most colonial ventures by other countries. In any case, once nations learn to evaluate their colonial possessions in money terms—and find them a losing business—Southworth assumes that some semblance of rationality will begin to be found in the actions and policies of nations. Perhaps he forgets that beautiful women have a habit of wanting to look their prettiest regardless of the statistics and that men are still willing to pay the bills.

As these studies indicate, it is not difficult to show that imperialism costs the colonial power more than it gets in return, even though certain groups or individuals profit, either at the expense of the native population, the domestic population, or both. Leaving special groups or individuals out of the reckoning, the question is whether the state viewed as a corporation has a good investment, as shown by its balance-sheet of trade, the interest returns on capital

[53] Melvin M. Knight, *Morocco as a French Economic Venture*, pp. 196, 222. See also Priestley, *France Overseas*, for similar conclusions: "Colonialism is an inveterate habit of the Western peoples, which involves pride of possession and activity, a yearning for prestige, regardless of success or profit" (pp. 396–97); "The determination was to hang on to imperialism in spite of the cost, let alone the debt" (p. 400); "It is obvious that the possession of colonies is a political liability rather than an asset" (concluding remark, p. 435).

[54] Southworth, *The French Colonial Venture*, p. 8.

sunk in productive enterprises, and its various outlays for administration, "pacification," and other such expenditures which may be
regarded as overhead costs.

The answer depends to a large extent upon whether the colony
is an open-door one or assimilated. If the former, the country
which acquires it, presumably at some cost, and spends money on
its administration, in all sorts of ways, may have a less favorable
balance to show from its exploitation because of these expenses
than the other countries which exploit without cost to themselves;
it may even have a negative balance in contrast to another country's
positive balance. The only economic justification which the mother
country would have in such a case would lie in the hope that in the
future it could recoup its losses. Failing this, it must fall back on
nationalistic sentiment—the desire to possess a colony regardless
of the cost or to keep another power from seizing it—in which case
it can easily be convinced that the open door was a mistake from the
first, to be rectified as soon as possible. Rectification would entail
the adoption of a domestic protectionist policy by the mother
country if it had previously had none.

If a country decides in the beginning to protect its investment
by restricting or excluding participation by other countries, it may
still remain questionable whether it can make the venture pay.
This depends partly on the richness of the possession, but whatever
gains are realized because of its exclusive control may be shared
in part, though indirectly, by the countries with which it trades.
If a colony makes the owner country richer, the benefits will be
disseminated in the course of trade; it can buy more from
other countries and thus enable other countries to buy more from
it.[55]

If it is assumed that some benefit would accrue even if the colony
were owned by another country, or if it were open equally to all
countries, the problem is not to determine the total benefit from
possession, but the benefit accruing from possession over and above
the benefit from nonpossession or nonexclusion. "It is the special
advantages derived from possession that make a colony an asset;
without these, the objections raised by the Manchester school in

[55] John A. Hobson observes that "it is not difficult to conceive cases where another
nation might enjoy a larger share of the results of a trade than the nation which
owned the private markets of this trade."—*Imperialism*, p. 72.

the last century against the cost of maintaining colonies once more become valid." [56]

The study from which the above quotation is taken also observes that it is practically impossible to isolate all the items of profit and loss to the various participants in the development of a colony, and that "the possession of a colonial empire will orientate the whole of the economy of the metropolitan Power, and its repercussions will be correspondingly hard to estimate." [57]

A private enterprise may willingly undergo a period of outlay and no income if it can foresee, after the developmental period, a period of prosperity at least enduring enough to compensate for the cost. But if the enterprise in a reasonable time fails to pay for itself, it is abandoned. Here the balance sheet rules, and not even pride and sentiment can delay an accounting. However, if the state decides to step in and save this or that enterprise (which soon creates an inescapable precedent for extending like favors to other enterprises) it can do so, but only at a cost, and the cost is measured in the levies made on more prosperous enterprises in order, to subsidize the less fortunate. By a leveling-down and a leveling-up process the state can save industries from failure, and by regarding colonies as enterprises worth saving by the same means, the state can keep on indefinitely convincing itself that it pays to do so. A balance sheet is of some use to a firm that knows that its fate depends upon what the balance sheet shows, but it is of no account if the decision has already been made to perpetuate the enterprise regardless of what the balance sheet shows. An imperial balance sheet, like that of a planned economy, might serve as a guide for certain shifts in policy, but it is never intended to serve as an evaluator of the policy as such. Empires and planned economies are not run that way.

If a country's colonial trade shows an increasingly profitable trend relative to its trade with the rest of the world, it might be deduced that here is evidence of a paying tendency at work. But if the colonizing country assimilates its colonies into its own economic system by imperial preference and a closed-door policy, obviously trade with the colonies must increase, whether or not it is more advantageous than trade with outside countries.

[56] Royal Institute of International Affairs, *The Colonial Problem*, p. 42.
[57] *Ibid.*, pp. 40, 43.

As Knight remarks,[58] a colony such as Morocco may itself be an economic liability to France, and at the same time be an inseparable part of a French economic asset—meaning by "asset" the entire French possessions in North Africa. Taken alone, such a liability, when considered as a supplementary part of the larger economic asset which is France itself, must certainly seem a justifiable luxury to the imperialist. At any rate, he is unlikely to be impressed by appraisals by economists who decide, on the basis of statistics, that this or that colony should be kept or dropped according to whether it pays its way. One might as well try to decide the fate of Savoy on such grounds—Savoy having been taken from Italy—or the fate of New Mexico, this state having been taken from Mexico. But if these territories should be given back to the original owners because they are a drain on the present owners, the problem of drain is not necessarily solved. To speak of a colony as a liability is to say that more money is being spent to hold and develop it than it yields in return; but obviously it must be an actual or potential asset to somebody, whether it is a "possession" or not, if it has any inhabitants and resources at all. Colonies are not regarded as liabilities when they are free, or held as open-door possessions in which anyone is free to invest capital or sell goods if he sees any profit in it. They become liabilities only when a state, which is more likely than a private enterprise to try to get blood out of a turnip, either tries to make them pay (usually meaning only that it is undertaking to create a self-contained empire regardless of the cost) or spends huge sums in order to keep someone else from getting them, or both.

Even if it is possible to gauge the absolute worth of a colony and also its relative worth in comparison with other possessions—and usually trade statistics will give a rough idea of this—there is no assurance that this will have any effect on the policy of the state: it may spend millions on a poor economic investment to pacify natives or build up defenses, to thousands spent on a richer colony where these problems do not exist or are less pressing.

It is easy enough to guess why private individuals invest in, go to, or trade with colonies, or for that matter with any other country. By far the greater part of such activity stems from the profit motive,

[58] *Morocco as a French Economic Venture*, p. 180.

just as investing, moving about, or engaging in business is motivated within a country. But there is very little evidence which permits us to assume that a state is primarily concerned with making profits when it enters upon colonial ventures. It may hope that its activity in this direction will help its own nationals in the quest for wealth and thus indirectly benefit their country; it may trust that its own enterprises will pay their way, and more; it may justify present losses in the hope of future gains; it may even be paternalistic and generous towards the native populations—all of which is to the good. But the study of the colonial question is likely to lead any objective observer to the conclusion that such thoughts are mainly afterthoughts and that imperialism is practiced regardless of the cost, and for much the same reasons that military preparedness is supported regardless of cost. As institutions, both imperialism and militarism constitute the sort of enterprise which uses the resources and every favorable aspect of the economic system—even the economic system as a whole—to further ends which are not themselves economic.

## DISSENT FROM THE ECONOMIC INTERPRETATION

The tendency so apparent a few years ago for historians and others to interpret the course of events in terms of economic concepts shows a few signs of weakening. Reluctance to use the term "imperialism," especially "economic imperialism," was apparent in Jenks's study of Cuba and in Knight's study of Santo Domingo. Increasingly in recent years there has been strong criticism of this particular type of economic interpretation of history, in some cases from historians, but more particularly from economists. Much of this criticism has appeared in reviews.

Professor Blakeslee, in reviewing Moon's *Imperialism and World Politics*, found so many (he counted seventeen) different uses or meanings of the word "imperialism" that he was moved to declare that "it is certainly misleading to describe by the same word, imperialist, both the European statesman who plans cold-bloodedly to seize 1000 square miles of territory in Africa and the university instructor who invests $1000 in a French government bond." [59]

[59] Blakeslee [Review of Thomas Parker Moon, *Imperialism and World Politics*], *American Historical Review*, XXXII (April, 1927), 597–99.

Professor Jacob Viner, in reviewing a study of imperialism,[60] says of the author's use of the term "imperialism":

He has acquired an undue attachment to the elastic concept of "imperialism," and he has used it as if it were a mystic formula whose mere reiteration, if in sufficiently derogatory tones, will reveal the keys to all the riddles of the history of European relations with backward peoples in the last half-century. The term as it has come to be used by many historians is so elusive of definition and covers practices and procedures of such variant and even contradictory character that it has become a downright nuisance.[61]

In his own studies in the field of international relations, Viner has studiously avoided the term.[62]

Another economist, likewise, in an extensive analysis of foreign investments and war, remarks that "imperialism" is a word to be avoided;[63] and still another avoids it because "it is difficult to assign it any precise meaning at all."[64] Occasionally criticism is directed against drawing parallels between European and American types of imperialism. If the term "economic imperialism" is used "to connote a deliberate and self-seeking policy of territorial or financial aggrandizement deliberately practised by the United States government without any particular regard for the prior rights, interests and desires of the foreign peoples affected—as was true of much of the expansion of the European countries in Africa —then the term is used erroneously, when applied to the generality of our relations with the Latin American regions just named" (the countries of the Caribbean and Central America and Mexico).[65]

In his study of Morocco, Knight declares that " 'economic imperialism' is not an economist's expression, and does not lend itself to economic calculations. In a commercial appraisal, past outlays are written down or off to fit market value or prospects. Save for that, and for guide posts and warnings by analogy, they are dead

---

[60] Blaisdell, European Financial Control in the Ottoman Empire.

[61] Viner [Review of Donald C. Blaisdell, European Financial Control in the Ottoman Empire], Journal of Political Economy, XXXVII (December, 1929), 746.

[62] See, for example, Viner, "International Finance and Balance of Power Diplomacy, 1880–1914," The Southwestern Political and Social Science Quarterly, IX (March, 1929), 407–51.

[63] Staley, War and the Private Investor, p. 416. In a later book (World Economy in Transition, p. 115), Staley does not avoid the term.

[64] Angell, Financial Foreign Policy of the United States, p. 5.

[65] Ibid.

issues." [66] But imperialism does not cease to be a dead issue merely because the costs are great.

An outstanding historical work which shows a keen appreciation of the new point of view and its criticism of the old is Professor Langer's *Diplomacy of Imperialism*. In one succinct paragraph he contrasts the old views with the new, and gives his own.

Imperialism is a word which is now in bad repute, partly because of a psychological reaction to what it was supposed to stand for, partly because it is generally used in so loose a sense that it means nothing to the historian or the political scientist. As everyone knows, the term was originally connected with the word *Imperator*, and was frequently associated with the ideas of dictatorial power, highly centralized government, arbitrary methods of administration, and in general with the ideas of Caesarism and Bonapartism. In this sense it is now almost obsolete. For our purposes it may be taken to mean simply the rule or control, political or economic, direct or indirect, of one state, nation or people over other similar groups, or perhaps one might better say the disposition, urge or striving to establish such rule or control.[67]

Professor Langer has here merely presented a working definition of imperialism, stated in terms of control, without commitment as to "fundamental causes." Thus defined, it is equally applicable to ancient and modern control of the kind described. "Taken in this sense, imperialism is probably as old as recorded history." [68] As for the "purely theoretical side of the problem," Langer remarks:

The historian . . . is apt to feel that the abstractions of the political scientist are of little help in reconstructing or understanding the past. Suffice it to say, then, that there is no agreement among those who have analyzed imperialism as to what the motives are that impel a state or people to expand its territory or control.[69]

After this cautious beginning the study proceeds without recourse to those concepts which to many other writers have become

66 Knight, *Morocco as a French Economic Venture*, p. 184. In "Water and the Course of Empire in North Africa," *Quarterly Journal of Economics*, XLIII (November, 1928), 44–93, Knight speaks in a similar vein; speaking of the economic advantages and material improvements resulting from French influence in North Africa, with equal stress on the evils involved, he says (p. 93): "Once we outgrow the delusion that 'economic imperialism' is a simple or uniform process, susceptible of dramatization by the use of a few stage monsters stuffed with imaginary virtues and vices as if they were persons, we perceive that very little is known about the subject."
67 Langer, *The Diplomacy of Imperialism, 1890–1902*, I, 67.
68 *Ibid.*
69 *Ibid.*, pp. 67–68. There follows a brief discussion of various viewpoints.

indispensable, and it covers a period of time which fairly bristles with the stuff of which imperialism is made. It is significant that the author deals with the *diplomacy* of imperialism during this period. He does not, however, neglect to point out the connection between national policy and its industrial background. Anti-imperialism in England, and its concomitants, laissez faire and Manchester free trade, "was the direct reflection of England's industrial supremacy in the mid-century. . . . In this scheme of things there was no place for empire or expansion." [70] But after 1870 England's real economic difficulty arose "from the steady accumulation of capital and the ever more pressing need for opportunities for profitable investment." [71] Therefore, as Langer says later, he has paid special attention to British imperialism because the British, while not alone imperialistic, were, "of all peoples, the most imperially minded" and "because the political and economic structure of Britain of itself brought the imperial movement to its most perfect flower." [72]

It is not clear from such words just how far Langer has broken away from the influence of those who emphasize the economic factors in imperialism. What seems clear from his whole treatment, however, is that he is merely talking about the economic *aspects* of imperialism, whereas others talk about its economic *causes*.

More and more the evidence accumulates that historians are aware that the economic interpretation of history has been over-emphasized and that it has often spoiled that sense of proportion which should distinguish good historical writing. To some extent historians were driven to overemphasize this particular formula by being made to feel, by the physical and social scientists, that they were old-fashioned and unscientific in not grasping the opportunity to make use of modern tools of analysis and interpretation. Some historians are now beginning to feel that they were misled and that the writing of history must regain or acquire a better sense of balance. It must deal with causes and effects, but it must proceed with caution. "The old overemphasis on political materials is practically ended," says a historian of the new persuasion, but he cautions that "our own age is apt to think that economic interest is the most obvious motive for men of any period and the historian who

[70] *Ibid.*, p. 70.  [71] *Ibid.*, p. 73.  [72] *Ibid.*, p. 96.

is not careful may find himself overemphasizing the profit motive in his study of the past." [73] An economic historian, writing in the same work, points out that although the economic interpretation is still with us, it is already old-fashioned, and we are now being asked to pass on to "approaches"—such as "the cultural approach"—which may carry historians too far in some other direction.[74]

In none of this criticism do the writers mean to imply that imperialism does not exist or that governments or business interests are guiltless of some of the worst charges made against them in dealing with backward races and regions. The criticism is directed against loose and inconsistent usage of the terms, especially the expression "economic imperialism"; drawing parallels between European and American practices where little or no parallelism exists; and assuming economic motives when a more careful appraisal of the facts would describe the motives and causes as political. At the same time there is usually evident a vague feeling that there is still room for the concept of economic imperialism if only the words can be properly defined.

[73] Strayer, ed., *The Interpretation of History*, pp. 22, 25 (The quotations are from Strayer's introduction).

[74] Heaton, "The Economic Impact on History," in Strayer, ed., *The Interpretation of History*, p. 104.

# IV ·

## THE SEARCH FOR A FORMULA

IT IS now the fashion to deride the old simple unilateral explanations of imperialism and war—those which single out the sinful nature of men, their wickedness and pure cussedness, the fighting instinct, race hatreds—because they are too vague, too general, and give no practical clues as to remedies. They are regarded as almost, but not quite, as naïve as the reasons supposedly assigned universally by primitive man—that supernatural forces such as gods and devils impose war upon sinful man. From the external and supernatural, emphasis shifted to natural causes, and from this to social forces.

### WAR AS A SOCIAL FORCE

At this stage the matter of analyzing how social forces create war appears to become the special province of the sociologist. To take a recent study [1] as an example, the treatment is to list the various explanations which, unlike the discarded beliefs of earlier times, now have some standing in the court of students of social problems: biological causes (having to do with the "competitive subsistence" of peoples); psychological causes (a matter of the emotions rather than, we might say, of the belly); social or cultural factors; religious and moral causes; political causes, and finally, but usually not least, economic causes, culminating in "imperialism" as the modern expression and center of all the imaginable economic factors and special-interest groups, such as monopolists, bankers, and their creatures the politicians. Here, at last, if we are to accept a common judgment, is the real culprit. A quotation will indicate how firm this judgment can be.

Economic causes [says the author of *War and Its Causes*] are especially potent in the making of modern wars, and they always have been impor-

[1] Bernard, *War and Its Causes.*

tant. They are in many ways closely related to the biological causes, since they frequently become dominant in the effort of a people to find food or food-producing resources (such as land, raw materials, and markets) as means to the subsistence of a people. Those modern causes of war known as imperialism and mercantilism are highly prominent among the economic causes. In fact, any other cause or set of causes of war which can be translated into economic terms or in which economic motives become dominant may, when thus transformed, be called economic causes, as when an overpopulated group seeks to supply its subsistance needs by means of the conquest of foreign territory.[2]

How jealously this view can be defended comes out in the further statement that the recent reaction against attributing wars to economic causes is partly the preference of the conservative historian to emphasize political causes.

But one of the chief causes of this trend away from an economic explanation [says the author] is the opposition which the arch materialists, the industrialists and the financiers manifest toward it. They will not willingly allow any theory to stand in the way of their untrammeled pursuit of the gains arising from the far-reaching economic exploitation in which they are engaged. They recognize the uncomfortable implications of this theory for their own practices and they condemn and make counter propaganda against it.[3]

In contrast with the potency of social forces, of which economic factors are declared to be the most important in causing war, the idea of war being caused by forces which have no conceivable dependence on economic activities and motives must, indeed, seem blind and superficial. And from this point of view the thesis that "the cause of war is war," or that war and imperialism are ancient behavior patterns appearing as atavisms in a modern society, where the weight of economic activity is against such conflicts, or that political causes can stand independently of economic motives, is likely to be dismissed as a thesis to be shunned by the scientific mind.

Yet precisely because it is possible to define economic activity in terms of something more than human selfishness and deadly rivalries, it is also possible to consider the interpretation of imperialism and war in terms other than economic terms. In the modern age, regardless of how much economic causation there may

[2] *Ibid.*, pp. 229–30.   [3] *Ibid.*, p. 325.

have been at first, imperialism and war may represent behavior patterns which have little or nothing to do with economic activity in the sense of cause and effect. It is entirely possible to think of them as institutions capable of standing independently as ends in themselves. That they use economic resources is another matter, entirely different from the question whether imperialism and war are caused by the desire to acquire economic resources.

Much as we may be forced to criticize the economic interpretation of history, the fact remains that it marked a big advance over the notion that war and conquest are mere visitations upon man for his wickedness—catastrophes ordained by God and carried out by the devil; it was "a healthy antidote to some of the romantic, political, military, or other unilinear or surface interpretations; it was even a good antidote to the refusal to interpret at all." [4] But in going all out for the theory that man's actions can be traced to the fact of his dependence on material things, the new interpreters of history went too far in the other direction and forgot that the pursuit of power can arise from a number of causes in which economic motives play no evident or conceivable part. Fear, the father of hate, has certainly played an enormous role in sending armies and navies against an enemy possessed of similar emotional qualities, across lands and seas which of necessity become the pawns of conquest. And those familiar stand-bys of the history books (which generally are given a place considerably below the economic factors)—love of adventure, prestige ("face"), strategy, civilizing missions, and political and ideological clashes—have certainly been potent causes of imperialism and war. Nor is there any conceivable economic cause in the vicious circle wherein war itself engenders more war. Militarism as a profession, feeding upon and perpetuating itself, combined with the love of power can be a delight and an end in itself, an all-consuming passion capable of perverting the material bases of welfare to the services of war and conquest. And there is truth also in the simple conclusion which history has taught some of its chroniclers, that imperialism is a demonstration of the principle that the more you have the more you have to have to hold what you have. Simplest of all, yet who can deny it some hearing, is

[4] Heaton, "The Economic Impact on History," in Strayer, ed., *The Interpretation of History*, p. 105.

the blunt view that imperialism and war are results of pure human cussedness.

These powerful, yet uncomplex, motives and vicious circles, simple as they are, seem somehow to elude most of the modern interpreters of history. Their place has been so largely taken by the economic—essentially capitalistic—interpretation of modern imperialism and war, that one can only conclude that the scientific mind feels obliged to foreswear obvious causes and seek the underlying and mysterious, the hidden and complex forces. This would be all right were it not for the danger that these forces, particularly the economic ones, may be imagined rather than real—supplied by the interpreter rather than merely uncovered. As such they may also be dangerous in that they create conflict and cause war, for these are the stuff of which ideologies are made; the clash of nations over ideological differences itself attests to the reality and power of ideas and notions, compared with which real economic forces may be as nothing.

It is not easy to accept the idea that power is an effective end in itself; it is much easier to regard it as a means to some other end. Power regarded as an end leaves nothing more to be said except that its users employ all available means to accomplish the end. But power regarded as a means opens up enormous possibilities for identifying it with political power, economic power, and every other field of human activity which strengthens the hand of the seekers after power. There is a great confusion here in the tendency to identify economic power with "naked power," yet nearly all the interpretative history written in the past two or three generations has been based on the assumption that economic power and naked power are identical. This assumption, erroneous though it is, gives the interpreter of history something tangible to grasp, because the concept of economic power adds to the general concept of power a dimension which enables the interpreter to talk in terms of tangibles such as economic surpluses, the struggle for markets, and the defense of territory, with a feeling that he is on the track of real and analyzable forces. Armed with these concepts, the interpreter of history has much to talk about; he can go far beyond the simple thesis that power as an end in itself uses all available means to accomplish the end.

If the theory of war and conflict were as simple as this, and if it were accepted by historical writers as a self-evident truth, there would be no need to bolster it with an economic formula. If men fight for perfectly obvious reasons, the historian can hardly be expected to supply the reasons. It would hardly occur to him to account for every battle in a war; therefore, why should it seem any more necessary to account for every war in the universal business of fighting?

Through its doctrine of class warfare, based on the clash of economic rivalries between capitalist and worker, and its accompanying parading of economic "inevitables" flowing from the operation of the profit motive and the accumulation of capital, plus the grinding movement of its business-cycle mechanism, which transmutes competition into monopoly, the economic interpretation of history, regardless of whether or not it describes and explains real events, has captivated the minds of untold millions and set them marching towards the socialist victory which from the first is promised as the inevitable end. The climax of this view of history, growing inevitably out of its doctrine of the class struggle, is the doctrine of the struggle between nations. The logic from here on, granting all the past assumptions, is so powerful as to convince its numberless devotees that there can be no other assumptions and no further argument. The whole thing behaves like a law of nature, and who is man to question it, let alone to oppose it?

Once the class struggle is made to appear incontrovertible, it is only a step to the struggle of nations for supremacy. There have been class struggles and international wars, ever since there were classes and nations, but whether they were inevitable or not is immaterial. The whole force of the modern economic interpretation is that they are made inevitable once all the forces which spring from hunger, the scramble for the earth's resources, and human selfishness converge and congeal in capitalist society. Therefore, modern imperialism, say these economic interpreters, is unavoidable, because it is a natural consequence of capitalist institutions. War is, in turn, the inescapable end-product of this imperialism.

Even if it be granted that all wars have had some sort of imperialistic base (they have been fought mostly on land, if not over it), the point made is that only modern imperialism has had a capitalistic base. Consequently, it is not sufficient to answer the economic interpreters by saying that because imperialism and war are eons older than capitalism their modern manifestations cannot be blamed on capitalism. This may have a point, but it is not their point, which is that capitalism not only has not prevented imperialism and war, but indeed at long last has made both inescapable. The final pay-off is that capitalism must be abolished and socialism must become triumphant before we can hope to see an end to these troubles.

The philosopher of history who created this astonishing way of looking at history was, of course, Karl Marx. Neither he nor the majority of his disciples were professional historians; they were practitioners of economic analysis. Not "economists" in the traditional and classical sense, but—in their own minds—endowed with a special insight which the orthodox economists never dreamed of. What they invented and preached was a formula of history regarded by them as a key to its complete understanding. It was left to the historians to make use of the key, and curiously enough many historians who were far from professing any attachment to Marxism or any other brand of socialism have been its most energetic advocates. At least, many have used an interpretation which looks very much like that of Marx, probably without in the least being conscious of the kinship. We need not be too surprised at this, however, because, shorn of all the mysteries and convolutions of Marx's underlying reasoning, the economic interpretation of history is one of the easiest ways of thinking that modern man can acquire. Surrounded as he is with industrialism, money-making, and aggressive business practices, all of which seem to be readily identifiable with capitalism, modern man in general and the historian in particular have reason to be impressed by the impact of these forces upon history.

## RUDIMENTS OF THE ECONOMIC FORMULA

The idea that war and conquest are simply the expression of man's passion to acquire "more" of everything—more goods, more territory, more trade, more opportunity—and the accompanying conviction that there is no stopping place in such acquisition, but that more repeatedly calls for more, is one of the trains of thought leading to the theory of economic imperialism.

The belief that conflict in all its manifestations arises out of man's economic desires is, in some form or other, as old as philosophy and probably almost as old as recorded history itself. Plato, in discussing in what part of the state justice and injustice spring up, contrasts the conditions in a simple and static society with those in a "luxurious State," or "a State at fever-heat." In the latter, people keep adding to their personal possessions until they acquire an appetite for all sorts of exotic things, after which "we must enlarge our borders";

Then a slice of our neighbours' land will be wanted by us for pasture and tillage, and they will want a slice of ours, if, like ourselves, they exceed the limit of necessity, and give themselves up to the unlimited accumulation of wealth. . . . And so we shall go to war . . . we have discovered war to be derived from causes which are also the causes of almost all the evils in States, private as well as public.[5]

From Plato to early modern times there was in intellectual circles wide acceptance of the general view that imperialism and war represent the simple fact that in the exercise of power there is no limit and that the more an imperialist acquires, the more he has to have to hold what he has.

Machiavelli knew very well what this meant: "Men never think they hold what they have securely, unless when they are gaining something new from others." [6] And Thomas Hobbes, in considering the various desires of man, considers first of all the desire for power, which, he says, is

a general inclination of all mankind, a perpetuall and restless desire of Power after power, that ceaseth onely in Death. And the cause of this, is not alwayes that a man hopes for a more intensive delight, than he has already attained to; or that he cannot be content with a moderate power: but because he cannot assure the power and means to live well, which he hath present, without the acquisition of more. And from hence it is, that Kings, whose power is greatest, turn their endeavours to the assuring it at home by Lawes, or abroad by Wars: and when that is done, there

---

[5] *The Republic*, Book ii. See Plato, *The Dialogues*, 3d ed., tr. by B. Jowett, III, 53–55.

[6] Machiavelli, *Discourses on the First Decade of Titus Livius;* tr. from the Italian by Ninian Hill Thomson, Book I, chap. v, p. 26.

succeedeth a new desire. . . . Competition of Riches, Honour, Command, or other power, enclineth to Contention, Enmity, and War.[7]

William Penn, in a remarkably succinct and uncomplex passage, singled out the self-appointed "judges and carvers" of dominions as the chief enemies of all rational plans of international government.

There appears to me [he says] but three things upon which peace is broken, viz., to keep, to recover, or to add. First, to keep what is one's right from the invasion of an enemy; in which I am purely defensive. Secondly, to recover, when I think myself strong enough, that which by violence I or my ancestors have lost by the arms of a stronger power; in which I am offensive. Or, lastly, to increase my dominion by the acquisition of my neighbour's countries, as I find them weak and myself strong. To gratify which passion there will never want some accident or other for a pretence: and knowing my own strength, I will be my own judge and carver.[8]

Rudiments of the economic interpretation, as it is generally understood, clearly reside in these passages, especially those of Machiavelli and Hobbes. The "acquisition of more" of this world's goods is the essence of economic activity, providing things are acquired through the process of production and exchange, but the kind of acquisition these writers evidently had in mind was not characterized by economic activity, but by more direct and forceful means. It seems clear that they regarded expansionism more as an end in itself than as a means to a fuller life, inasmuch as apparently men are never satisfied with what was the original end, but use it as a means or stepping stone to acquire more, so that the great end and ambition of their life is to keep going, to keep on acquiring, and to increase their power at the expense of others.

In ancient literature there are enough observations such as these to satisfy anyone seeking to verify the antiquity of and the high authority for the economic interpretation of imperialism and war. They proceed from the commonsense observation that "we," the state, are merely the individual, with all his cupidity and selfishness writ large. Such statements involve no attempt to define the word "economic" in terms of a particular kind of human activity which

---

[7] Hobbes, *Leviathan*, Everyman's Library edition, pp. 49–50.

[8] Penn, "An Essay towards the Present and Future Peace of Europe by the Establishment of an European Diet, Parliament, or Estate," in his *The Peace of Europe* (Everyman's Library), p. 8.

is concerned with economizing scarce resources, producing economically through the division of labor, and exchanging through a price mechanism. Nor do they involve looking into economic activity to see if it differs from the kind of activity which proceeds from ethical judgments. These are modern modes of thought, worlds removed from either the ancient or the modern view that "economic" is a synonym for cupidity.

Alongside the view that the desire for more and more of this world's goods leads to conquest and war, there developed another line of thought, which held that acquisition *per se* is not sinister and that the excuse or necessity for war must be looked for in bad political arrangements. This is pre-eminently a modern idea, and it arose out of the fact that modern economic enterprise and competition operate through a mechanism of cost-price relationships which enables acquisition to depend on the prior act of production, not merely on the ancient and imperialistic technique of going out and grabbing whatever is wanted. Not that grabbing was the sole method of the preindustrial era or that modern gains are all made through economic processes; the point is that grabbing by conquest predominately characterizes the imperialistic approach to the problem of acquisition in all ages, especially in the pre-industrial age, while gaining by industry characterizes the economic approach to the problem of acquisition in all ages, especially in the industrial era.

The belief that the excuse or necessity for war must be sought in bad political organization usually implies that if the political system were arranged so as to fit into the peaceful ways of the economic system there would be no danger of conflict. This brings us down to the view that capitalism not only is opposed to the ill-fitting political clothes in which it is obliged to work, but is anti-imperialistic as well. Such ideas as these, of course, do not lead to a theory of economic imperialism. The kinds of criticism of the economic system which provide the basis for such a theory are discussed in the next section, but it is relevant to say a few words about the views of the various schools of economic thought regarding the more general question of the relation of economic activity to war.

As a rule we can expect that those who are least critical of the economic system, or think of the capitalist order mainly as an ideal pattern of economic behavior, are also least likely to regard greed, competition, the profit motive, the search for markets, the law of diminishing returns, or any other economic law as the proper place to look for the causes of war. Adam Smith spent nearly all his criticism on mercantilist and colonial policies, which to him were political policies, and apparently he had no inclination to regard the free system which he advocated as containing in it the seeds of war. Ricardo makes the rather casual remark that "wars are entered into for the sake of private advantage," [9] but he did not say this in his *Principles of Political Economy and Taxation,* and in any case this is not quite the same as saying that greed is a general cause of wars. Malthus was, of course, responsible for the idea that misery is the chief cause of war [10] and Proudhon regarded pauperism as the principal factor.[11] But, again, this is not placing the blame on economic motives or on the working of any economic law.

Other economists, however, have quite positively expressed the opinion that war is not caused by economic motives. James Mill was certain that foreign trade was not a source of war,[12] and John Stuart Mill put the same idea positively in proclaiming that international trade has become the principal basis of peace.[13] Nor could Say regard war as the product of the kind of economic world in which the equilibrium of production and consumption was capable both of creating perfect harmony and of convincing the world that such harmony should be given full expression.[14] Bastiat [15] and Laveleye [16] held similar views.

Given a world of free trade in a political atmosphere which permitted free enterprise to flourish between nations as it existed within the more advanced countries, with a minimum of governmental interference, it was indeed difficult to see why nations would have any economic reasons for going to war with each other.

---

[9] Rather than cite primary sources for this and the following brief statements regarding the views of various economists on war and economic motives, I refer the reader to the following excellent review of their opinions: Edmund Silberner, *The Problem of War in Nineteenth Century Economic Thought;* tr. by Alexander H. Krappe. For the statement by Ricardo, see Silberner, p. 36. No attempt has been made in the present discussion to do more than give a few examples of the opinions of well over one hundred writers mentioned in Silberner's book.

[10] *Ibid.,* p. 15.          [11] *Ibid.,* p. 222.          [12] *Ibid.,* pp. 39–40.
[13] *Ibid.,* p. 65.          [14] *Ibid.,* p. 14.          [15] *Ibid.,* pp. 94, 99.
[16] *Ibid.,* p. 199.

In this kind of world there was no need for international peace machinery, and the liberals could see no excuse for a world state or federation or a league to enforce peace. To them the indivisibility of peace was inherent in the one world of free trade. If nations refused to accept this kind of world order and insisted upon following a protectionist and separatist policy, the liberal could find no explanation except that rulers, democratic or otherwise, of such nations, were the victims of perverted economic reasoning. Failure to see the truth in such obvious economic principles as the law of comparative advantage and the benefits of the international division of labor meant that they were mistaking the very fallacies of economics for its eternal verities.

It is not surprising that views quite opposite to those just considered are to be found both among the critics of capitalism and among the opponents of the classical-orthodox school of economic thought. Marx, whose doctrines we shall examine at some length in a later chapter, was the great outstanding critic of capitalism and opponent of "bourgeoise" economics, and to him capitalism and war were inseparable evils. Most of the members of the German Historical School of Economics were opposed to the doctrine of free trade and equally inclined to reject the classical view which associated war with protectionism and other political interferences with economic life. Most of them also held the view that wars are inevitable.

Roscher had only scorn for the idea that the unprofitableness of war presages its disappearance.[17] Knies believed that wars arise chiefly from economic (territorial, commercial, industrial) motives.[18] Von Stein blamed war on human nature and dismissed it as a natural phenomenon.[19] Schäffle viewed it as part of the social struggle inherent in human behavior—as a manifestation of overpopulation, greed, religious fanaticism, and the love of military glory, and he thought that it would be impossible to suppress war merely by disarmament.[20] Schmoller took a similar view of war as a necessary international factor, comparable to the necessity of internal national strife.[21] Hildebrand, otherwise an adherent of the views of the Historical School, did not share the view that war is in-

---

[17] *Ibid.*, p. 174.
[18] *Ibid.*, p. 178.
[19] *Ibid.*, p. 180.
[20] *Ibid.*, pp. 183–84.
[21] *Ibid.*, p. 190.

evitable. He held that war, like other social institutions which give way to the march of civilization, is destined to disappear.[22]

Non-German adherents of the historical method in economics, such as Cliffe Leslie [23] and Thorald Rogers [24] in England, Laveleye [25] in France, and Levasseur [26] in Belgium, were generally closer to the English classicists on the question of war than to their German colleagues. They were free traders, opposed to militarism and optimistic that economic rationality would in time make war untenable. Cunningham, on the other hand, was closer to the Germans.[27]

List's fame rests on his defense of protectionism rather than on his adherence to any special school other than his own. He blamed wars on man's uncivilized nature, his greed, and his love of power and dislike of subservience to others. Since the most highly industrialized nations are also the most civilized, List argued, the protective system, by raising nations to this higher level, is a historical process which points the path to universal peace—and eventually to free trade among equals. If war comes in the leveling process, as List admitted it might, that would not be the fault of protectionism. Rather, it would have to be credited to man's savage nature, still untamed by the civilizing mission of the protective system.[28]

Characteristically, while the liberal free-trader regarded "international organization" as no substitute for sound economic ideas and policies to solve the problem of war prevention, the protectionists and adherents of the historical school turned to international organization and leagues to enforce peace as the right solution, assuming that a solution is desirable. At least one writer of the nineteenth century, Charles Fourier, was driven to the unwelcome thought that world unity would come about only by the conquest of the whole world by one great power.[29] Perish the thought, but if there was no hope for free trade, if the protectionists regarded war as inevitable, and if they and the lovers of power were to dominate the ideas and policies of the world, the thought could not be downed forever.

[22] *Ibid.*, p. 207.  [23] *Ibid.*, pp. 196, 208.  [24] *Ibid.*, pp. 197, 208.
[25] *Ibid.*, pp. 199, 208.  [26] *Ibid.*, pp. 194, 208.  [27] *Ibid.*, pp. 201–4.
[28] *Ibid.*, pp. 145, 152, 162.  [29] *Ibid.*, pp. 239–40.

Apparently little more than a substitution of the word "imperialism" for "war" is required to turn most of these views into some kind of theory of imperialism. But the fact remains that eighteenth- and nineteenth-century writers did not make this transposition; even when we do it for them, the resultant theory of imperialism is still a long way from the detailed cause-and-effect mechanism visualized by the economists and socialists of the twentieth century who became responsible for the theory of imperialism as we now know it.

## BASES OF A THEORY OF "CAPITALIST IMPERIALISM"

The bearing of eighteenth- and nineteenth-century economic thought on the problem of imperialism is to be found—implicit rather than explicit—in ideas about the mechanism of trade which could be used to connect the trade itself, especially exports, with some "necessity" at home to dispose of surpluses or the desirability of gaining and retaining access to foreign sources of supply. This is not exactly a corollary of the general view that protectionism leads to conflict, but it is related to this view, for it was never difficult to argue (if need arose) that somehow protectionism (or any other form of state interference in favor of monopoly) or lack of interference to preserve free enterprise and trade necessitated following an aggressive foreign policy.

Out of the economic theorizing which followed Smith's *Wealth of Nations* there gradually emerged two trends of thought which are germane to the theory of economic imperialism—one in a negative, the other in a positive way. The first, represented by Say and Ricardo, was that capitalism can remain in perfect equilibrium and that underconsumption is not a threat to the stability of the system. In these ideas there is no basis for the theory that capitalist imperialism is the outcome of absolute necessity. But the second trend of thought, initiated by Sismondi and Malthus, in departing from the first view, laid the basis for the theory of imperialism which culminated nearly a century later in the work of John A. Hobson. But the latter views, as Keynes has remarked, lived on "furtively, below the surface," while those of Ricardo triumphed.[30] This explains why, as we shall see, the capitalist theory of im-

[30] Keynes, *The General Theory of Employment Interest and Money*, p. 32.

perialism came from sources not in line with the accepted economic orthodoxy of the nineteenth century.

J. B. Say, whose influence on English thought was for a time second only to that of Smith, gave the first impetus to the idea that capitalism can be self-contained and independent of outside markets in the formulation of his celebrated "law of markets." This unwitting target of the pessimists and of the critics of capitalism represents the high-water mark of optimism in economic thought. Say held it to be self-evident that supply creates its own demand and that general overproduction or general disequilibrium is impossible.[31] From the idea that products pay for products came the conclusion that no country can overproduce, nor can it suffer from the production of other countries. All gain together by increasing their production and exchanging their surpluses, which, of course, disappear in the exchange itself. If this theory of markets were lived up to, he thought, the whole policy of the world, especially its colonial policy, would be changed for the better, and the brotherhood of man would be within sight of realization.

In Say's system there was no room for either mercantilism or imperialism. He was opposed to the colonial policies of his day because colonialism is "built upon compulsion, restriction, and monopoly." [32] It is detrimental to the colony because the mother country can force it to buy its products at a higher price than would prevail under free trade, and at the same time compel it to purchase from the mother country everything it requires. He regarded the loss of the American colonies as a positive gain to England, and in proof he cited the increase in trade between the two countries after the Revolution.[33] Say considered free trade superior because it would permit the "law of markets"—and therefore capitalism—to work perfectly. Thus, he was a free trader without any of the reservation or equivocation which characterized some of the ideas of Adam Smith. No one would ever find grounds for calling him an imperialist, not even a "liberal imperialist." To Say, and to all the economists of his tradition, colonies were an anachronism, destined to disappear—at least if the "right policy" were pursued.

Ricardo accepted Say's dictum that supply creates its own demand:

---

[31] Say, *A Treatise on Political Economy* (Princep's edition), I, 107 ff.
[32] *Ibid.*, p. 220.          [33] *Ibid.*, pp. 222 ff.

No man produces but with a view to consume or sell, and he never sells, but with an intention to purchase some other commodity. . . . By producing, then, he necessarily becomes either the consumer of his own goods, or the purchaser and consumer of the goods of some other person. . . . Productions are always bought by productions, or by services; money is only the medium by which the exchange is effected.[34]

Conversely, of course, there could be no underconsumption. Since there is room for neither overproduction nor underconsumption in this sort of reasoning, Ricardo can be ruled out as a contributor to the later view that because of lack of equilibrium between supply and demand capitalism must seek a solution to such lack of balance by resorting to foreign trade.

On the other hand, however, Ricardo lent heavy support to an idea which later turned out to be an alternative approach to connecting capitalism with imperialism. This is found in his theory of profit. Smith had argued that a monopoly of colonial trade, being itself a more profitable field of investment, would in turn have the effect of raising the rate of profit of all trades by increasing the competition for capital. In turn, high profits, combined with high wages, would raise the price of commodities, thus injuring the mother country by diminishing its power of selling manufactured commodities as cheaply as other countries. Conversely, free trade would decrease the competition for capital, thus keeping profits and wages low, which in turn would lower the price of commodities, to the advantage of the mother country.[35]

Ricardo, armed with an entirely different theory of the relation between profits and prices ("prices being regulated neither by wages nor profits"),[36] took emphatic exception to Smith's reasoning. He agreed with Smith that free trade would be advantageous. On the other hand, he held that the injury from trade restrictions is not (as Smith suggests) that they first raise profits and wages and thus cause prices to rise, but that they cause a lessening of production (by diverting capital to less profitable uses), which in turn leads to higher food prices, higher wages, and lower profits.[37] Wages, according to Ricardo, must remain stationary at the level necessary

---

[34] Ricardo, *Principles of Political Economy and Taxation* (Gonner's edition), pp. 273, 275.

[35] *Wealth of Nations* (Cannan's edition), pp. 99 ff.

[36] Ricardo, *Principles of Political Economy and Taxation*, p. 333.

[37] *Ibid.*, pp. 325, 331–33.

for subsistence; but as existing land becomes more completely utilized, rents will rise and profits will decline.[38] Therefore, the way to arrest both these tendencies is to resort to foreign trade as land becomes scarce at home.[39]

The kinship of this theory to Marx's thesis that the declining tendency of the rate of profit within a country must be offset by foreign trade—or by imperialism, to use a later phrase—will become apparent in subsequent chapters.

What Ricardo had to say on the question of colonies was concerned solely with the matter of colonial trade as it related to his general theory of international trade. In the opening remarks of his chapter "On Colonial Trade" Ricardo agrees that Smith "has shown, most satisfactorily, the advantages of a free trade." Nevertheless, Ricardo thought that "the trade with a colony may be so regulated [by monopolistic restraints] that it shall at the same time be less beneficial to the colony, and more beneficial to the mother country, than a perfectly free trade." [40] But this was a little exercise in logic, and a reminder that even Smith—who had admitted that a nation which would give another nation a monopoly as supplier of its imports would thereby permit the latter to sell its goods at a better price than if it were selling in competition with other countries—had been guilty of inconsistency in denying the same principle where colonial trade and restraints were involved.

It is significant that we find in Ricardo none of the crusading zeal regarding the colonial question to be found in Adam Smith, or Say, or James Mill. Economics, for Ricardo, had become a matter of almost "pure theory," and until economists like Hobson and the Marxists again became concerned with the old political aspects of political economy, we must look for ideas which, like Ricardo's theory of profit, bear only indirectly on the theory of imperialism.

The century and a quarter between Adam Smith's attack on mercantilism and J. A. Hobson's attack on imperialism was marked by some curious changes of opinion regarding the source of economic ills and the causes of conflict between classes and nations. The earlier theory that capitalism would work perfectly and remain in equilibrium through the operation of cost-price relationships

[38] *Ibid.*, pp. 47, 70, 98.     [39] *Ibid.*, p. 112.     [40] *Ibid.*, pp. 325, 330.

and the law of supply and demand was followed by emphasis upon the tendency towards unemployment owing to the substitution of men by machines, the tendency towards underconsumption because of the substitution of profits for wages, and the tendency towards falling profits associated with the accumulation of capital.

On the optimistic side, it could be admitted that the tendency towards unemployment might be mitigated if the machine creates more work than it displaces, that the tendency towards underconsumption could be counteracted if all savings were immediately invested, and that the falling tendency to the rate of profit might be offset by various counteracting factors, including foreign trade. But foreign trade, which the earlier economists looked upon as beneficial, later came to be regarded with suspicion as a cause of international conflict and at best as a stop-gap antidote to the forces of underconsumption and falling profits which, in the long run, nothing could stay. These constituted the theoretical details around which controversy raged, while above them, as larger and more comprehensive symbols, stood such emotional terms as mercantilism, capitalism, and imperialism.

Among none of the predecessors of the early classicists, and in fact among few of their contemporaries, is there any systematically developed idea that the evils of the world are due to the "economic system." The trouble, as Adam Smith and his followers saw it, was bad political interference with natural (and therefore good) economic processes. But Sismondi and Malthus saw the economic processes themselves as sinister because of the inability of the economic system to satisfy the conditions of effective demand. Capitalism runs into difficulties from which it tries to save itself by foreign expansion. Such was the real beginning of the theory of economic imperialism.

Sismondi, in contrast with Say, was convinced not only that the machine would result in a displacement of labor but also that it would lead to a dead level of chronic underconsumption and stagnation. He regarded Say's Law as a ridiculous assumption, entirely at variance with the facts. At every crucial point the capitalists fail to do the thing that would keep "revenue" and production in balance, and what appears to be in the interest of labor as well as themselves turns out to be the contrary. Capitalists have it within their power to use the "revenue" as they choose; if they consume too much, laborers suffer from getting too little to spend on themselves; if they go to the other extreme and save and invest too much in labor, the population increases and tends to put conditions back where they were before.[41] And they are likely to save and invest too much because of their ignorance of what the market will profitably absorb. They bolt ahead and adopt machines without relying on a pre-existing demand for goods, and the result is overproduction and crises.[42]

Furthermore, Sismondi believed that the adoption of labor-saving machines results in a shift from the production of staple necessities to the production of luxuries. Improved techniques for producing necessities will displace labor and at the same time displace a proportionate amount of demand for necessities. Concurrently, the higher profits anticipated and received from the adoption of new techniques will create an increased demand for luxury goods and the growth of industries producing such goods. This calls for a shift of labor, which may be effected but slowly, and it requires new capital, which may not be available at all.[43] Sismondi concedes that the expansion of foreign trade would replace to some extent the markets lost by the replacement of men by machines. Because luxury-producing industries fail to keep up with the demand, part of the income of the rich is thus left free to be sent abroad. Wealth becomes concentrated in the hands of a few, says Sismondi, and this causes the domestic market to contract and forces industry to seek outlets in foreign markets.[44] But this can be no permanent remedy because demand is also restricted by the same forces in other countries, all of which will soon have access to any improved techniques which are developed elsewhere.[45] Thus, in Sismondi we find a foreshadowing of the criticism of capitalism that was later to be made with much greater skill and force by Marx and his followers, and at least a mild anticipation of the "necessary" and "imperialistic" role of foreign trade.

Rodbertus, too, anticipated Marx—and also Hobson—in carrying the Sismondian ideas a step further. Writing of the crisis of 1857, Rodbertus contended that it was not due to a money shortage,

---

[41] Simonde de Sismondi, *Nouveaux Principes d'économie politique* (2d ed.), I, 104–9.
[42] *Ibid.*, II, 312 ff.
[43] *Ibid.*, II, 417–26.
[44] *Ibid.*, I, 361.
[45] *Ibid.*, I, 346–48.

as was widely held, but to a maldistribution of income, resulting from too much capital being invested in productive equipment, leaving too little to be spent on consumption; hence disequilibrium and crisis.[46] The only way to prevent the recurrence of such disequilibrium in the future, he reasoned, was to find outlets for surplus capital in foreign markets, thus preventing productivity at home from outstripping the purchasing power of the consumers, which remains constant. Thus was first developed the famous underconsumption theory of the business cycle. Whenever and wherever new markets can be found, or when the population is reduced by colonization, says Rodbertus, the great social problem is eased by that amount; but the time will come when neither of these temporary palliatives will be workable, and then society must try to find a solution in some other direction. It was left to his successors to turn this idea into a capitalist theory of imperialism and to state in great detail why socialization of the means of production is the only remedy.

Because of the high level of his reasoning in pursuit of the problem of effective demand,[47] Malthus enjoys a much higher place in the estimation of many modern economists than either Sismondi or Rodbertus, or even Ricardo. In a spirited controversy with Ricardo he maintained, in the face of Ricardo's refusal to see any sound reason for questioning Say's Law, that the vast powers of production are not put into action because of the lack of a proper distribution of the produce of industry. A general glut and stagnation in the demand for labor, he maintained, was inevitable from any attempt to accumulate rapidly, unless accumulation is accompanied

[46] Rodbertus, *Die Handelskrisen und die Hypothekennot der Grundbesitzer* (Berlin, 1861). See also Rodbertus, *Overproduction and Crises;* tr. by Julia Franklin, with an introduction by John B. Clark; the German original of this translation was *Soziale Briefe an Von Kirchmann*, Berlin, 1850–51.

[47] Cf. Keynes, *General Theory*, pp. 32, 362–64. There is a good discussion of classical doctrines in this connection in Gourvitch, *Survey of Economic Theory on Technological Change and Employment.* Keynes's influence in reviving the discussion of underconsumption and effective demand is of course well known. Numerous articles have been written to show the similarity between Keynes's views and those of Marx, but while Marx certainly anticipated much that is in Keynes, the direct influence of Malthus is much more apparent. See Keynes's own remarks on Malthus in the *General Theory* and also an article, "Malthus and Keynes," by James J. O'Leary, *Journal of Political Economy*, L (December, 1942), 901–19. O'Leary points out that Malthus depended heavily on such terminology as "habits of saving," "consumption habits," "passion for consumption," and "passion for accumulation," and even used the term "propensity to consume" made famous by Keynes.

by an adequate proportion of unproductive consumption by landlords and capitalists.[48]

Malthus declared that Adam Smith was wrong in holding that there is no danger of pushing saving too far,[49] and that Say's Law is "utterly unfounded." [50] It was wrong in theory, because it viewed commodities only in relation to each other, whereas to Malthus the significant consideration is their relation to consumers. This identifies Malthus with that long line of economists who have maintained that the end of production is consumption, but he was not a critic of production for profit. He was only concerned lest too much saving and a wrong distribution of the product blunt the profit motive, and to him the chief function of the economist is to discover how these dangers can be avoided. He saw clearly that employment, and therefore consumption, depends upon investment and that the latter depends upon the profit motive and the existence of profitable business opportunities and a ready market.[51]

Although Malthus considered the possibilities of excessive capital accumulation, with its depressive effect on profits, investment, and employment,[52] and worries more or less about the temporarily depressive effect of the introduction of machinery on employment and wages,[53] he believed that the long-run effects of accumulation and technological progress are bound to be good. The effect of the machine will be to cheapen production and increase output, which will in turn open up new markets, both at home and in foreign countries.[54] He does not avoid giving the impression, however, that the tendency towards falling profits is an ever real and important threat. This tendency is inherent in the accumulation of capital, because too great an accumulation causes money to become stagnant in the circulation process, that is, to be saved or hoarded at a greater rate than it is invested; it is also inherent in the law of diminishing returns, which reduces profits by first raising agricultural costs.[55] It is only when he ceases to regard demand as static and takes into consideration the great possibilities of technology, increased labor efficiency, reduced costs, and expanding markets

[48] Letters from Malthus to Ricardo, dated July 7, 1821, and July 16, 1821 (as quoted by Keynes in *Essays in Biography*, pp. 142–44).
[49] Malthus, *Principles of Political Economy*, pp. 6–7.    [50] *Ibid.*, p. 315.
[51] *Ibid.*, pp. 238, 312.    [52] *Ibid.*, pp. 314 ff.    [53] *Ibid.*, pp. 351 ff.
[54] *Ibid.*, p. 360.    [55] *Ibid.*, pp. 271–98, *passim;* 314 ff.

that Malthus approaches the solution of removing "under" from "underconsumption" and of making demand fully effective by creating purchasing power on the side of supply. In other words, he saw in this a vindication of Say's Law, but he arrived at his conclusions after a great deal of worrying about short-run matters of which Say was never conscious.

When we take leave of Sismondi and Malthus and turn to the followers of Ricardo, who from now on hold the stage, we hear no more of the dangers of underconsumption and can find no further indication in classical economics of how this particular factor might be turned into a theory of economic imperialism. Marx, as we shall see, revived the doctrine, and Hobson definitely associated it with imperialism, but neither belong firmly in the tradition that produced Ricardo, Mill, Marshall, and the great American classicists. We do, however, find in Ricardo's successors a continuing concern with the falling tendency of the rate of profit and with foreign trade as a counteracting factor to this tendency, which presages an important aspect of later theories of imperialism.

Classical economics reached its zenith in John Stuart Mill. Henceforth the crusading zeal against mercantilism and the "monopoly of the colony trade," which had been declining with each generation of economists following the appearance of the *Wealth of Nations*, gave way almost completely to matters of "economic theory." The hated system of mercantilism seemed to have been routed sufficiently so that it could be ignored for more intellectual exercises.

Mill elaborated the Ricardian theory of international trade and had the customary things to say against mercantilistic restraints on trade, although he regarded the infant-industry argument in favor of protection as valid. Profits tend towards a minimum, not, as Smith had it, because capital competes with capital, but because, as Ricardo held, the growth of population means progressively poorer opportunities of investment for capital as a whole. This tendency can be arrested by commercial crises (which temporarily diminish the supply of capital and raise the rate of profit), by improvements in production, by importations of food (which retards recourse to poorer lands and therefore to the no-profit margin), and by the export of capital, which (reverting to Adam Smith) eases the competition for the investment of savings at home.

There are, perhaps, more ideas in Mill on which a theory of economic imperialism might be based than in the writings of any other nineteenth-century classical economist. "The expansion of capital," says Mill, "would soon reach its ultimate boundary, if the boundary itself did not continually open and leave more space." [56] This quotation, taken from Mill's chapter entitled "Of the Tendency of Profits to a Minimum," was an echo of Ricardo, who had held that the extension of foreign trade or improvements in machinery would cause profits to rise (or keep them from falling) because it would mean cheaper food and necessaries for the laboring class. [57]

Mill arrived at the "fundamental proposition" that "the rate of profit is habitually within, as it were, a hand's breadth of the minimum, and the country therefore on the very verge of the stationary state," as a result of capital accumulation, with no reserve of fertile land to fall back on. The latter prospect appeared so hypothetical, however, that Mill saw no immediate chance of a no-profit society being realized. The hypothesis further assumed

an entire cessation of the exportation of capital for foreign investment. No more capital sent abroad for railways or loans; no more emigrants taking capital with them, to the colonies, or to other countries; no fresh advances made, or credits given, by bankers or merchants to their foreign correspondents. We must also assume that there are no fresh loans, for unproductive expenditure, by the government, or on mortgage, or otherwise; and none of the waste of capital which now takes place by the failure of undertakings which people are tempted to engage in by the hope of a better income than can be obtained in safe paths at the present habitually low rate of profit. We must suppose the entire savings of the community to be annually invested in really productive employment within the country itself; and no new channels opened by industrial inventions, or by a more extensive substitution of the best known processes for inferior ones. [58]

Mill then declares that this would not lead to a general glut, as most people would suppose, or that commodities would be produced and remain unsold or be sold only at a loss.

The difficulty would not consist in any want of a market. If the new capital were duly shared among many varieties of employment, it would

[56] Mill, *Principles of Political Economy*, p. 731.
[57] Ricardo, *Principles of Political Economy and Taxation*, p. 112.
[58] Mill, *Principles of Political Economy*, pp. 731–32.

raise up a demand for its own produce, and there would be no cause why any part of that produce should remain longer on hand than formerly. What would really be, not merely difficult, but impossible, would be to employ this capital without submitting to a rapid reduction of the rate of profit.[59]

Mill is even more emphatic later, when he asserts that one of the principal causes by which the decline of profits in England has been arrested is "the perpetual overflow of capital into colonies or foreign countries, to seek higher profits than can be obtained at home." This draining off of capital, he continues, "does what a fire, or an inundation, or a commercial crisis would have done: it carries off a part of the increase of capital from which the reduction of profits proceeds." Exported capital is not lost, he hastens to add, but is used to keep up a supply of cheap food, etc., "thus enabling an increasing capital to find employment in the country." [60]

In his discussion "Of the Stationary State" Mill points out that in the preceding chapters (in which foreign trade and other factors are presented as counteractions to the tendency of profits to decline to zero in industrial countries) he was merely presenting "the general theory of the economical progress of society." He then significantly remarks:

But in contemplating any progressive movement, not in its nature un-limited, the mind is not satisfied with merely tracing the laws of the movement; it cannot but ask the further question, to what goal? Towards what ultimate point is society tending by its industrial progress? When the progress ceases, in what condition are we to expect that it will leave mankind? [61]

Mill was convinced that at the end of what economists call the progressive state lies the "stationary state" and that this goal

is at all times near enough to be fully in view. . . . The richest and most prosperous countries would very soon attain the stationary state, if no further improvements were made in the productive arts, and if there were a suspension of the overflow of capital from those countries into the uncultivated or ill-cultivated regions of the earth.[62]

Mill surmises that the impossibility of ultimately avoiding the stationary state must have been an unpleasing and discouraging prospect to the political economists of the last two generations (to

[59] *Ibid.*, p. 732.          [60] *Ibid.*, pp. 738–39.
[61] *Ibid.*, p. 746.          [62] *Ibid.*

Adam Smith, Malthus, McCulloch); but Mill declares that he cannot regard such a prospect with so much aversion. On the whole, he believes that a stationary society would be "a very considerable improvement on our present condition" of struggling to get on, and of "trampling, crushing, elbowing, and treading on each others' heels."[63] Under a better system of distribution, such as socialism seemed to promise, no one would be poor and no one would desire to be richer than his neighbors. But Mill was convinced that in order to reach this happy goal society would have to do everything in its power to restrain the growth of population.[64]

Not the least reason for Mill's influence on his generation is to be found in the view—which is curiously inconsistent with his more pessimistic outlook—that economic progress presages peace. In an oft-quoted passage he says:

It is commerce which is rapidly rendering war obsolete, by strengthening and multiplying the personal interests which are in natural opposition to it. And it may be said without exaggeration that the great extent and rapid increase of international trade, in being the principal guarantee of the peace of the world, is the great permanent security for the uninterrupted progress of the ideas, the institutions, and the character of the human race.[65]

Another matter related to the later theory of imperialism which Mill considered at great length was colonization. This was one among a half-dozen or so cases, he thought, in which the state should abandon laissez faire and adopt a positive program. To Marx and his followers it was about the last place where the ideal state should take a hand, and they identified Mill with the reactionaries who would force masses of workers, in the name of helping the indigent, to settle in new lands under conditions practically amounting to slavery.

The source of Mill's inspiration for the state to adopt a positive program of colonization was E. G. Wakefield, a publicist and member of Parliament, who was instrumental in persuading the British Government to adopt an orderly scheme of sending settlers to Australia and New Zealand. In brief, it was a great scheme of "outdoor relief," based on the conviction that something should be done to insure that each colony, instead of consisting entirely of landowners and farmers, should have an adequate supply of ordinary

[63] *Ibid.*, pp. 749–50.    [64] *Ibid.*, p. 750.    [65] *Ibid.*, p. 582.

laborers available for building roads, canals, and other improvements, which would create a balanced economy and at the same time enhance the value of the land admitted to private ownership. Therefore Wakefield proposed to prevent the loss of this productive power in the early stages of colonization by placing on all unoccupied land a price high enough to discourage its purchase by people with very small means and, furthermore, to use the proceeds from the sale of such lands to import laborers from the mother country.

In commenting on this self-supporting scheme of colonization, Mill tried to maintain some of the judicious objectivity of the economist, but in the end he declared that in spite of many difficulties and much mismanagement, it had "produced a suddenness and rapidity of prosperity more like fable than reality." [66] Back of Mill's enthusiasm was his happy discovery that Wakefield was a very good economist and understood the implications of the tendency of profits to fall; moreover, he knew what to do about it. Paraphrasing Wakefield, Mill remarks:

On a limited extent of land, only a limited quantity of capital can find employment at a profit. As the quantity of capital approaches this limit, profit falls; when the limit is attained, profit is annihilated; and can only be restored through an extension of the field of employment, either by the acquisition of fertile land, or by opening new markets in foreign countries, from which food and materials can be purchased with the products of domestic capital. These propositions are in my opinion substantially true . . . [concluded Mill, and he declared that they were in accord with] the best school of preceding political economists. [67]

Amplifying his belief that this was an area of endeavor in which the state might exercise good economic statesmanship, Mill made it a matter of world concern by declaring that colonization "should be considered in its relation, not to a single country, but to the collective economical interests of the human race," and should not be viewed merely as a means of relieving an overcrowded labor market (such as England) and supplying another. [68] The problem was to increase the world's production as well as to redistribute its population. From the economic point of view colonization is a business matter—in fact, the best "in which the capital of an old and wealthy country can engage. It is equally obvious, however,

[66] Ibid., p. 973.     [67] Ibid., pp. 727–28.     [68] Ibid., p. 970.

that Colonization on a great scale can be undertaken, as an affair of business, only by the government, or by some combination of individuals in complete understanding with the government." [69]

Marx was to regard this scheme to "effect the manufacture of wage-workers in the Colonies" with alarm and derision.[70]

Economists after Mill gave less and less attention to those problems which border on power politics. Despite the resemblance of the nineteenth- and early twentieth-century colonialism or imperialism to mercantilism, economists were able to make historical references to the latter without being moved to make some further obvious comments about the modern imperialism that was all about them. The closest most of them came to it was in the use of such terms as "neo-mercantilism" and "neo-protectionism." But they were not fired by these mild words as Adam Smith and his immediate followers had been fired by the "mercantile system." The most evident reason, of course, is that they became more interested in developing the theoretical side of economics as a science of value than in investigating the political implications of the very movements which were rapidly rendering many of their theoretical assumptions untenable. They were challenged more by Mill's bland assertion that "the theory of the subject is complete" than by the assumption, much more widely held, of the permanency of freedom, liberty, free competition, and capitalism.

While Marx and successive generations of socialists continued the early classical interest in the problems of colonialism and imperialism, the orthodox economists took little notice of this aspect of socialist doctrine but confined their criticism to the more vulnerable socialist theory of value. By and large the economists of the classical tradition have believed with Smith, Ricardo, and Mill that the wealth of nations and economic progress are injured by a mercantilistic policy and by attempts at national self-sufficiency or autarchy. They have tended to regard these interferences with economic life as political and transitory, dictated by the desire for national power or by motives that cannot properly be called economic. It was easier to identify imperialism with mercantilism and let it go at that than to break new ground. At the same time, there was enough substance in classical economic thought on which a theory

[69] *Ibid.*, p. 971.          [70] See below, pp. 119–20.

of economic imperialism could be based, given the stimulus to develop it. The "economic man" of classical political economy had been invented as a symbol for every man who has wants, knows what they are (or at least by his conduct indicates to the economist what they are), and knows how to satisfy them; and it was only a step from the economic man to the equally rational "economic class" or "economic nation."

The socialists found their stimulus in the labor-cost theory of value and the doctrine of the class struggle, and it was an easy matter to extend these ideas into the field of international relations. But it required the jolt of war and the threat of disturbance in the international field—the field in which orthodox economists had shown the most interest—to stimulate any serious attempts at interpretation. Even then it required a strong strain of the old orthodoxy, combined with a highly critical attitude towards capitalism, to permit an economic interpretation of such disturbers of the peace as imperialism and war. This combination is found at its best in the work of John A. Hobson.

# V .

## HOBSON AND THE THEORY OF

## ECONOMIC IMPERIALISM

WE ARE now ready to begin bringing into focus the various theories which find the roots of modern imperialism in the operation of the capitalist system of production and distribution. In the preceding chapter an attempt was made to compress the trends of thought of certain economists which presaged the conception that a highly competitive, overproducing, and under-consuming economic society would be forced to seek outlets for its goods and capital and to find new sources of raw materials. The general tenor of most of this thought was still not socialistic. Rather, it looked towards reforms which would free capitalism from the monopolistic and other tendencies which prevented it from distrib-uting goods and services on an equitable basis. These economists, even though critical of the system, could still see that free-enterprise capitalism, if properly directed, need not produce undesirable (i. e., imperialistic or mercantilistic) results. This point of view came to a head in Hobson's theory of economic imperialism.

For general purposes, it makes little difference whether we speak of "economic imperialism" or "capitalist imperialism." Yet there is a subtle difference worth noting in any attempt to under-stand the two main schools of thought which use these terms.

"Economic imperialism" is, of course, the more general term. It can be applied to every suspected attempt, no matter how ancient or how modern, of any group to further its economic interests by expansionist policies. Thus used, it appears to fit the ambitions of Caesar as well as those of the modern capitalist seeking foreign markets or concessions, and to apply equally to the self-seeking people of Plato's day who were bent upon obtaining "a slice of our neighbours' land" and to a present-day schoolmaster buying a foreign government bond.

But the term is also used in a narrower context. One may not wish to go so far as to denounce capitalism *in toto* as the source of imperialism, as the Marxists do, and yet go far enough in this direction to ascribe imperialism to certain workings of the capitalist system. From this it follows that it is not necessary to abolish capitalism in order to eliminate imperialism—it is necessary only to "reform" capitalism in such a way as to eliminate from it the roots of "economic imperialism."

"Economic" best describes the kind of theory of imperialism discussed in this chapter, namely, that of Hobson; and it is implied in most of the criticisms of capitalism which formed the background of Hobson's theory. "Capitalist imperialism," on the other hand, while of course "economic," comes closer to suggesting the sort of theory which emanates from the analysis of capitalism at the hands of Marx and his followers.

## THE "UNORTHODOXY" OF HOBSON'S THEORY

While economists of the classical and orthodox tradition became absorbed in the theoretical niceties of their science, assuming that mercantilism had given place to a system of free enterprise and free trade, old phenomena, which were never really dead, were creeping back in the form of neo-protectionism and empire-building. But it never came easy to a true follower of the classical tradition to develop a theory of "economic imperialism." Had it not been for their preoccupation with other matters the classical economists might have assailed imperialism as Smith had assailed mercantilism, but such reforming zeal was never one of their notable attainments.

The attack on imperialism was left for the new radicals, who were dissatisfied with orthodox economics and embittered by the capitalism which the orthodox school, almost with awe, sought to describe and explain. These new radicals, by a process of association, condemned not only capitalism but also imperialism (which they regarded as one of its works) and orthodox economics (which they believed had been so degraded that it was merely an apology for capitalism and imperialism). But it took more than a feeling of rebellion against this trinity to produce a theory of economic imperialism. It required some measure of belief in the economic interpretation of history and the stimulus of some modern dramatic sign of imperialism in action. The "imperialistic" wars which came at the turn of the century, particularly the Boer War and the Spanish American War, supplied the necessary stimuli.

By all logic, the Marxists should have been ready first with a theory to explain imperialism, for Marxism possessed not only the hatred of capitalism and imperialism but also belief in the economic interpretation of history. But the Marxists, too, had been preoccupied, not so much with theoretical controversies as with the practical problems of socialist organization and tactics. If the orthodox economists were more or less inclined to regard certain evils of capitalism and the evil of imperialism as temporary phenomena which would soon blow over, the socialists regarded them as evils which would soon be overthrown by the long-expected revolution.

As it turned out, an English economist who was a heretic from economic orthodoxy and yet not a socialist, but in a somewhat intermediate position, was the first to develop a theory of imperialism. John A. Hobson (1858–1940) published his *Imperialism* in 1902. No other book has been so influential in spreading the doctrine of economic imperialism. Not only did Hobson influence the writing of history by English and, even more strikingly, American historians, but he also anticipated the Marxian socialists in the same field of thought and even had considerable influence on their theory.

To Hobson economic imperialism is merely one kind of expansion, representing a particular type of motive, which operates—although with a lion's share of influence—alongside the military, sentimental, religious, and other "non-economic" motives. It is a product, not of capitalism as such, but of certain faults in capitalism which, were they removed, would spell the doom of imperialism. Correct the excesses and abuses of capitalist production, says Hobson, and there will be no motive for outward expansion. Private property will still endure, and capitalism will continue to be capitalism, but on a much higher moral plane after its conversion. Other motives for imperialism may go on as before, but once a reformed capitalism begins to move in a more social direction, these other motives will still be too weak, as they were before, to have a decisive influence. In short, Hobson thought that finding the key and opening the door was a more intelligent way to get inside the house of capitalism than to burn it down.

The more radical socialists, as we shall see, regard all this as bourgeois nonsense. In the first place, many of them believe, all motives, once they are traced to fundamentals, are economic, and any thoroughgoing theory of imperialism must be an all-embracing economic theory; the singling out of one kind of imperialism and calling it economic and another kind and calling it noneconomic is to them both unscientific and untrue to history. Furthermore, capitalism, as the dominant economic system or mode of production, with the greed for profit as its breath of life, must expand or die. It is not only that capitalism has "faults"—it is all one great social evil, bringing in its wake exploitation, the class struggle, violent crises, a fratricidal struggle for markets, and war. It will not reform itself from within, because it has no inner will or motive to do so; the only hope for social salvation is that the kind of society which it has created—the proletariat—may destroy it. Capitalism cannot be remodeled and still remain capitalism. The edifice must be burned, for there is no magic key that will ever unlock it. In its place will be erected a new social order which will harbor no motive for imperialistic behavior and universal exploitation. The problem is not, as Hobson thought, the removal of the causes of imperialism so that capitalism can survive. To the socialists the whole concern is to remove capitalism; once this is done there will be no imperialism to worry about.

Hobson was unsympathetic to most of the orthodox economic views of his time, but also he confesses that he never felt at home with full-blooded socialists. He had no use for Marx's labor-cost theory of value or for the Hegelian dialectic, which, he says, "used an empty intellectual paradox to impart an air of mysticism into quite intelligible historic processes." [1]

The central idea in any theory of economic imperialism is "surplus value." Hobson's conception of surplus value differs from that of Marx and his followers. Whereas Marx regarded it as the exclusive product of labor, Hobson regarded it as issuing from the

[1] *Confessions of an Economic Heretic,* pp. 35–36; cf. also p. 126.

existence of various hindrances to perfect equality of bargaining power among the owners of land and capital, that is, from the economic superiority of certain persons or classes over others in the market.[2] Here there emerges the idea of "forced gains," wherein lies the root of the economic evil which Hobson sees flowering into the deadly plants of imperialism and war.

Hobson preferred free enterprise and capitalism to socialism, but the Boer War [3] convinced him that English capitalism had made the war inevitable, and his economic studies led him to the conclusion that capitalism could be changed for the better and still stop short of socialism by curbing the excesses of international finance and by correcting the inequalities of wealth in industrial countries so that great pools of private funds would not pile up and seek investment elsewhere.

Not only was Hobson an underconsumptionist, but he was the first economist of the classical tradition to revive the doctrine after its long period of hibernation following the triumph of Ricardo over Malthus and Sismondi [4] In *The Physiology of Industry*, by A. F. Mummery and J. A. Hobson, which appeared in 1889, the traditional view that saving enriches and spending impoverishes a nation was vigorously assailed. In language strongly reminiscent of Rodbertus the authors said:

> Our purpose it to show that these conclusions are not tenable, that an undue exercise of the habit of saving is possible, and that such undue exercise impoverishes the Community, throws labourers out of work, drives down wages, and spreads that gloom and prostration through the commercial world which is known as Depression in Trade . . . any undue exercise of this habit must . . . cause an accumulation of Capital in excess of that which is required for use, and this excess will exist in the form of general over-production.[5]

Hobson dwelt on this theme with very little variation for the rest of his life. Underspending, underconsumption, and underemploy-

---

[2] Hobson, *The Economics of Distribution*, pp. 351–54, 357, 360.

[3] In his *Confessions of an Economic Heretic* (pp. 59, 62), Hobson tells how, as a result of an article on "Imperialism" which he contributed to the *Contemporary Review* of March, 1899, he was sent by the *Manchester Guardian* to South Africa on "a voyage of political enquiry." This trip increased Hobson's understanding of the "real relations between economics and politics." After his return he published *The War in South Africa* (1900), followed by *The Psychology of Jingoism* (1901), and in 1902 by his famous *Imperialism*.

[4] Keynes, *General Theory*, p. 364. See also below, pp. 106–10.

[5] Mummery and Hobson, *The Physiology of Industry*, pp. iv–v.

ment, oversaving, overinvestment, and overproduction—all these are aspects of a bad distribution of income, which is made progressively worse by technological change, which in turn makes possible the more rapid growth of large incomes. Hobson assumes that income spent on capital goods is potentially lost to consumption by being diverted into unused capacity for production beyond the requirements of consumption. He was not concerned with the kind of underconsumption that may result from failure to invest less than the amount of saving because of the habit of hoarding. He simply concentrated on the thesis that under conditions of prosperity people of wealth save their surplus income and invest it in enterprises which produce and throw onto the market goods for which there is no adequate purchasing power. This condition initiates a state of depression under the stress of which incomes are reduced until over-saving is checked, thus allowing consumption to catch up with production and bring the crisis to an end. Then the whole cycle starts over again.[6]

Hobson's preoccupation with this theory of the business cycle led him to his "most destructive heresy"—the conviction that markets, even under competitive conditions, are intrinsically unfair methods of distribution.[7] His purpose was to educate people regarding the "fundamental 'immorality' of a business system in which all markets were morally damaged by differences in bargaining power and the settlement of market prices alike for goods and services by the play of selfish interests."[8] For Hobson the remedy lay in a system of planning whereby the Government should interpret and administer the popular will.[9]

"Forced gain" was an early Hobsonian idea (closely related to Marx's "exploitation") which later influenced his views on imperialism. Capitalism, with its chaotic competitive conditions, leads to a forced gain or toll on the weaker members of society by the more economically powerful. If competition worked perfectly and smoothly, as the laissez-faire doctrine assumed, there would be no hard-driven bargains or differential gains of this sort.[10] As it is, such forced gains determine the character of the economic system and drive it along the road to imperialism, which

---

[6] Hobson, *The Industrial System*, chap. iii; see especially pp. 52–53.
[7] *Confessions of an Economic Heretic*, p. 168.　　　　[8] *Ibid.*, p. 64.
[9] *Ibid.*, p. 171.　　　[10] Cf. Hobson, *The Economics of Distribution*, passim.

is but a new phase of the desire to find and reap still other forced gains. "Everywhere," says Hobson, "appear excessive powers of production, excessive capital in search of investment. . . . It is this economic condition of affairs that forms the tap-root of Imperialism." [11] Imperialism he defines as "the endeavour of the great controllers of industry to broaden the channel for the flow of their surplus wealth by seeking foreign markets and foreign investments to take off the goods and capital they cannot sell or use at home." [12] Thus, the most important factor in the economics of imperialism, says Hobson, is foreign investments, and the great banking houses are the sinister elements which promote imperialistic policies, from which they gain at the expense of the manufacturing and trading interests and those cat's-paws of the banks, the small investors.[13]

In a rather bewildering mixture of metaphors, however, Hobson says that finance is not really the "motor-power" of imperialism or the fuel of the engine. These are supplied by such noneconomic factors as patriotism, adventure, military enterprise, political ambition, and philanthropy, while finance is the "governor of the imperial engine," manipulating to its own ends the patriotic forces which politicians, soldiers, philanthropists, and traders generate. The enthusiasm for expansion emanating from these sources, though strong and genuine, is irregular and blind, whereas the financial interests have precisely those powers of concentration and calculation which are needed in the business of imperialism. Statesmen, soldiers, missionaries, and the like may take the first steps in imperial expansion and act as agents in the education of a public opinion favorable to such enterprise, but the final decision is made by the financial interests.[14] Therefore Hobson concludes that it is idle to attack imperialism or militarism unless the axe is first laid to the economic root of the tree.[15]

[11] Hobson, *Imperialism*, p. 86.    [12] *Ibid.*, p. 91.
[13] *Ibid.*, pp. 59–60, 63–65.    [14] *Ibid.*, pp. 66–67; see also p. 381.
[15] *Ibid.*, p. 99. At a much later date, in his essay on *Veblen*, pp. 138–41, Hobson criticizes Veblen ("On the Nature of Peace" and "Imperial Germany") for finding the causes of "national-imperialism" in the psychology of patriotism instead of in the overproduction tendencies of capitalism. He says that he had expected to find Veblen much closer to Marx on this question, but thinks his deviation from Marx was due to his devotion to the idea of "financial sabotage," or the restriction of output, which "demands a non-expansive market as a condition of its profitable application," thus leading to the view that peace, or effective internationalism, is blocked

But how is the axe to be laid to the economic tap-root of imperialism? Hobson's answer is to make a direct attack, not on the financial interests, but on the underlying conditions which make them resort to imperialism. First of all, there would be no economic basis for imperialism in a sound and progressive economic society. Imperialism would be impossible in a socialistic state, he says, or in "an intelligent laissez-faire democracy which gave duly proportionate weight in its policy to all economic interests alike," because from a general social point of view imperialism does not pay.[16] Imperialism "pays" only when it benefits certain groups at the expense of others.

In answer to those who argue that industrial progress demands new markets, Hobson replies that such is not the case. Rather, the conditions of industrial progress can be found in utilizing markets which already exist. Under prevailing conditions it is a problem, not of finding markets, but of distributing purchasing power in such a way that demand can absorb the supply. In his own words, it is

maldistribution of consuming power which prevents the absorption of commodities and capital within the country. The over-saving which is the economic root of Imperialism is found by analysis to consist of rents, monopoly profits, and other unearned or excessive elements of income, which, not being earned by labour of head or hand, have no legitimate *raison d'etre.*

Thus, he disposes of the "fallacy of the supposed inevitability of imperial expansion as a necessary outlet for progressive industry."[17] Like certain socialists, whose views we shall note later,[18] Hobson contends that there is no need for outside markets, provided that

---

"by obsolescent feelings of patriotism based not on economic but on distinctively sentimental or emotional lines."

[16] *Ibid.*, pp. 52–53. Why, he asks in another place (p. 72), are the lessons of enlightened common sense and the economics of free trade forgotten? "The answer is that Imperialism repudiates Free Trade, and rests upon an economic basis of Protection."

[17] *Ibid.*, p. 91. In his *Confessions of an Economic Heretic* (p. 34) Hobson declares that had Britain been an isolated economic community it would long ago have reached the limit of effective saving. It failed to reach the limit earlier only because it was the only advanced industrial country with an exportable surplus. "It was only when Germany, America, France, and Japan began to encroach upon our practical monopoly of the world market for the export of staple manufactures and for the capital development of backward countries, that the fallacy of unlimited saving became apparent."

[18] See below, pp. 158–69.

the over-savings of unearned or excessive elements of income are used at home to raise the "wholesome standard of public and private consumption." Under these conditions there would be no "parasites," such as the financial interests, to feed upon patriotism, and

no excess of goods or capital clamorous to use Imperialism in order to find markets: foreign trade would indeed exist, but there would be no difficulty in exchanging a small surplus of our manufactures for the food and raw materials we annually absorbed, and all the savings that we made could find employment, if we chose, in home industries.[19]

This is to say that in a closed economy capitalism can expand indefinitely on its own resources.

Hobson believes that he sees a statement and solution of the whole problem of imperialism in the analogy of extensive *versus* intensive cultivation. An ignorant farmer, he says, will use land prodigally when it is plentiful and cheap, spreading his capital and labor over a large area, constantly taking in new tracts and cultivating them poorly. But a skilled and scientific farmer will concentrate on a small parcel of land, using his knowledge to get everything possible out of it.[20] The moral, as applied to world economy, is obvious, for "everywhere the issue of quantitative *versus* qualitative growth comes up. This is the entire issue of empire." [21]

## COMPARISON OF EARLIER WITH LATER VIEWS

Hobson later confessed that his heretical view of capitalism as the source of unjust distribution, over-saving, and an economic impulsion to adventurous imperialism led him for a time to an excessive

[19] *Imperialism*, pp. 64, 86.

[20] This, of course, is not true. The only rational conduct is to exploit both the intensive and extensive margins up to the point of equa-marginal returns; and a nation's reasons for "quantitative growth" are certainly not to be interpreted as if they were a matter of economic calculation, especially when one can marshall as many noneconomic motives as Hobson does. Putting Hobson's various thoughts together he is really saying that a country does not have to expand for economic reasons and that when it does expand it violates an economic principle; both statements are nearer the truth for a nation than for an "economic man." Hobson does not accept the argument that "the cause of war is as permanent as hunger itself; since both spring from the same source, the law of diminishing returns." Edward Van Dyke Robinson, "War and Economics in History and in Theory," *Political Science Quarterly*, XV (December, 1900), 622. Hobson replies (*Imperialism*, pp. 184–86) that the validity of this argument is contestable because man can avoid the necessity of war and expansion by mitigating the law of diminishing returns and by limiting the rate of growth of population. "The tendency of rational civilization is to employ both methods." It would have been pertinent to add that it also employs both the extensive and intensive margins.

[21] *Imperialism*, pp. 97–98.

and too-simple advocacy of the economic determination of history.[22] Even in his *Imperialism* Hobson used the word "imperialism" with some reluctance—more, in fact, than is evident among his disciples. At the outset he says:

Amid the welter of vague political abstractions to lay one's finger accurately upon any "ism" so as to pin it down and mark it out by definition seems impossible. . . . A certain broad consistency in its relations to other kindred terms is the nearest approach to definition which such a term as Imperialism admits. Nationalism, internationalism, colonialism, its three closest congeners, are equally elusive, equally shifty, and the changeful overlapping of all four demands the closest vigilance of students of modern politics.[23]

Further on Hobson concludes that quibbles about the modern meaning of the term "imperialism" are best resolved by reference to concrete facts, and forthwith he examines the facts of history in an attempt to put new stuff into a vague concept. In drawing distinctions between nationalism, colonialism, and imperialism he accepts Mill's characterization of the nature and limits of "true nationalism" as consisting not only of geographical limits but also of community of race, descent, language, religion, historical recollections of pride and humiliation, pleasure and regret, etc.[24] But when this genuine nationalism overflows its natural banks and attempts to "absorb the near or distant territory of reluctant and unassimilable peoples, that marks the passage from nationalism to a spurious colonialism on the one hand, Imperialism on the other."[25]

Nationalism [he says] is a plain highway to internationalism, and if it manifests divergence we may well suspect a perversion of its nature and its purpose. Such a perversion is Imperialism, in which nations trespassing beyond the limits of facile assimilation transform the wholesome stimulative rivalry of varied national types into the cut-throat struggle of competing empires.[26]

Civilized governments, Hobson says, may quite properly and legitimately undertake the political and economic control of the

---

[22] *Confessions of an Economic Heretic*, p. 63. "When I wrote my volume on *Imperialism*," he says, "I had not yet gathered into clear perspective the nature of the interaction between economics, politics, and ethics," adding that practical experience with movements and "causes" (one of which was anti-imperialism) gave him a clearer perspective.

[23] *Imperialism*, p. 1.       [24] *Ibid.*, pp. 3-4.
[25] *Ibid.*, p. 4.       [26] *Ibid.*, p. 9.

lower races, but such interference with their affairs must be directed primarily to secure the safety and progress of civilization, not for selfish interests. Here was the idea of stewardship, later to be adapted to the mandates system. But Hobson could not be very optimistic in 1902, because no sign was in evidence that nations would exercise such a trust.[27] In his *Imperialism,* as previously noted, he had said that high finance was the greatest single factor in the economics of imperialism. But at a later date Hobson thought he could see a ray of hope. By 1911 he had reached the conclusion that international finance might be a guarantee of peace.[28] Imperialism, he thought, was changing its character, especially with regard to the Far East and South America. It no longer merely concerned political control and national domination over backward areas; this was weakening, and the old primary desire for profitable trade and investment was giving way to an economic internationalism exercised only with enough political supervision to afford good security. "Inter-imperialism," or international capitalist co-operation for the exploitation of labor, was to Hobson still a danger in 1930, but his emphasis had shifted.[29]

As time went on Hobson talked less and less about economic imperialism, stressing rather the theme that something better was about to take its place. During the first World War he wrote a book on international government—the antithesis of imperialism—in which "raising the consuming power of the public" is not mentioned as a remedy for imperialism.[30] The solution Hobson here presents is some sort of international council, or league of nations, in which democracy would replace the old system of alliances and federations in international affairs. Although he did not abandon his original idea that the fundamental causes of imperialism and international conflict are economic,[31] his later emphasis, after all, seems to be more on political causes and cures than on economic.

Hobson's later views, as well as some of his earlier remarks, clearly indicate that he thought imperialism was a passing phase of modern capitalist society because of the prospects for the realiza-

[27] *Ibid.,* pp. 245–50.

[28] Hobson, *An Economic Interpretation of Investment,* pp. 116–17. There is a striking parallelism between this idea and that of Kautsky; cf. p. 157, below.

[29] Hobson, *Rationalisation and Unemployment,* p. 115.

[30] Hobson, *Towards International Government.*          [31] *Ibid.,* p. 130.

tion of a reformed capitalism and a genuine international government. The old system, in other words, is an "atavism"—although Hobson did not call it that—going back to certain primitive instincts of mankind. In one place he says that imperialism is made to flourish "by playing upon the primitive instincts of the race," particularly the "trek" habit and the passion for land. The nomadic habit, bred of necessity, "survives as a chief ingredient in the love of travel, and merges into 'the spirit of adventure' when it meets other equally primitive passions." Again he says:

The animal lust of struggle, once a necessity, survives in the blood, and just in proportion as a nation or a class has a margin of energy and leisure from the activities of peaceful industry, it craves satisfaction through "sport," in which hunting and the physical satisfaction of striking a blow are vital ingredients.[32]

Again, at the very end of his *Imperialism,* Hobson speaks of imperialism as "a depraved choice of national life, imposed by self-seeking interests which appeal to the lusts of quantitative acquisitiveness and of forceful domination surviving in a nation from early centuries of animal struggle for existence." [33] This view also fits in with another, in which Hobson remarks that "the gravest peril of Imperialism lies in the state of mind of a nation which has become habituated to this deception and which has rendered itself incapable of self-criticism." [34]

The thing that is anachronistic, in Hobson's opinion, is not capitalism, as such, but only those elements in it which make for imperialism. The socialists, on the other hand, regard both imperialism and capitalism as anachronisms, destined to disappear together as one inseparable system of exploitation. Even Marx, writing before the modern theory of economic imperialism was developed, regarded colonialism as a purely precapitalist phenomenon, of which only vestiges remain. But in the case of both Hobson and the socialists the atavistic character of imperialism is incidental and implied, rather than worked out. It was left to an economist, Joseph Schumpeter, to take this idea and develop it into a well-rounded body of theory.[35]

[32] *Imperialism*, pp. 224–25.
[33] *Ibid.*, p. 390.
[34] *Ibid.*, p. 223.
[35] See below, pp. 229–36.

## BACKGROUND AND INFLUENCE OF HOBSON'S IDEAS

It was shown in the preceding chapter that certain ideas of such writers as Malthus and Sismondi contributed the sort of criticism of capitalism which readily could be turned into a theory of economic imperialism. Hobson stood in the direct tradition of these criticisms and was the first to draw the logical conclusions which they implied. Yet there is little direct evidence in his writings that he owed intellectual debts to these earlier critics. The idea of surpluses seeking outlets—indeed, the whole problem of effective demand, of which such ideas are the center—seems to arise spontaneously in the minds of a great many students of economics seeking the reasons for capitalism's failure to maintain an equilibrium between production and consumption. There is little point, therefore, in trying to find definite evidence of the various sources of influence which may have contributed to Hobson's theory of economic imperialism.

It is interesting, however, to note that an American financial writer, Charles A. Conant, has been suggested [36] as a possible source of his ideas on imperialism. It seems more probable, however, that the influence was in the other direction, inasmuch as Conant quotes Hobson with approval,[37] while Hobson does not mention Conant

[36] By Langer, "A Critique of Imperialism," *Foreign Affairs,* XIV (October, 1935), 102–19.

[37] See Conant, *The United States in the Orient.* This is a collection of articles by Conant which previously appeared in various journals. In chap. VI, "The United States as a World Power—Nature of the Economic and Political Problem" (which had appeared in the *Forum,* July, 1900), Conant (pp. 172–73) agrees with Hobson's observation in *The Evolution of Modern Capitalism* that international finance is a power which disregards boundaries and dictates to nations. In an earlier article, with a much more pointed title, "The Economic Basis of Imperialism" (chap. i of the collection; printed in the *North American Review,* September, 1898), Conant emphasized the importance of naval power as the advance agent of commercial supremacy, which he declared was not a matter of sentiment, but "the result of a natural law of economic and race development" (p. 2), the economic aspect being determined by the excess of savings under modern machine methods of production, which must find an outlet in order to prevent the economic order from being shaken by social revolution (pp. 2, 3). He also remarked that he was not an advocate of "imperialism" from sentiment, but had no fear of the term if it meant that the United States would assert its right to free markets in the world (p. 30). Since it was not the policy of other countries to permit free markets, Conant believed that the United States would be compelled by the instinct of self-preservation to engage in the scramble for commercial supremacy, abandon the policy of isolation, and enter the field of international politics (see chap. iii, "The Struggle for Commercial Empire," pp. 63, 79, 86; previously printed in the *Forum,* June, 1899).

in his study of imperialism. There is little evidence that his theory of imperialism was suggested by any particular writer, although he was familiar with Marx's writings, and this may have quickened his own feeling that capitalism had evolved to a bad position, from which it could not easily be extricated; [38] but he was highly critical of some of Marx's basic ideas, such as the labor-cost theory of value and Marx's conception of surplus value.

Even John Stuart Mill, who represented the brand of orthodoxy against which Hobson rebelled, nevertheless entertained ideas closely akin to those to be found in Hobson's *Imperialism*. Long before Hobson speculated on the conflict between expanding production and relatively static markets, Mill had observed that "the expansion of capital would soon reach its ultimate boundary, if the boundary itself did not continually open and leave more space." [39] Mill might not have moved on from this generalization to agree with Hobson that the home market itself could grow indefinitely without resorting to external or imperial expansion, but he undoubtedly would have agreed that there was some relation between capital export and what writers of Hobson's day were to call imperialism.

The mercantilism which Adam Smith had attacked as the product of monopolizing business was not far removed from the imperialism which Hobson was to regard as the consequence of financial and industrial monopolies. From Smith to Hobson the lesson was that men must be watched and curbed lest they turn enterpise from social to personal ends and foreign commerce from free trade to monopoly, protectionism, mercantilism, and imperialism. There was nothing in traditional economic thought, at least in plain sight, to make one aware that there is a vast gulf of difference between economic and noneconomic competition and economic and noneconomic motives and power. There was no entrenched body of thought to discourage ordinary commonsense reasoning from reaching the conclusion that the pursuit of economic power, motivated by the desire for profits, results in an exclusive form of competition in which one side must emerge victorious and the other a victim. The economic motive and im-

[38] Hobson first read Volume I of Marx's *Capital* a considerable time before his *Evolution of Modern Capitalism* appeared, in 1894.

[39] Mill, *Principles of Political Economy*. See also above, p. 86.

perialism, as Hobson saw them, seemed most obviously to be linked together. Neither Smith nor Mill could have found much fault with Hobson's reasoning about this relationship. The phenomenon seemed to verify the old fear that competition might turn into monopoly, and the search for profits into mere greed and avarice. It was no great leap from these concerns of classical economists to the conclusion reached by Hobson and the socialists that capitalism as a whole was degenerating into state enterprise and becoming the "tap-root" of imperialism.

Much clearer than the sources of Hobson's theory of imperialism is his influence on those who followed him in writing on this same subject, including even the socialists. His theory has had a more direct and apparent influence on the writing of history, at least in the English language, than that of Marx and the Marxists, because after all Hobson was English and wrote primarily for an English-speaking audience about a phenomenon that was almost exclusively British at the time he wrote. But the historians of international relations, whether English-speaking or not, were concerned with the same spectacle and were ready to become interested in any contribution that a penetrating and original scholar might make. The great modern historians, furthermore, had for the most part been cloistered and conservative and therefore very little inclined to listen to what a man of Marx's reputation had to say. What he had to say was not only radical but also terribly complex. Hobson wrote with a direct simplicity that sounded like common sense, and his ideas were not too theoretical to put into the history books.

## NOTE ON THE SIMILARITY OF KEYNES AND HOBSON

Keynes, of course, has been the chief influence in reviving the underconsumption theory. In common with other underconsumptionists, he does not see as a problem the enormous productive capacity of modern capitalism, and in common with the neglected heroes of the underconsumption theory—Malthus, Marx, Hobson, and others—he believes that the problem centers on consumption. To Keynes the insufficiency of effective demand may not be passed off as the result of a wrong distribution of wealth, a lag of population growth, or the failure to pay higher wages, but is ascribable to the failure to provide full employment.

Thus [says Keynes in summarizing the outline of his theory] the volume of employment is not determined by the marginal disutility of labour measured in terms of real wages [as the old analysis had it], except in so far as the supply of labour available at a given real wage sets a *maximum* level to employment. The propensity to consume and the rate of new investment determine between them the volume of employment, and the volume of employment is uniquely related to a given level of real wages—not the other way round. If the propensity to consume and the rate of new investment result in a deficient effective demand, the actual level of employment will fall short of the supply of labour potentially available at the existing real wage, and the equilibrium real wage will be *greater* than the marginal disutility of the equilibrium level of employment.

This analysis supplies us with an explanation of the paradox of poverty in the midst of plenty. For the mere existence of an insufficiency of effective demand may, and often will, bring the increase of employment to a standstill *before* a level of full employment has been reached.[40]

In the end Keynes reaches the conclusion that for various reasons, which need not be repeated here, full employment will not be attained under present conditions of private enterprise and that the state should step in to provide employment which private investors are unwilling or unable to provide. Such a solution, in itself, would be of no special interest to the theory of imperialism (which has come to be largely a theory of capitalist expansion) were it not for the fact that Keynes in his concluding pages in substance presents his solution of the unemployment problem as an antidote to imperialism in much the same way that Hobson had argued a similar case, and at the same time he definitely relates imperialism to the operation of the old laissez-faire economic system and the gold standard.

The mercantilists, he says, knew perfectly well that their nationalistic policies tended to promote war, because they were striving both for national advantage and relative strength. Nevertheless, Keynes believes that the mercantilists, though indifferent to the consequences of their system, possessed an intellectual realism which is much preferable to the confused thinking of present-day advocates of an international fixed gold standard and laissez faire in international lending, who believe that such policies will promote peace.

[40] Keynes, *General Theory*, pp. 30–31.

For in an economy subject to money contracts and customs more or less fixed over an appreciable period of time, where the quantity of the domestic circulation and the domestic rate of interest are primarily determined by the balance of payments, as they were in Great Britain before the war, there is no orthodox means open to the authorities for countering unemployment at home except by struggling for an export surplus and an import of the monetary metal at the expense of their neighbours. Never in history was there a method devised of such efficacy for setting each country's advantage at variance with its neighbours' as the international gold (or, formerly, silver) standard. For it made domestic prosperity directly dependent on a competitive pursuit of markets and a competitive appetite for the precious metals. When by happy accident the new supplies of gold and silver were comparatively abundant, the struggle might be somewhat abated. But with the growth of wealth and the diminishing marginal propensity to consume, it has tended to become increasingly internecine.[41]

It comes as no surprise after these words to have Keynes declare that of all the causes of war the economic causes are the greatest—"namely, the pressure of population and the competitive struggle for markets."[42] What is the remedy? Full employment, for if nations can learn to solve this problem by domestic policy, there will be no important economic forces left to set one country against another.[43] At this point Keynes sounds like Hobson, especially when he adds:

There would still be room for the international division of labour and for international lending in appropriate conditions. But there would no longer be a pressing motive why one country need force its wares on another or repulse the offerings of its neighbour, not because this was necessary to enable it to pay for what it wished to purchase, but with the express object of upsetting the equilibrium of payments so as to develop a balance of trade in its own favour. International trade would cease to be what it is, namely, a desperate expedient to maintain employment at home by forcing sales on foreign markets and restricting purchases, which, if successful, will merely shift the problem of unemployment to the neighbour which is worsted in the struggle, but a willing and unimpeded exchange of goods and services in conditions of mutual advantage.

[41] *Ibid.*, pp. 348–49.
[42] *Ibid.*, p. 381.
[43] The same point is made by Alvin H. Hansen in the opening page of his introduction to *Fiscal Policy and Business Cycles*, p. vii. The present war, says Hansen, has "an economic basis—the inability of the great industrial nations to provide full employment at rising standards of real income."

Like Hobson, Keynes wants to reform the capitalistic system instead of uprooting and destroying it. The influence of the *General Theory* has been enormous, and the new note which it strikes, namely, the necessity of solving the problem of unemployment (thereby solving the problem of the insufficiency of effective demand) is far superior to Hobson's feeble cry that all capitalism has to do to save itself from international conflict is to pay higher wages and keep most of its surpluses at home.

But something is lacking in Keynes which is not lacking in the writings of the orthodox economists with whom he has broken. That is, the emphasis on monopoly as the cause of capitalism's trouble and the resultant emphasis on the suppression of monopoly in all its forms and manifestations as the price of intra-national and international harmony. It is entirely foreign to Keynes, and to his many followers, that the pattern of imperialism and militarism, or for that matter of mercantilism, is to be found in the growth and power of great monopolies. Rather, these forces are to be recognized and somehow made to work for the common good. This is a curious omission in view of Keynes's unusual insight into the role of investment, for it keeps him from stressing the necessary conflict between investment and the sort of resistance to investment that is associated with monopoly and sticky costs and prices. Investment is essentially a cost-reducing process; it is what makes the free-enterprise system function and produces economic progress, while at the same time making possible the sufficiency of effective demand. But instead of associating the insufficiency of demand with such obvious barriers to investment as monopolies and tariffs, Keynes looks for it in the psychological propensity to consume and to invest.

Why, we may ask, is there reason to think that nations will try to solve their unemployment problem by strictly "domestic" measures? Keynes criticizes the old system because it sets neighbor against neighbor through the process of international trade, that is, because each country tries to solve its "surplus" problem by forcing its exports on unwilling markets. This is another way of saying that it tries to export its unemployment in exchange for a higher standard of income than could be done by trying to solve the problem by domestic means, such as state-promoted public works. But if nations continue to strive for national advantage and relative strength, what surety is there that they will submit voluntarily to a policy which appears only to purchase full employment at the price of that greater relative strength nations have always worshiped? Indeed, it is quite conceivable that Keynes's theory might supply the scientific basis (assuming that such a basis is possible) for a *Volksimperialismus,* or popular imperialism. In contrast to the Marxian idea that the cause of trouble resides in the existence of unemployed capital and in the attempt of the state to come to the rescue by forcing its export, a mass movement in favor of imperialism might be created should a highly nationalistic state undertake by similar means to come to the rescue of its own unemployed labor. Such an idea could never occur to Marx, because he conceived of the state as being the tool of the capitalist class, but it is implicit in Keynes's insistence that the state should do something for the working class, assuming that the state continued to regard national advantage and relative strength as the primary aim of policy.

The central problem is still how to solve the problem of effective demand without the intrusion of the state into economic life and without the backing of national policies which stir up the internecine strife so deeply regretted by Hobson and Keynes. Unless a solution can be found and applied, it will continue to be recorded that international conflict is what economists like Hobson and Keynes—and, we may add, Marx and his followers—say it is, the product of a bad or a badly working economic system.

# SOCIALISTIC THEORIES
# OF IMPERIALISM: MARXIAN
# BACKGROUND

IF Imperial Britain and other imperial powers of the seventeenth century illustrated William Penn's observation that peace is broken by the attempt "to keep, to recover, or to add," modern Imperial Germany could be used as the leading example of this truth in the late nineteenth and early twentieth centuries. Here, under modern industrial conditions, was a late-comer which first added, then lost, tried to recover, and lost again in the great game of empire. Realizing her strength, she tried the old policy of being her own "judge and carver" in a world that was far more resistant to carving than it had ever been before.

## IMPERIALISMUS—MADE IN GERMANY

Although Germany became an imperial power, there arose in that country while the process was going on one of the strongest anti-imperialistic movements to be found anywhere, and out of this movement developed the modern theory of imperialism which has found such wide currency throughout the world. Modern imperialism originated in Great Britain, but the theory of *imperialismus* reached its highest development in Germany. The theory developed as a reaction not only to British imperialism but also to the imperial ambitions of Germany. These ambitions, in turn, were stimulated by the British example.

Imperialism has always been associated with activity that takes place across salt water rather than across fresh water and most of what can be said about it is found in the history of sea power. Nations without sea power or overseas possessions, and yet with a tradition of land power, are easily made conscious of their inadequacies in contrast to neighbors having vast possessions and power. Unless the trading spirit has developed to a point where it is more forceful in politics than the military or naval spirit, the latter, with its tradition of getting things by force rather than by bargaining, can easily set a nation on ambitious schemes of expansion. When this tendency is thwarted, either by opposition from abroad or from lack of a residue of rich lands to exploit, it is easy to stimulate in the people as well as in their leaders a feeling of inadequacy. At this stage anxious speculation about imperialism—usually the imperialism of the sated powers—comes into its own. But this in turn arouses speculation from those at home, especially among the masses, or their leaders, who may feel that in any grandiose scheme of imperial expansion they would be the ones exploited.

In Germany the most ardent anti-imperialists were found among those Social Democrats who were opposed to expansion because they associated it with the capitalistic system which they were trying to overthrow. Because the various national Social Democratic parties had strong international connections and were constantly educating their people to the dangers and iniquities of imperialism, it is not strange that the "radicals" of all nations soon learned to express the same thoughts about it. And since scholarship and the press are not monopolies of any one group, it was only a matter of time before these radical ideas began to permeate more traditional cloisters and to produce serious studies under the exciting label of imperialism.

In old Germany we find a tradition of historical scholarship and philosophy entirely different from the thought of the English. Highly abstract, it placed great store on "system building" and the development of ideologies, from which come such powerful conceptual symbols as capitalism and imperialism. While the English built an empire on the earth, the Germans built theirs in the air, long before the German Empire became a reality. The growth of German nationalism, a certain sense of inferiority, combined with a feeling of jealousy towards England, prompted Germans to speculate about the meaning of Britain's greatness and their own insufficiency.

In Fichte, for instance, this produced a rabid anti-imperialistic surge of emotion, powerful enough to make him outstanding as one of the first proponents of "economic nationalism." Indeed, it would be difficult to find a more pronounced statement of the essential conflict between nationalism and imperialism than that found in Fichte's arguments for a closed commercial system.[1] List, with much less emotion, but nevertheless looking in the Fichtean direction, believed that the German states, like the United States, must show and maintain their unity and independence by adopting protectionism. In his opinion this was the road to power, and Germany not only followed his advice, but went far beyond it.[2]

Marx, influenced by Hegel, came out of his saturation in German philosophy to preach the doctrine of still another kind of system—the classless society. Here, for the first time, we find a professedly scientific view of history being used in an attempt to prove that economic forces determine the conflicts of society and that the conflicts are all headed in the same direction—the end of private property, over which the class struggle takes place, and the appearance of common ownership of the means of production.

By the end of what was to have been "Marx's century," the socialists were beginning to realize not only that the Kingdom of Heaven on earth, which Marx had so earnestly believed to be at hand, was still in the future but also that capitalism, far from being in its last throes, was taking a new lease on life. It appeared, however, to be developing all those warlike tendencies which its critics regarded as inherent in the system, and there was always hope that revolution might follow the Boer, Spanish-American, and Russo-Japanese wars of imperialism. These and a series of international

[1] Fichte was a thoroughgoing cosmopolite until Napoleon's humiliation of Prussia at Jena in 1806. This roused him to a "powerful anti-imperialist blast," in which he said: "May we at last recognize that while the airy theories about international trade and manufacturing for the world may do for the foreigner, and belong to the weapons with which he has always invaded us, they have no application to Germans, and that, next to unity among ourselves, internal independence and commercial self-reliance are the second means to our salvation, and through them to the welfare of Europe."—"Reden an die Deutsche Nation, 1807–1808, Lecture 13," in Engelbrecht, *Johann Gottlieb Fichte*, p. 120.

[2] Friedrich List's *The National System of Political Economy* (first published in 1841), long neglected even by the Germans after its first period of popularity, is the classic opposite of Adam Smith's *Wealth of Nations*. List professed a belief in free trade as an ultimate goal, but desired protectionism as a means of raising Germany to a position where she could afford it. He wanted a strong German nationalism, because protectionism was unthinkable without it, but he had no intention of encouraging Germany to go beyond nationalism to imperialism.

"incidents" all seemed to point towards further conflict, and socialist writings of the decade before 1914 were full of warnings of a general war of great magnitude and violence.

The signs that capitalism was taking on new vigor could not go unnoticed. The relative peace and quiet of the era of "industrial capitalism" and of laissez faire and free trade had obviously passed, and something more sinister and powerful was taking its place. "Economic nationalism" was in full stride, as evidenced by increased protectionism, the growth of powerful trusts and cartels behind tariff walls, and the rise of powerful banking institutions. But it was also evident that economic nationalism was not enough to satisfy the capitalists, who were beginning to look beyond their tariff walls for greener pastures of exploitation, and soon the great cartels and banks were becoming "international." Having exploited their domestic markets to somewhere near the maximum, they were now "dividing the world between them," as the socialists liked to put it.

Leadership in this new type of enterprise fell to the great banks, which were regarded as overlords of the industrial capitalists and their cartels and trusts. Old-fashioned industrial capitalism had turned into "finance capitalism," and the "international bankers" were beginning to be suspected of fomenting wars in order to reap the profits of war; at least they were regarded as following policies which inevitably would lead to imperialism, which in turn would lead to war. If "economic nationalism" described the earlier stages of this new development, "economic imperialism" seemed to be the appropriate term for the more advanced stage in which nationalism was giving way to empire building.

Socialist speculations about this new turn of events were not at first so much concerned with projecting the theory of capitalism into a theory of imperialism, although that was what it now appears to be as we look back. Rather, the rise of imperialism led to speculation about its relation to capitalism. But it soon became apparent that the new imperialism did not fit squarely into the old concept of capitalism, and this forced a re-examination of Marxian doctrine to see what had happened. The conclusion which finally emerged was that, while peaceful industrial capitalism might give rise to the class struggle, it could hardy be conceived as the producer of international war. Only when socialists began to hit upon the idea that *financial* capitalism develops a new ideology making for expansion, conflict, and war were they able to speak with confidence of "capitalist-imperialism." The Boer War and the Spanish-American War gave them this confidence, but before they could formulate their ideas and present the world with a new theory of imperialism, Hobson had already pointed the way.

In a very true sense the concept of *imperialismus* is German in origin and typically German in its philosophical base and its relation to the economic interpretation, and most of the history of the theory of imperialism revolves about German writers. Although the development of the concept became almost a monopoly of the Marxists and was as much a reaction to German capitalism and imperialism as it was to British, the idea of economic imperialism commanded more attention in Germany (and Austria) than in any other country, and earlier than in any other country. While British scholars either ignored the concept or at most talked in straightforward and uncomplex terms about the realities of empire building, German scholars, whether Marxian or not, pursued it with the zeal of men on the track of the key to all history, politics, and economics.

Imperialistic as Great Britain's policy had been in the heyday of her empire building, and continued to be, but in a somewhat more enlightened way, during the nineteenth century, it was scarcely a match either in zeal or singleness of purpose to German imperialism from the time of Bismarck. From the German point of view it was necessary in a world of power politics to outmatch the British, and from this same point of view Germany was no more a troublemaker for the world than Britain had been. In the crudest terms, it was a question of who would be boss, and Germans were not inclined to think that their ends and means were any different from or any worse than those of other imperialistic powers. Even the severest critics of imperialism in the two countries could agree with this as a generalization.

And yet there was a certain spirit of liberalism abroad in the world which tried to say that by-gones should be forgotten, that the *status quo* should be accepted, and that in this atmosphere all rivalry and power politics might be submerged in the interest of the common goal. If this sounded good to English imperialists as well as to liberals, it was not convincing to German imperialists and militarists, and the judgment of the rest of the world against them has been all the harder because they refused to accept it.[3]

## THE ROLE OF "BRUTE FORCE" IN THE RISE OF CAPITALISM

We shall look in vain in the writings of Karl Marx for a theory of modern imperialism as such. Yet Marx is the father of the idea that capitalism is responsible in modern times for the creation of surplus products for which it must find ever-expanding markets or die, and in seeking them fight to the death. It makes little difference whether he called this out-thrust of the national capitalist systems "imperialism" or not. "Capitalism" was the all-embracing term to Marx, and he had no need for any other concept.

Although in one place Marx used the term "imperialism," he had in mind merely a political system called an empire, supported by bourgeois elements for the purpose of exploiting labor. His specific reference is to the aims of Napoleon III in the Franco-Prussian War, with the implication that defeat was the just price of imperial ambitions and the opportunity for the French proletarians to stage the long expected counter-revolution.

Imperialism [he says in this connection, is] the most prostitute and the ultimate form of the State power which nascent middle class society has commenced to elaborate as a means of its own emancipation from feudalism, and which fullgrown bourgeois society had finally transformed into a means for the enslavement of labor by capital.[4]

Few socialists have singled out this particular statement as indicative of Marx's foresight in anticipating the nature of future imperialistic developments, although Leon Trotsky thought that it had "a wider significance than for the French Empire alone, and includes the latest form of imperialism, born of the world conflict between the national capitalisms of the great powers."[5] There are

---

3 Of the enormous literature on the subject of Germany's share in the blame two books may be mentioned as characteristic, one by an Englishman, the other by a German: Hearnshaw, *Germany the Aggressor throughout the Ages*, and Foerster, *Europe and the German Question*.

4 "The Civil War in France," from *The Paris Commune*, p. 173. Marx used the word *Imperialismus* in the original, *Der Bürgerkrieg in Frankreich*, pp. 25–26.

5 Trotsky, *Dictatorship vs. Democracy*, p. 34.

many more suggestive passages in Marx—or Marx and Engels—for those who are looking for sources of the modern socialist ideas of imperialism: in what Marx and his collaborator thought about the nature of conflict, "collisions," and force; in Marx's remarks on "the theory of colonization"; and finally in what he had to say about the more mechanical aspects of capital expansion.

In the *Communist Manifesto*, which appeared in 1848 as a preview of what was to come later in more detail in *Capital*, Marx and Engels speak of how the discovery of America opened new territory for the rising bourgeoisie to exploit, created new markets, increased exchange, and gave commerce and industry an impulse never before known. They pictured a new world—the bourgeois world—whose conquerors, ever in "need of a constantly expanding market," covered the face of the earth, to "nestle everywhere, settle everywhere, establish connections everywhere," in order to make the "barbarian and semi-barbarian countries dependent on the civilised ones." [6] This made it appear that capitalism was already a world-wide system—"everywhere established," as Marx was to put it again later—and that the next step was for the proletariat of each country to settle matters with its own bourgeoisie and then join forces throughout the world independently of all nationality, in order to abolish countries and nationality. Indeed, "national differences and antagonisms between peoples are daily more and more vanishing" (owing to the spread of capitalism), and "the supremacy of the proletariat will cause them to vanish still faster." [7]

In some articles written by Marx about British policy in India, Ireland, and elsewhere there are many passages which have been cited as evidence that he had a complete understanding of the nature of imperialism. [8] Likewise in *German Ideology*, by Marx and Engels, and in Engels' *Feuerbach* and *Anti-Dühring* [9] there is much

[6] Marx and Engels, *Manifesto of the Communist Party*, pp. 17–18.
[7] *Ibid.*, p. 38.
[8] "The deep analysis of the economic and political factors underlying Indian events make these articles particularly important for the understanding of Marxist theory on the development of imperialism and colonial revolt," says Emile Burns, *A Handbook of Marxism*, p. 179. In speaking of British policy towards Ireland, Marx says that "England is at present what ancient Rome was, in even greater degree. A people which enslaves another people forges its own chains."—*Ibid.*, p. 196.
[9] These and other works (some of them abbreviated) are found in the *Handbook of Marxism*. For complete editions see the authorized German and English publications.

discussion of the theory of conflict, "collisions," and force, and there are expositions of the materialistic interpretation of history. But through it all runs the thought that the era of conflict and force was nearly ended.[10]

Capital accumulation and capitalist expansion obviously had to begin somehow and somewhere, and in Volume I of *Capital* [11] (especially Part 8) Marx describes the earlier stages as "primitive" accumulation, with colonial expansion and exploitation taking a leading part in the unsavory business of separating the producer (worker) from the means of production and making profit out of human misery by the simple process of robbing, looting, enslaving, and carrying on other such "idyllic proceedings," all of which combined to usher in the "rosy dawn" of capitalism. Whatever the methods, they all "depend in part on brute force," says Marx, singling out the colonial system as a special example.[12] Added to this "brute force" was the organized and concentrated force of society embodied in the state, whose function was to hasten the transition from feudalism to capitalism. But the chief point which Marx, in many a flaming passage and in some of his best word pictures, was trying to make was that *force*—brute force and a somewhat more refined political force—was the lever of progress from feudalism to colonialism to capitalism and that in each succeeding stage the newly emancipated became the exploiters of those still on the lower rungs of the social ladder. The great lesson was that in the end the worm would turn—the proletarian class which a capitalist society, itself newly emancipated from feudal domination, had enslaved would soon become the master by its own numerical superiority and force. "Force is the mid-wife of every old society pregnant with a new one. It is itself an economic power." [13]

----

10 While Marx could not justify what was going on in India, he could at least regard it as inevitable: "The bourgeois period of history has to create the material basis of the new world," just as "geological revolutions have created the surface of the earth" (*Handbook of Marxism*, p. 194). This sort of talk was later used by certain socialists to excuse the imperialism of their day as a necessary stage of capitalist development in its march towards socialism. They would have nothing to do with it as a policy, but they seemed to feel that it was not their business to oppose it— the policy itself would bring a retribution far greater than any they were able to impose.

11 Ernest Untermann's translation of Volumes I–III of Marx's *Capital* is used throughout this book.

12 *Capital*, I, 823.                    13 *Ibid.*, p. 824.

Force implies weapons, and Marx saw the weapons of capitalism to consist of the great trading monopolies in the "primitive" or colonial stage, of great banking institutions, heavy taxation, protectionism, and "commercial wars" in the later stages. The use of credit enabled the masters of the new society to endow "barren money with the power of breeding"; [14] they could turn it into capital, establish banks, gamble on the stock exchange, and even make loans to the state. The state in turn, to bolster its credit, must be able to repay what it borrows, and out of this necessity grew the modern system of taxation, itself an enormously powerful weapon of expropriation, especially when it takes the form of protective tariffs. [15] Yet Marx regarded the banks as mere handmaidens of the capitalist class. Capitalism still meant "industrial capitalism"; "financial capitalism" was not to be heard of until the great banks rose to the peak of the pyramid, a generation after Marx's death, when the neo-Marxists found it necessary to revise the old doctrine.

Although Marx generally spoke of colonialism as if it were a thing of the past, belonging to the age of primitive accumulation, there was enough of this anachronism left in the world to take serious notice of, especially the various schemes, such as that of E. G. Wakefield, "to effect the manufacture of wage-workers in the Colonies." [16] Wakefield's scheme, which he preferred to regard as a plan for "systematic colonization," was a program for sending settlers to the colonies, particularly to Australia, under regulations designed to check the premature occupation of new land by placing an arbitrarily high price on it, the proceeds to be used to transport laborers from the mother country. Thus, it was hoped, there would be no rush to take up new land, with the result that an adequate supply of labor would be made available. [17] As Wakefield pointed out, people had learned that capitalist production was impossible without a division of society into capitalists and workers, and if capitalism were to be maintained in the colonies, a plentiful supply of labor must be created by artificial means.

Such a proposal was enough to convince Marx that capitalists and their governments would stop at nothing to maintain their

[14] *Ibid.*, pp. 826–27.      [15] *Ibid.*, pp. 826, 829–30.      [16] *Ibid.*, p. 839.
[17] See above, p. 89, for Mill's favorable estimation of Wakefield's ideas.

system, going even to the point of establishing slavery; "systematic colonization" would not work with free men, and Wakefield's scheme was evidence that the only natural basis of colonial wealth is forced labor.[18] Marx did not call this sort of thing "imperialism." In his day it was sufficiently damning to call it "capitalism," buttressed with such descriptive terms as "forced labor," "wage-slavery," "exploitation," and "expropriation." Nor was it exactly imperialism in the modern neo-Marxian sense. It was a scheme to export surplus population rather than a policy of exporting surplus products. Marx also considered the latter without calling it imperialism; it was simply the foreign-market aspect of capitalist expansion.

But despite his apparent opposition to colonialism, as it was carried on by capitalists, Marx nevertheless thought that it was necessary and not only inevitable but also part of the dialectic process whereby capitalism conquers the world before socialism can conquer it. Though some of his remarks and attitudes seem quite imperialistic,[19] they must be taken as arguments of Marx in the role of devil's advocate, not of Marx the socialist. He believed that Germany was destined to put an end to the dream of "Czechian nationality," since "Bohemia could only exist, henceforth, as a portion of Germany"; as for Schleswig and Holstein, they were "unquestionably German by nationality, language and predilection [and] are also from military, naval, and commercial grounds necessary to Germany."[20] He wanted to see France defeated by Prussia in 1870–71: "The French need a thrashing. If the Prussians win, the centralization of the state power will be useful for the centralisation of the German working class."[21] Further evidence of his militant Germanism is seen in a passage in which he praises "the historical tendency, and at the same time the physical and intellectual power of the German nation to subdue, absorb, and assimilate its ancient eastern neighbours," adding that "this tendency of absorption on the part of the Germans had always been,

18 *Capital* I, 840–46.
19 One of Marx's critics points out that "there are to be found in Marxism all the elements which were afterward to be combined, according to a different formula, in Naziism."—Parkes, *Marxism*, p. 264.
20 *Selected Works*, II, 91, 94; see also Parkes, *Marxism*, pp. 16, 263 ff.
21 Marx and Engels, *Correspondence*, p. 292.

and still was, one of the mightiest means by which the civilisation of Western Europe had been spread to the east of that continent." [22]

Once Marx leaves the question of primitive accumulation and turns to the operation of modern capitalism, he has finished with the word "force" in the sense of naked power. As he says, "Direct force, outside economic conditions, is of course still used, but only exceptionally." [23] Although force is still at work in the background, it is a more highly rarefied thing, the power of exploiting human beings for profit, operating through "the natural laws of production" and the price mechanism. But as Marx saw it, the capitalist mode of production was also working swiftly towards its own end and on into socialism, and not even temporarily towards what his followers were to call "imperialism" and later "fascism."

## THE BASIC ELEMENTS IN MARX'S IDEOLOGY

Marx's conception of brute force constituted part of his explanation of colonialism as a breeding ground for accumulation and the rise of capitalism, but it is not amenable to an explanation of modern imperialism. According to the Marxian theory modern imperialism is to be found only in the development and expansion of capitalism itself, which is largely a matter of technological development with emphasis on a particular "mode of production," namely, that of machines as distinct from that of handicraft.

But before turning to this part of the analysis we need to sketch briefly some background conceptions without which the mere mechanics of development seem rather tasteless and gritty. Marx added the spice for a purpose, and we cannot leave it out, although we need not go so far as to think that these ingredients are essential to an understanding of what Marx was driving at on the more mechanical level, for the latter analysis stands or falls depending upon whether it fits the facts.

First of all, there is the materialistic interpretation of history, or "historical materialism," which is important because it introduces the idea of inevitability and imparts that air of finality which distinguishes Marx from all other writers. This view of history simply reduces to the proposition that *cause*, not purpose, rules men's

[22] *Selected Works*, II, 120.          [23] *Capital*, I, 809.

behavior,[24] which means that they act as they do because they are earthlings in a world that keeps them tied down to its own physical laws; given their animal and physical nature and requirements, they cannot do otherwise than obey the law of the natural environment of which they are a part.[25] In short, they are subject to forces which make their action inevitable, and all attempts to *purpose* to do otherwise are doomed to failure, no matter how high or low the end or aim. The earth, not heaven, helps those who help themselves—always in accordance with its laws—and Marx made this idea most pointed in the sarcasm he poured upon the Utopian Socialists for thinking that heaven on earth could be attained by wishful thinking. Capitalism, he said, will dig its own grave, because by nature it is a digging and gouging social system. That it could not survive, because it was fundamentally dishonest, was the essential idea, and among the purposeful ideas that have influenced history this has been one of the most powerful. But Marx would have insisted that it was not the idea that made history, but history which made the idea inevitable.

Compared with the Malthusian theory of what the world is coming to, Marx's dialectics, by which he explains the "laws of motion" in society by the conflict of forces, of which capitalist class conflict is the latest and most important, seem mild indeed. Marx leads us to the fateful end of capitalism and leaves us with the comforting thought that history has accomplished its purpose and that under socialism all will be sweetness and light. But the Malthusian law of population growth and the law of diminishing returns on which the fate of humanity rests is a kind of supereconomic interpretation of history, as forboding for a world of socialists as for a world of capitalists. To use the language of a typical Malthusian, the law of decreasing returns is at once "the source of the origin and de-

---

24 The Marxian viewpoint is well presented in Bukharin, *Historical Materialism*, especially pp. 21–22. For a good brief statement of both views see Allyn A. Young, "Economics and War," *American Economic Review*, XVI (March, 1926), 1–13; reprinted in Young's *Economic Problems New and Old*.

25 Marx did not mean that the economic motive is the only motive, but he nevertheless believed that the fundamental economic motive conditions religious and ethical motives so that they are made harmonious with it. This is quite different from "reducing" everything to economic causation, which is the same as denying the existence of noneconomic motives. Many of Marx's followers, including Engels, have gone much farther than Marx and have in fact "reduced," where Marx only correlated or pointed out conditioning relationships.

velopment of civilization . . . and for the same reason, the source of poverty and war." [26]

Population growth held no terrors for Marx except as it operated under capitalism, which had its own peculiar law of population. Not the absolute surplus population in the Malthusian sense of too many people for the earth to support, but a "relative surplus population" (the labor reserve army) in the sense of more people than capitalism could support and still retain the capitalistic conditions of profit. In the process of competing for profits, which entails replacing men by machines and forcing the weaker capitalists to become workers, capitalism always has at its command more workers than it requires, and it is this, not the sheer increase of the birthrate, that equates wages and the value of labor. Remove capitalism, and this kind of surplus population will disappear; or, let the labor reserve army of unemployed wax strong in numbers, and revolution will remove capitalism. Here, then, was the seed of revolution and war.

The conflicts engendered between capitalist nations in their struggle for markets was likewise the seed of war, but this, too, would disappear once the world is united under the banner of socialism. Thus, while Malthus held out no hope of peace unless people reformed and learned to control their numbers, which he regarded as by no means inevitable, Marx could say peace was inevitable because socialism was inevitable. Marx held an economic interpretation of war, but it is just as clear that he believed in an economic interpretation of peace; prevailing economic conditions were the final determinant in each case. Neither did the law of diminishing returns hold the terror for Marx that it did for the classical economists, who held that because of this law, which reflects the niggardliness of nature, profits will decline eventually to zero, and the owners of capital will suffer extinction. Thus the economic system will be brought to stagnation from lack of saving, for without profits capitalists will not accumulate. Marx accepted this conclusion, but instead of basing it on the niggardliness of nature or upon land's refusal to yield subsistence in proportion to the growth of population, he blamed it on the capitalists, who for love

[26] Edward Van Dyke Robinson, "War and Economics in History and in Theory," *Political Science Quarterly* (December, 1900), 619–20.

of profit force a change in the organic composition of capital, resulting in the replacement of men by machines. Thus, where the classicists held out no hope because men could not change nature, Marx was able to suggest that it was not a matter of mastering nature, but of gaining mastery over the machine, or technology. And the logic, as applied to imperialism, is that capitalists plus machines mean expansion, conflict, and war. On the other hand, *producers* —the workers—plus machines mean higher wages, a lack of incentive for outward expansion, and therefore co-operation and peace.

Marx accepted uncritically and with no attempt at proof the classical doctrine of the labor-cost theory of value, which to Ricardo had been a questionable hypothesis at best. This was the basic error in the whole Marxian theoretical system. Marx knew that it "contradicts all experience based on appearance," [27] but he persisted in trying to make the facts fit the theory. It was an obvious falsehood, and like all falsehoods it called for more falsification, until its author was finally enmeshed in a whole train of untenable positions. Yet we must not accuse Marx of seeking to perpetrate a fraud. He honestly (and rightly) believed that somewhere in the system of capitalist production there was a loose screw, for obviously somebody for some reason was getting something for nothing. It was capitalism more than Marx that was perpetrating a fraud; Marx was only trying to discover in what the fraud consists. He was dimly aware—and yet at times acutely near the truth—that it might have something to do with credit created by the banks, but he could not force himself to think that this was fundamental, because credit, being a monetary phenomenon, is only a veil which hides what goes on in the field of production and exchange.

Obviously consumers were not to blame either, and therefore Marx was always forced back to the mode of production in his search for this elusive something-for-nothing. The labor-cost theory supplied the only promising clue: labor produces all value, but the capitalists, by virtue of their legal ownership of capital, were in a position to exact a tribute in the form of surplus products, which constituted their source of profits. Therefore, to Marx, the loose screw was production for profit, and the real villains were the capitalists. But the owners of capital were not really to blame; it

[27] *Capital,* I, 335.

was the "system." They could not even control the system, but rather the system controlled them. It forced them to compete, and the inevitable decline of the rate of profit forced them to compete ever more fiercely until, in desperation, they would be obliged to organize themselves into monopolies. They were obliged, in pursuit of profits, to substitute machines for men, but whereas the machines could not strike back, the growing army of displaced workers could—and eventually would.

It was a majestic and intoxicating thought. It was one of the world's great original ideas, and that its author was carried away by it was to his credit, for at least he was sincerely trying to reform a world that was badly out of joint. His mistakes were largely the mistakes of the generation of economists which had preceded him, pushed to their logical conclusion, while his insight into new problems was the result of his own reasoning and industry.

## FOREIGN TRADE AND THE PROBLEM OF CAPITALIST EXPANSION

Any economic argument involving modern capitalism in imperialistic expansion obviously must say something regarding foreign trade and finance. Likewise, any theory of capitalist development which excludes the foreign trade and financial aspect leaves no room for a capitalistic theory of imperialism; in fact such treatment would establish the basis for denying that capitalism has any economically necessary connection with imperialism.

Both types of treatment are to be found in Marx, and from this curious lack of consistency has sprung the confusion of method among Marx's followers (to be considered in the following chapter) in handling the theory of imperialism. In saying that both types of treatment are to be found in Marx, it must be emphasized that he had no theory of foreign trade, but only some scattered remarks about it. In some places he stresses the dependence of capitalism on foreign trade, and in others he rejects the relevancy of foreign trade to his analysis of capitalism. The confusion goes back to his failure to develop a consistent theory of capitalist development. Marx's failure to develop a consistent theory of capitalism is in part due to basic errors in his assumptions and analysis, and partly to the fact that he did not live to round out his theory and settle upon some one of the various hypotheses which he considered.

We shall in particular examine two lines of argument bearing on foreign trade. First, Marx's theory of the falling tendency of the rate of profit, in which foreign countries become important to the capitalist economy as a source of cheap raw materials and foodstuffs. Second, his theory of underconsumption, with its implication (to some of Marx's followers rather than to Marx) that foreign markets for exports are essential as a means of disposing of goods for which no market can be found at home. On either of these hypotheses a theory of capitalist imperialism might be based, but not on both at once, because they are mutually contradictory. Actually, neither, without considerable qualification, has been acceptable to Marx's followers as a basis for a theory of imperialism.

Then there is an entirely different line of thought in Marx which appears to deny that foreign trade is essential to capitalism. This is particularly significant, because it leaves no room for a theory of imperialism, and the cogency of the argument has led certain socialists to regard imperialism as a policy of capitalism rather than an absolute essential. And what is more significant, perhaps, it has been used by these same socialists to show, on Marxian grounds, that capitalism need not collapse, but can go on indefinitely as a self-contained and self-equilibrating system, provided the correct proportions are maintained between the industries producing consumers' goods and those producing producers' goods. This, however, is regarded as theoretically possible only, since Marx makes it clear that capitalism lacks a plan for controlling investment and production. Such equilibrium as may appear is due to an accident, in which newly mined gold plays the central part as the accidental equilibrating factor.

In those parts of his theory which bear most heavily upon profits, Marx undertook to show that the rate of profit has a continuous tendency to decline.[28] Obviously, if it should fall to zero there no longer would be any motive for the profit-seeking capitalist to produce, and capitalism would die. But it does not have to fall to zero in order to injure capitalism; Marx is clear that it merely has to fall below the level to which capitalists are accustomed, or to the point where it no longer pays them to remain in business. For capitalism as a whole this tendency means that the source of savings,

[28] *Capital*, Vol. III, Part III.

or capital accumulation, dries up, causing the system to stagnate from lack of capital for expansion.

In the face of what actually went on in the capitalist world, Marx could not say that the rate of profit showed any imminent signs of falling to zero. In fact it held up so well, and even showed such a strong tendency to rise, that he was obliged to explain both why there should be a declining tendency and what circumstances were always arising to offset this tendency. The rate of profit tends to fall, he explained, because capitalists, each acting independently in his own interests, substitute labor-saving devices, or machines, for labor, thus causing the organic composition of capital, or the amount of capital per man, to rise. This in turn means spreading the resulting surplus value, derived alone from the men employed, over a widening capital base, causing the ratio of income to capital to fall. If capitalists were all banded together in a common purpose they would not do this, because according to Marx only labor is the source of the surplus value from which profits arise, and the common capitalist purpose could be served only by preserving for their constant use the source of surplus value, which is also the source of profit. But each one alone, faced with rising wage rates, can reap a temporary advantage over his competitors by expanding his production through the use of machines. When all do the same thing independently at once, however, the total result is overproduction —a greater output of consumer goods than can be taken off the market at the "profitable" price, inasmuch as the wage earners fail to receive the necessary purchasing power in the form of wages, while the capitalists who thus receive this foregone purchasing power do not spend it all on consumer goods, but save it for further investment. The result is a crisis of overproduction; values —from the capitalists' point of view—have to be destroyed because the surplus goods have to be sold for less than their value. They cost the equivalent of a certain amount of labor power, but must be sold for less.

Marx failed to show that the destruction of capital depends on the falling rate of profit, because he assumed an unchanging rate of exploitation, which in turn requires that wage rates rise as productivity increases. Such an outcome, however, was entirely out of harmony with Marx's whole system of thought. Modern economists, by ascribing productivity to capital as well as to labor and by bringing the discussion of profit in line with the problem of effective demand, do not emerge with a unique law of profits, but relate profits as well as wages to the total productivity of society under given conditions. By this sort of analysis it can be explained how both wages and profits can rise with productivity. But Marx, faced with this fact, was forced to turn to the underconsumption theory to explain the destruction of capitalism—a matter which we shall discuss presently. To explain the fact most glaringly contradicting his theory of declining profits, namely, that profits actually rise, he was obliged to resort to a set of "counteracting causes" which should have been taken into account in the first place. Having already committed himself, he could patch up his mistake by belatedly recognizing the facts. Thus, he proceeds to list six counteracting factors which intervene to keep the rate of profit up.[29] Only one of these, however, namely, "foreign trade," has any claim to being a connecting link between a capitalism in distress from falling profits and its attempt to solve its problem by "imperialistic" methods.

In the same way that capitalists find it profitable to invest in cheap labor or in cheap substitutes for labor in the form of machines, they also find it to their advantage to invest in the cheapest possible raw materials. Anything that results in "cheapening the elements of constant capital" (which is Marx's expression for everything except labor, which he calls "variable capital") raises the rate of profit. Foreign trade has this result because it brings into the country both cheaper raw materials and cheaper foodstuffs, thus lowering costs. Therefore, whenever capitalists have an opportunity to import raw materials and foodstuffs which are cheaper than those obtainable at home, they do so; and a capitalist country—which to Marx always means a country dominated by profit-seekers—will seek out and exploit foreign sources of supply even if it has to conquer them by forceful methods.

However, there is a flaw in this argument which has forced Marx's followers to seek the cause of imperialism in other aspects of international relations. The question is: How can a capitalist coun-

---

[29] They are (1) raising the intensity of exploitation; (2) depression of wages below their value; (3) cheapening the elements of constant capital (raw materials, etc.); (4) relative overpopulation; (5) foreign trade; and (6) increasing stock capital.—*Capital*, III, 272–82.

try exchange goods containing a given amount of surplus value for goods containing a greater amount?

It is implicit in Marx's theory of value that it is impossible within a country for one capitalist to gain in this way at the expense of another, assuming the complete mobility of labor, because goods produced under such conditions must exchange at their full value, and their full value must represent the same amount of labor for all producers who are drawing upon the same homogeneous and mobile labor supply. Assuming the same conditions to prevail between countries as within countries not only would mean that international trade merely gives the interrelationships a wider sphere and a "greater latitude," [30] but it would also mean that the whole world is considered as one unit, no different except in size from any component part. In other words, there is no unique gain from foreign trade.

On the other hand, if there is not complete mobility of labor between countries, it follows that commodities can be produced in one country with a high composition of capital (that is, more capital per man, as in highly industrialized countries) and in another with a lower composition. It would therefore be to the advantage of the highly developed country, which produces less value and reaps less profit because it uses relatively less labor, to exchange its products for those of a country which produces more value because it uses relatively more labor. But since it is obvious that it would be equally to the disadvantage of the latter to make the exchange, the presumption must be that there is no basis for a free and mutual exchange under such terms and that it would not take place. If, however, the highly developed country owns the less developed, or if capitalists in the one have investments in the other, it is clear that the exchange might be forced. Therefore, on Marx's general assumptions, there must be an export of capital before there can be any basis for foreign trade. But this Marx did not see, and it has escaped some of his followers, who even thought that Marx provided the proof that trade will naturally and automatically take place between highly developed and less developed countries. [31] It will take place, of course, but not on the conditions set up by Marx.

---

[30] *Capital*, II, 546; see also p. 548.
[31] See Sweezy, *The Theory of Capitalist Development*, pp. 289–92.

Foreign trade as a counteracting cause to the falling rate of profit turns out to be a delusion.

Since Marx failed to make it clear that his assumptions require an export of capital before there can be any gain from imports of raw materials and foodstuffs, he left no basis for imperialism in his analysis of the declining rate of profit. Certain of his followers were to elevate the international "finance-capitalists" to the role of empire builders, but they had to support their theory on better grounds than they could find in Marx and to make a special point of the fact that the international movement of capital creates ties which the trade in goods cannot possibly create.

In the underconsumption theory of crises, which develops in Marx as a rival of the theory of the falling tendency of the rate of profit, there is even less on which to base a theory of imperialism. Rosa Luxemburg and other neo-Marxists made underconsumption the cornerstone of capitalism's need of imperialism, but they did so only by adding ideas which Marx never worked out and perhaps never entertained. As thus developed, the thesis is that capitalists are constantly engaged in a struggle for foreign markets on which to dump that part of their product which the workers are unable to purchase and therefore unable to consume (hence "underconsumption") because they always receive less than the value of the products which they create. They are chronically underpaid and perpetually unable to take off the domestic market all that is produced there. In other words, exports appear in this neo-Marxian theory as an offset to underconsumption at home.

So far as Marx's treatment is concerned, exports are never definitely presented as an offset to underconsumption in the way that imports were presented as an offset to declining profit rates. In fact, he presented no counteracting forces to underconsumption, emphatically denying the most obvious one, namely, the popular idea that underconsumption could be offset simply by the payment of higher wages.[32] Such action, said Marx, is entirely alien to the nature of capitalism, and impossible besides, so long as the competitive drive for profit constitutes the only economic motive. In the same vein, he undoubtedly would deny that exports can be a remedy for

[32] See *Capital*, II, 475–76. Marx's underconsumption thesis is well stated in *Capital*, III, 568.

underconsumption. Such counteracting forces may be imagined,[33] but they are not to be found in Marx.

It is true that Marx often speaks of the dependence of modern capitalism "on the markets of the world" and states that "except in periods of prosperity there rages between the capitalists the most furious combat for the share of each other in the markets," [34] and he might have called this imperialism, with exports providing the connecting link. But the fact remains that exports are never given this important task. Indeed, Marx abstracts exports and foreign trade generally at the very points of his analysis where they might be expected to play a part.

Thus it becomes obvious that if imports cannot be regarded as an offset to the declining rate of profit which threatens capitalism, on the one hand, and if exports are no remedy for the underconsumption which threatens it, on the other, there is nothing left in Marx on which to base a theory of capitalist imperialism. The spirit of such a theory undoubtedly exists in Marx, but not the body. What he said, in effect, was that capitalism is planless, and because it is planless there can be no remedy against falling profits, except in the most makeshift sense, and none at all against underconsumption, which springs from the wrong distribution of the product of industry between wages and profits.[35] Because of their lack of planned co-ordination in production and distribution, capitalists invest too much in capital-goods industries and not enough in consumer-goods industries, thus creating a chronic state of "disproportionality" which finds expression in such phenomena as underconsumption. Marx's central thesis was that only a planned

[33] See, for example, Sweezy, *The Theory of Capitalist Development*, pp. 218 ff. Sweezy lists the following "forces counteracting the tendency to underconsumption": (1) new industries; (2) faulty investment; (3) population growth; (4) unproductive consumption; and (5) state expenditure. Certain Marxists, notably Rosa Luxemburg (see p. 175), have tried to make out a case for exports as the principal counteracting force to underconsumption, but such attempts at correction or amplification of Marx's theory are not justified by what is found in Marx.

[34] *Capital*, I, 495; see also *Capital*, III, 278.

[35] In a very cumbersome passage Marx makes the point that the conditions governing the production of surplus value are entirely different from those which govern its sale. The first is limited by the productive power of society—no more can be produced than the supply of labor and capital permit. The selling, or "realization," of surplus value, however, depends on the consuming power of society, which in turn is not related to what actually can be produced or to what actually could be consumed, but is limited by "the proportional relations of the various lines of production."—*Capital*, III, 286.

economy, for which he used the word socialism, can maintain the correct proportions in industry and prevent underconsumption. In effect, therefore, he was saying that socialism is the antidote not only to capitalism but also to imperialism.

## ARGUMENTS WHICH APPEAR TO DENY THE NECESSITY OF CAPITALIST BREAKDOWN AND IMPERIALIST ACTIVITY

*That capitalism can be self-contained as a producing mechanism—* Marx's line of reasoning which appears to affirm the ability of capitalism to exist as a self-contained and self-equilibrating mechanism without foreign trade and under balanced proportionality and therefore seems to deny the necessity of imperialist expansion, is to be found in that part of his analysis which considers the conditions of effective demand. He failed to solve the problem, but he came closer to solving it than did his contemporaries, and in the process he laid the groundwork for the thesis that capitalism can exist without imperialism—indeed, that it can exist without succumbing to socialism.

One rather out-of-the-way statement by Marx has been used by some of the neo-Marxists to show that he believed it possible to regard capitalism as a continuing self-contained system. In that part of Volume I of *Capital* where he discusses savings and the process by which surplus value is converted into capital in order for an expansion of production to take place, Marx makes the assumption that there are no capitalist nations to compete with each other, but that the whole world is a closed and fully developed system of capitalism.

We here take no account of export trade [he says] by means of which a nation can change articles of luxury either into means of production or means of subsistence, and *vice versa*. In order to examine the object of our investigation [the conversion of surplus value into capital] in its integrity, free from all disturbing subsidiary circumstances, we must treat the whole world as one nation, and assume that capitalist production is everywhere established and has possessed itself of every branch of industry.[36]

Marx knew, of course, that capitalist production is not everywhere established, and he believed that foreign trade can be highly

[36] *Capital*, I, 636n.

exploitative, and he certainly would not have objected to regarding imperialism as a necessary accompaniment of capitalist expansion in the real world. But we must give him credit for realizing that under quite different assumptions, which he regarded as justifiable theoretically, if not in practice, a case can be made for equilibrium in the realm of the circulation of goods produced under capitalistic conditions.

It was always a challenging thought to Marx that Say and the classical economists so easily disposed of the problem of effective demand simply by saying that general overproduction is impossible, inasmuch as every producer is also a consumer, and every act of production creates its own demand.[37] Marx expressed his opinion of this facile economic theorizing early in the first volume of *Capital*. "Nothing can be more childish," he says, "than the dogma, that because every sale is a purchase, and every purchase a sale, therefore the circulation of commodities necessarily implies an equilibrium of sales and purchases."[38]

In challenging Say's Law of Markets, Marx was primarily exercised about the implication that such perfect equilibrium is possible under capitalism. That it is possible under assumed conditions of perfectly balanced factors, whether under capitalism or any other system, was an entirely different matter to Marx, and he proceeded to state what those conditions are. In other words, he constructed his own Say's Law, if for no other reason than to show that this sort of thing must be handled right if it is to be handled at all. He had no doubt that socialism would be able to solve the problem of effective demand because production and consumption would be so planned that there would be an equilibrium of sales and purchases at all times, not sporadically or accidentally as under capitalism. It is only a matter of finding and maintaining the correct proportionality between the producers of producers' goods and the producers of consumers' goods;[39] and while such a solution Marx

---

[37] Say, *A Treatise on Political Economy*, Vol. I, chap. xv, and Vol. II, chaps. ii, v; Ricardo, *Principles of Political Economy*, chap. xxi; J. S. Mill, *Principles of Political Economy*, Vol. II, Bk. III, chap. xiv, secs. 2–3. See also Nugent, *Consumer Credit and Economic Stability*, pp. 152–55.

[38] *Capital*, I, 127.

[39] Marx discusses this problem with the help of his famous *schema*, or arithmetical illustrations, in which he tries to show what takes place between the capital goods industries, which he calls "Department I," and consumer goods industries, or "De-

regarded as theoretically possible even under capitalism, he was convinced that proper proportionality could never work in practice without a plan. As thus visualized, the question is whether capitalism can exist theoretically as a self-contained system, can create its own markets, can make the ideal of every sale a purchase into a reality, and thereby solve the problem of effective demand.

It is where Marx discusses the operation of capitalism under monetary conditions that he comes nearest to solving the problem of effective demand. He failed to solve it, to be sure, and fell back with all the more earnestness to the conviction that capitalism can never solve the problem of selling profitably all that it produces, because of its lack of plan and proportionality.

Marx visualizes a production-consumption circle within which, without money, there are many things which may go wrong and cause disequilibrium; with money, or the circulation process, superimposed on the production-consumption circle, many more things may go wrong. One of these is that people hoard. For one reason or another money becomes "clogged up" on its way from capitalists to workers, and into consumption and investment, and back again to its starting point.

With this observation we can have no quarrel, nor with the equally obvious corollary that there would be no problem if all the money income received were immediately spent by those who received it. The flow of goods and money would be in equilibrium. The trouble, as Marx visualizes it, resides in the investment process. In order to replace old capital as it wears out, and in order to expand capital equipment, capitalists must save part of their income— again an unassailable fact with which everyone is familiar. But aside from the relatively minor fact that money becomes lost, remains idle for awhile in pockets and tills, and is even hoarded by misers, Marx greatly—and unjustifiably—adds to these hoards by assuming that the accumulation of capital for investment purposes

partment II." No explanation of what these *schema* purport to show can be a substitute for actually looking at them and reading Marx's accompanying comments (see especially *Capital*, II, 591 ff.). However, since this is one of the dullest assignments in all economic literature, the task can be abbreviated somewhat by consulting some of the popular abridgments of his works, such as Marx, *Capital, the Communist Manifesto and Other Writings*, ed., with an introduction by Max Eastman, pp. 293–314. For an able criticism of Marx's analysis see Joan Robinson, *An Essay on Marxian Economics*, chap. vi.

involves the hoarding of funds, like pennies in a child's bank, until time to use them.

In many a passage [40] Marx makes it perfectly clear that, in his view, both amortization funds for replacement and investment funds represent actual money withdrawn and withheld from circulation until old machines are replaced by new ones or until enough has been accumulated to enable the capitalist to expend it all at once on the equipment for a new enterprise. Marx mentions time and again that it is necessary for investment funds to reach a certain magnitude before being used and that this results in the money meanwhile being inactive, and he describes the way in which this interrupts the process of production and causes a crisis.[41]

But, "even aside from money matters," a crisis is bound to occur

unless a constant proportion between expiring (and about to be renewed) fixed capital and still continuing (merely transferring the value of its depreciation to its product) fixed capital is assumed, so long as reproduction takes place on a simple scale under the same conditions, such as productivity, volume, intensity of labor, the mass of circulating elements to be reproduced in one case would remain the same while the mass of fixed elements to be reproduced would have been increased. Therefore the aggregate production of [department] I would have to increase, or, there would be a deficit in the reproduction.[42]

The gap between production and consumption resulting from hoarding and resulting in crises posed to Marx the problem of how to close this gap. He was not in the least interested in finding an answer for the sake of telling capitalists how to run their system, but only in calling upon certain historical facts to explain how the gap actually has been closed (to the gratuitous advantage of capitalists, who, he assumes, are incapable of maintaining the correct proportions between departments I and II), and for the purpose of showing that any system based on saving and investment which fails to fill this gap will not work.

After repeatedly raising the question of "where the money comes from" [43] and giving the impression of really being on the trail of some great discovery, Marx ends by finding the solution to the

[40] *Capital,* II, 93–95, 136–37, 139, 142, 369–70, 396, 399, 411–12, 527–28, 571–73, 586, 589.
[41] *Ibid.,* pp. 94–95, 142, 545.                    [42] *Ibid.,* p. 545.
[43] As in *ibid.,* pp. 379–80, 383, 385–86, 397, 551, 583–84.

problem of underconsumption in *newly mined gold*.[44] Historically
this had been the answer, and Marx lets it suffice theoretically.[45]
Although a purely historical accident, for which capitalism can take
no credit, it is nevertheless the element which satisfies the requirement of equilibrium, for sales without equivalent purchases, which
results from hoarding, are now matched by "purchases without
sales," which are the result of a gratuitous dishoarding by nature;
the gold producers are the only segment of the capitalist class who
are always able to purchase commodities without having first to
get money by selling commodities. Here at least was one commodity which its producers, the gold miners, could give in exchange
for consumable goods without having to produce and supply consumable goods. Therefore it was conceivable that what otherwise
would be an overproduction of goods in general was prevented by
the creation of new general purchasing power with which its owners
could take title to goods which otherwise would be a drug on the
market.

Why could they not take title to them by the use of credit instruments? It is obvious that they could, but Marx specifically
rules out credit or the exchange of goods for promises to pay.[46]
He also considers the possibility that increased purchasing power
might come from "economizing" the money actually in circulation, "whether by means of balancing payments, etc., or by some
measure which accelerates the circulation of the same coins—or,
by the transformation of money from the form of a hoard into that
of a circulating medium," [47] but he does not intend to let this possibility have a deciding influence either. He understood perfectly
that increasing the velocity of circulation of money has the same
effect as an increase in the supply of money, but he rules this out.[48]
And, having also excluded hoarded savings as a source of purchasing power, there was nothing left but to conclude that "an additional production of gold must take place." [49] And to make his as-

[44] *Ibid.*, pp. 375–76, 387–89, 398, 547–51, 556, 573–74, 586, 610–11.
[45] Marx was very conscious of the stimulating effect of the gold and silver discoveries and the price revolution of the 16th century on the rise and expansion of commerce and industry, and states that "the increased supply of precious metals since
the 16th century is an essential factor in the history of the development of capitalist
production."—*Ibid.*, p. 396.
[46] *Ibid.*, pp. 128, 297, 370, 400, 557, 585.        [47] *Ibid.*, pp. 397–98.
[48] *Ibid.*, pp. 397, 584.                           [49] *Ibid.*, p. 398.

sumptions still tighter, Marx states that there is no foreign trade, so that the newly mined gold must come from within the country where it is needed; [50] he further reduces the area from which outside purchasing power might come by assuming that there are no "third persons" in the economy, but only capitalists and workers.[51] And the latter, it must be remembered, are not a source of money, or of savings, but only the temporary destination of the capitalists' money in the form of wages—and wages are assumed to be so low that additional money cannot be squeezed out by reducing them.[52] All in all, Marx excluded every source from which capitalists might receive payment for their output except the gold mines. Here was his answer to the ubiquitous question, "Where does the money come from?"

The relevancy of this reasoning to the problem of imperialism now becomes clear. Marx's type of analysis means that it is demonstrable that capitalism theoretically can exist without foreign trade, that it can go along indefinitely in equilibrium, and, what is more significant, that it can endure without collapsing into socialism so far as the mere mechanics of the economy are concerned.

But Marx's real conviction was that capitalists cannot maintain the correct proportions in industry because they have no planned scheme of production; that they, acting individually, substitute machines for labor power, thus changing the organic composition of capital, which results in a falling rate of profit, and that because of the wrong distribution of property chronic underconsumption is a constant threat to the capital-labor relationship. Capitalists save and invest without regard to consumer interests; they throw the mechanism of the monetary circulation out of balance by "hoarding," and nature has to rescue them fortuitously by yielding up gold.

Marx said nothing to indicate that the seeds of imperialism might reside in this process. Here, as well as in his failure to regard exports as an offset to underconsumption and in his silence regarding the crucial element of capital export, Marx left no basis for a theory of imperialism. The nearest he came to providing such a basis was in that part of his analysis in which he visualized imports as an off-

[50] *Ibid.*, pp. 399–400, 547.     [51] *Ibid.*, pp. 384, 429, 488, 531–32, 590.
[52] *Ibid.*, pp. 391–92, 594. Cf. Joan Robinson, "Marx on Unemployment," *The Economic Journal*, LI (June–September, 1941), 234–48.

set to the declining rate of profit. This provided a weak foundation at best.

*That capitalism can be stable if credit is controlled.*—The type of reasoning just analyzed points in the direction of a solution of the problem of how production and consumption, even under capitalist conditions, can find and maintain a position of equilibrium; from which it follows that theoretically capitalism in any given country can get along without foreign trade or any foreign economic contacts which are supposed to give rise to conflict.[53] But the joker which Marx inserts into this analysis is the necessity, as he regarded it, that capitalist production be planned—which means that it must be controlled, which in turn, to Marx, meant that it must be socialized. It also means that capitalism would no longer be capitalism, but socialism, and that there would be no more capitalist imperialism, because there would be no capitalism. So all this talk in Marx about the possibility of equilibrium under capitalism is a play on words, and his followers, in recognizing it as such, have gone ahead with their various views of how capitalism produces imperialism.

But there is still another line of argument in Marx which practically amounts to saying—and certainly points in the direction of saying—that the controlling or socializing emphasis need not be laid on production at all, but only on the monetary and credit side of the "circulation" process and that this control would at once save capitalism from getting out of equilibrium on the production side, would leave no room for imperialistic activities as a counteracting factor, and therefore no need for the socialization of the means of production. Since none of Marx's followers have seen this possibility, and since it does not turn out to be a play on words, as his other equilibrium thesis did, but gives a real insight into the one element of control which can be applied to capitalism without the socialization of production, it deserves particular attention. Here, perhaps, Marx (and other economists) might have found a real explanation of how capitalism can avoid being led into those paths which mean monopoly, protectionism, forced export policies,

[53] The emphasis here, of course, is on equilibrium, not on foreign trade, for obviously if a single country can maintain internal equilibrium without foreign trade, a world-wide capitalism could remain in equilibrium by virtue of "foreign" trade.

forced foreign lending, and all the other policies which are associated with "economic imperialism."

Marx stumbled upon the central idea (which he never developed and probably never saw in its true implications) in his long harangue against the banks and the credit system. We have already seen how he ruled out credit and then admitted gold in his search for an equilibrating factor between production and consumption, and we questioned why he failed to see that credit could have played the same part as newly mined gold. This, in turn, raises two questions with which we are immediately concerned. First, what is the place of money and credit in the whole process of production and exchange, and, second, having discovered that their role can be good or bad according to the degree of control exercised, what does this mean to the problem of socialization and control with which Marx was dealing?

There is obviously a good side to the institution of credit, and there is also a bad side. On the good side is the fact that it can serve as a temporary substitute for money, thus acting as a stabilizing factor in the monetary and price system. This Marx appreciated to some extent, although he failed to see that credit can play the same stabilizing function as newly mined gold. He was far more impressed by the bad side of the institution of credit—the ability of competitive banking to make it a substitute for real saving and therefore a highly risky addition to capital.

Proper control of the monetary system is so essential to the stability of a free enterprise economy that it becomes a practical alternative to and substitute for the socialization of production. It seems entirely possible that if the monetary side of capitalism had been properly controlled from the beginning there never would have been any reason for Marx or anyone else to advocate the socialization of production. And capitalism would never have displayed those breakdown tendencies which make it appear that it must of necessity resort to imperialism as a counteracting means of salvation and must in the end, when the frontiers of empire disappear, succumb to socialism.

The central point is that free enterprise in the competitive creation of bank credit is highly disastrous to free enterprise in the competitive creation of goods; that it overextends the field of production by substituting forced or false saving for real saving, resulting in false capital assets and in crises in the form of what the socialists have always described as crises of overproduction and underconsumption. This kind of capitalism, producing this kind of result, can very well be accused of forcing exports and following an imperialistic policy. At least it is understandable as somehow a bad and undesirable way of entering into international relations.

Clearly Marx was wrong in ruling out credit and the exchange of goods for titles, because he thereby excluded the one promising answer to the dilemma created by the slowing down or clogging up of money in the roundabout circulation process which, quite properly, he undertook to analyze as the monetary corollary of the roundabout production process. Here was an instrument already at hand which economic necessity had called into existence to meet the deficiencies temporarily created by saving and investment, but instead of admitting it at the front door, he excluded it and then opened the back door to newly mined gold, and got the same result as would have come from admitting credit.

Marx's prior commitment to the labor-cost theory of value, of course, was the strong factor in preventing him from conceding that either credit or paper money could serve the function of a lifesaver for capitalism in the way that newly mined gold was supposed to have done. These substitutes for gold had no real value in Marx's sense, and to admit that such valueless media could fill the gap between purchases without sales and sales without purchases would have meant abandoning the one basis of Marx's entire system.

Marx's blind spot regarding the function of credit can also be accounted for in terms of his general condemnation of banking and credit as the most artificial, illusory, dishonest, and disruptive institutions ever created. He was particularly harsh in his condemnation of "created" bank credit because of its part in the disastrous overexpansion and contraction of the economic system, and this prevented him from seeing any usefulness in any kind of credit. Yet in the process of discussing this question Marx anticipated much theory that is now regarded as enlightened; but most significant of all, he came very near to seeing that the control of the "circulation process," by controlling money and credit, is more important than controlling or socializing the production process.

In Volume III of *Capital*,[54] in a context far removed from the search for an answer to the problem of effective demand, Marx again moves towards the answer without seeing that the exchange of goods for credit might have the same effect in filling the gap and avoiding a crisis as the exchange of goods for newly mined gold. At great length he points out that the shortage of purchasing power resulting from the withholding of money from circulation calls for money substitutes to take its place in order to keep production moving at the rate at which it would move if the circulation process were not interrupted.

Marx's analysis may be interpreted to mean that it is the function of commercial credit in the form of bills of exchange and other documents of deferred payment to supply such a deficiency of purchasing power and to correct the correlative deficiency of effective demand.[55] Capitalists and merchants want such credit in order to enable them to "receive value without giving an equivalent," so that "they may not have to get rid of their commodities below price."[56] In other words, the function of commercial credit is to keep industrial and business activity going at an even and uninterrupted rate without the danger of a crisis, and it is the primary function of the banks to supply such credit.[57] Assuming that this credit actually fills the gap and no more than fills it, the effect is the same as if enterprisers and merchants granted each other book credit. It simply represents a postponement of payment. The banks in this way supply no capital for the expansion of production, but merely the means of maintaining production at a given rate.

The ordinary business man discounts [says Marx] in order to anticipate the money-form of his capital and thereby to keep his process of reproduction in flow; not in order to expand his business or secure additional capital, but in order to balance the credit which he gives by the credit which he takes. And if he wants to expand his business on credit, the discounting of bills will do him little good, because it is merely the transformation of capital, which he has already in his hands, from one form into another; he will rather take up a direct loan for a long time.[58]

Marx condemns the entire banking and credit system in the harshest terms, not so much because the banks supply commercial

[54] Especially chaps. xxv–xxviii.     [55] *Capital*, III, 562.     [56] *Ibid.*, p. 505.
[57] Cf. Valentin F. Wagner, *Geschichte der Kredittheorien*, pp. 454–56.
[58] *Capital*, III, 503.

credit, which appears to be a relatively harmless form of capitalist convenience, but because they create credit out of nothing, and out of this fictitious substitute for money make loans which capitalists can use as if they were real capital. What results is accelerated expansion and production, augmented exploitation and boom, followed by a collapse of the artificial credit structure, widespread ruination and unemployment.[59] If production were socially controlled, Marx would say, this could never happen. Failure to control production is bad, failure to control money compounds the failure, but failure to control credit is made to appear infinitely worse. Money gave rise to usury, and the credit system developed as a reaction to usury [60]—then proceeded to wreck the capitalist system by enabling capitalists to over-extend themselves on easy money and by making it inevitable that the structure built on credit will collapse as soon as people lose faith in the monetary reserves held by banks as the basis for credit.[61] Money and credit, in short, are responsible for injecting the circulation process, with all its opportunities for usury, hoarding, the concentration of wealth, and overexpansion, into the production process, thus preventing production from being carried on for the direct use of the producers.[62]

Although Marx believes that all credit is "fictitious" capital [63] and that it must eventually collapse and "slaughter" values in a welter of crisis,[64] he makes it clear that created bank credit (he had particularly in mind uncovered bank notes which cost the banker "nothing but paper and printing," [65] and for which the British Bank Act of 1844 was intended as a remedy) is the most illusory and disruptive element and that the banking system is "the most artificial and most developed product turned out by the capitalist mode of production." [66] By taking capital out of the hands of private capitalists and usurers, "banking and credit thus become the most effective means of driving capitalist production beyond its own boundaries, and one of the most potent instruments of crises and swindle." [67] That is, by leading to ease of speculation, the use of credit causes production to be extended far beyond the boundaries

---

[59] It was in the midst of his discussion of the effect of credit in over-extending production that Marx made his famous statement (*ibid.*, p. 568) that "the last cause of all real crises always remains the poverty and restricted consumption of the masses."
[60] *Ibid.*, p. 704.        [61] *Ibid.*, pp. 671, 673, 713.        [62] *Ibid.*, pp. 674, 697, 712.
[63] *Ibid.*, pp. 547-48, 552-53, 579-80.        [64] *Ibid.*, p. 298.        [65] *Ibid.*, p. 526.
[66] *Ibid.*, p. 712.        [67] *Ibid.*, p. 713; see also pp. 601-2, 606-7, 612-13.

of safety or the ability to find markets when the credit structure collapses. It collapses because of the superstructure of fictitious capital erected on a small reserve of money.

The development of the credit and banking business . . . tends on the one hand to press all money-capital into the service of production (or what amounts to the same, to convert all money incomes into capital), and . . . on the other hand reduces the metal reserve to a minimum in a certain phase of the cycle, so that it can no longer perform the functions for which it was intended.[68]

It is this small reserve which is the "pivot" that wrecks the system because of its insufficiency when a run on the banks occurs.[69]

Nowhere does Marx better summarize his case against credit than in the following passage:

The credit system appears as the main lever of overproduction and overspeculation in commerce solely because the process of reproduction, which is elastic in its nature, is here forced to its extreme limits, and is so forced for the reason that a large part of the social capital is employed by people who do not own it and who push things with far less caution than the owner, who carefully weighs the possibilities of his private capital, which he handles himself. This simply demonstrates the fact, that the production of values by capital based on the antagonistic nature of the capitalist system permits an actual, free, development only up to a certain point, so that it constitutes an immanent fetter and barrier of production, which are continually overstepped by the credit system. Hence the credit system accelerates the material development of the forces of production and the establishment of the world market. To bring these material foundations of the new mode of production to a certain degree of perfection, is the historical mission of the capitalist system of production. At the same time credit accelerates the violent eruptions of this antagonism, the crises, and thereby the development of the elements of disintegration of the old mode of production.[70]

Despite what appears to be the basis for the kind of monetary-credit theory of crisis which was behind the British Bank Act of 1844, and which had enjoyed some popularity in the United States,[71] Marx has no intention of being the author of any such

---

[68] *Ibid.*, p. 671.          [69] *Ibid.*, pp. 672–73.          [70] *Ibid.*, p. 522.

[71] A remarkable number of early American writers held a credit theory of trade cycles, while very few set forth an overproduction theory. They believed that banking reform was necessary (higher reserves, etc.) and the "hard money" advocates were of course even more critical of credit banking.—See Miller, "Earlier Theories of Crises and Cycles in the United States," *Quarterly Journal of Economics,* XXXVIII (February, 1924), pp. 294–329.

heresy. To do so would have meant a denial of his basic theory that it is the appropriation of surplus value in the process of production and its accumulation, not what happens in the "circulation" process, which constitutes the initial cause of crises. The most he will say is that credit is an important factor in causing crises, but never a cause in the fundamental sense. Entirely in keeping with this point of view is his warning that we "must not entertain any myths as to the productive power of the credit system"; [72] also his criticism of bourgeois economists (singling out Fullarton) for stressing the overproduction of money capital, when the emphasis should be on the overproduction of goods,[73] and his assertion that political economy is superficial in regarding the expansion and contraction of credit as the cause of the business cycle, when actually they are mere symptoms.[74] He was determined that the exchange of goods for titles is not to be regarded as the way out of the dilemma created by hoarding or the clogging of money in the circulation process.

Although to Marx hoarding was one of the fundamental weaknesses of capitalism, he took the phenomenon for granted and, assuming that it was necessary, never went far enough to ask if there was any other reason for hoarding. Modern theory has worked very close to the idea that hoarding has to do with the fear of investment which has been induced by the business cycle and that booms and depressions are caused mainly by the creation and destruction of bank credit. We have noted Marx's apparent insight into the nature of created credit and its destructive influence, but the fact remains that he made no further use of this clue. Had he done so, he might have reached the conclusion that people hoard because of the great instability and uncertainty resulting from the use of created credit and that they would not hoard—at least not enough to cause great and prolonged crises—if its use were suppressed or controlled.

But this is a highly sophisticated modern idea which is by no means widely accepted, and it is no discredit to Marx that he failed to grasp it. Had he become thoroughly convinced that created credit is the disrupting force in capitalism and the main source of ex-

[72] *Capital*, II, 399.

[73] *Ibid.*, p. 582. See also *ibid.*, p. 365: "That which appears as a crisis on the money-market, is in reality an expression of abnormal conditions in the process of production and reproduction."

[74] *Capital*, I, 695.

ploitation, he could still have found plenty of reasons for believing in socialism, but the emphasis certainly would have been on the socialization, or at least the control, of banking, not on the socialization of production.

Not knowing how to associate the something-for-nothing which he could see in capitalism with the element of created credit, he clung to his original suspicion that exploitation must be looked for in surplus value and that it can be turned to social account only by socializing production. He got a surplus value because his analysis was incomplete, not because the process of roundabout production and roundabout exchange was necessarily imperfect. To the extent that the process of roundabout exchange was imperfect, he had no clear idea how its tendency towards disequilibrium was related to created credit.

It was the nature of roundabout exchange that Marx failed to understand, not the nature of roundabout production, and the fact that he understood the nature of the latter narrows by that much the area in which his doctrine can be criticized. That he understood this process is indicated not only by his view that the function of investment is to shorten the process of production but also by his appreciation of the fact that the process does not mean the "simple reproduction" of the same kind and quantity of goods at constant cost, but the production of more goods of the same kind at lower costs, or of new kinds of goods at any cost that will permit them to be sold. He knew—and this was what disturbed him—that this transformation is effected by technological improvements or the introduction of labor-saving machines. While this implies a recombination of productive factors and the competitive bidding up of wages, Marx does not talk in such terms, although he occasionally speaks of labor getting higher wages through what is essentially this process. His failure was due to the entirely erroneous conception of costs as consisting only of "labor-costs," and this prevented him from making any use of the concept of expanded production, except to regard it as a means of thwarting the distribution of wealth, when its real function is both to increase and, when accompanied by an appropriate exchange mechanism, to distribute wealth to all classes of the population.

From this part of Marx's doctrine we can, without forcing the point, conclude that he came much nearer to finding reasons for not socializing production than did his orthodox contemporaries, simply because he came closer than they to solving the mystery of effective demand. Nor is it without significance that he used newly mined gold as the balancing factor under his assumed conditions. Although he refused to let gold be the final arbiter, he was worried by what it implied. It must not be forgotten that socialism as a program resulted from an attempt to find a remedy for crises and that the cyclical as well as the secular fall of prices was the index to the critical situation which cried for solution. Then came the great gold discoveries of the middle of the nineteenth century, and Marx realized that the resulting upswing of prices was bound to have a dampening effect on the socialist movement because of its stimulating effect on capitalism. He also recognized that the power of the banks to create credit could have a similarly stimulating effect, and that the sudden drying up of this credit can have a devastating effect, but instead of making competitive credit-making the object of social control, if not of socialization, he turned away from this promising clue to find his reasons for the inevitability of socialism in the field of competitive production. Between "created credit" and "created products" he chose the latter as the object of socialization.

Definite conclusions regarding any positive place for Marx in the theory of imperialism—even a socialist theory—are not easy to state. We are thrown off the track at the outset by his tendency to dismiss colonial expansion and exploitation as a pre-capitalist phenomenon, not a characteristic of highly developed industrial capitalism. Even in those parts of his general theory of capitalist development where he speaks of foreign trade, and even appears to emphasize its necessity, it was distinctly a side issue. He simply was not interested in this aspect of the problem. This is indicated by the way in which he excluded foreign trade in various important parts of his analysis, showing clearly that he regarded it merely as a complicating, not an essentially significant, factor. His portrayal of the capitalist world as a closed system, while no doubt never intended to be a picture of reality, could certainly be taken as evidence that he would not have held capitalism responsible for imperialism in the sense that the latter was absolutely necessary. This deduction is further strengthened by his construction of a new "Say's Law" of markets, his appeal to newly mined gold as the balancing factor between supply and demand, and finally by the impression, which he succeeded in creating whether he intended to or not, that the only thing wrong with capitalism is not lack of foreign markets, or lack of consuming power, or even falling profits, but lack of any plan for maintaining the correct proportion between producers' goods and consumers' goods industries.

Marx's followers inherited all this great jumble of ideas and theories, and one by one they showed their ingenuity in picking out those parts which for one reason or another most appealed to them. This process of selection is most clearly seen in the development of the neo-Marxian theories of imperialism.

# VII ·

# DEVELOPMENT OF THE THEORIES
# OF CAPITALIST IMPERIALISM:
# THE NEO-MARXISTS

MARX died in 1883, firm in the belief that capitalism was dying with him; at best it could be only a few years before his forecasts would come true. But by the nineties his followers were beginning to see that capitalism had still a long way to go and indeed seemed to be acquiring a new lease on life by reason of its rapid advance into fresh and noncapitalistic areas. In time, they could still believe, these new areas would themselves become capitalistic and diseased with the deadly virus of profit seeking which was the nemesis of capitalism, but until this poison had time to work, capitalism might expect to enjoy the fruits of its "new colonialism," or imperialism.

## EARLY SPECULATIONS

The earlier speculations on this phenomenon were naturally tentative, imperfectly worked out, and still too close to the old Marxian doctrine to be recognized as in any way novel. In retrospect, however, viewed from the vantage point of the World War of 1914–18, which every socialist could recognize as the fulfillment of the prophesies in which he had been nurtured, even the most casual observations of the older generation of Marxists took on the stature of unusual insight. The older socialists, who had lived both as contemporaries of Karl Marx and as more or less unwilling participants in the great conflict, could look back upon their earlier views and find in them the germ of those advanced ideas which they had later formulated into a theory of imperialism. In all cases the germ was unmistakably Marxian, but not in all cases were the ultimate formulations as easily recognizable, because those who called themselves Marxists could no longer agree unanimously on the earmarks of true Marxism and the characteristics of capitalism. Among the younger generation of socialists—a generation which was contemporary with the Great War, but not with Marx—there was a tendency to accept new ideas because they appeared reasonable rather than merely because they were found in the pages of *Capital.* There was, in short, a veritable confusion of tongues among the disciples, and it is now our task to try to understand the various Marxian dialects which gave rise to this confusion. As we have seen, there was confusion in *Capital* itself. Less wonder, then, that a confusion so ably begun should become worse confounded.

The various socialist theories of imperialism had their origin in the diverse speculations regarding the nature of capitalism which developed after the appearance of Volume III of *Capital*, in 1894. The revisionists, under the leadership of Edward Bernstein, began the assault on the citadel of old-fashioned Marxism with the well-known thesis that capitalism is not suffering from the signs of imminent breakdown which many had read in Marx, warning that socialists who relied on this catastrophe and the expected revolution were courting disappointment. This struck directly at the underconsumption theory of crises and made it appear that Marx was near the truth only in that part of his analysis where he developed the proportionality thesis. To Bernstein the insufficiency of effective demand was no problem, and there was no question of who absorbs surplus value. It is not "capital," he says, "but the working class itself that has the task of absorbing the parasitic elements of the social body." [1]

Tugan-Baranowsky, the Russian economist, although he disclaimed any affiliation with Marxism, did more to precipitate new developments in socialist theory than the revisionists. Rejecting both the overproduction and the underconsumption theories of crises, Tugan-Baranowsky maintained that Marx's disproportionality thesis alone made any kind of sense. [2] He was particularly

[1] Bernstein, *Evolutionary Socialism*, pp. 50–51.
[2] Tugan-Baranowsky, *Les Crises industrielles en Angleterre*. The French translation (1913) is from the revised Russian edition of 1900, the first edition having appeared in 1894. See also his *Theoretische Grundlagen des Marxismus*, pp. 226–31. An extensive discussion of Tugan-Baranowsky's theory and its relation to Marxism is found in Sweezy, *The Theory of Capitalist Development*, especially Chapter X.

critical of the underconsumption theory, and he used Marx's *schemas* of reproduction in a revised form to show that disproportionality need not develop from any lack of consumers.[3] Nevertheless, he believed, as Marx certainly did, that disproportionality and crises are inescapable under capitalism because by its very nature the unplanned and uncontrolled process of saving and investing for profit renders impossible a proportionate division of the product. Capitalists may hope to maintain a balanced system only by suppressing surplus producers, striving for monopoly, and doing other things that put an end to the competitive system.[4] A generation later such efforts to save capitalism were to be called "fascism."

Tugan-Baranowsky's demonstration of the theoretical possibility of equilibrium was used for the negative purpose of overthrowing the underconsumption theory and was never intended to be taken seriously as a picture of what really happens or can happen in the capitalist world. Like Marx, Tugan-Baranowsky did some theoretical equation stacking. Nevertheless, he strengthened the hands of those of Marx's followers who had a revisionist leaning away from the underconsumption theory towards something more realistic. But in leading to the conclusion that, theoretically at least, capitalism need not expand outside its own framework and become imperialistic, they were not for a moment trying to buttress the argument for capitalism. Rather, they were afraid that capitalists and capitalist countries would resolve their differences, since this had some theoretical possibility, and join forces in a kind of super-capitalism to maintain the correct proportions, solve the problem of crises, and thereby remain in power. This, however, was a remote possibility, useful only as a bogey-man for socialists to keep in reserve. The real question was not why capitalism need not expand imperialistically, but why, granting the lack of necessity, certain

[3] One of two things may happen: either surplus value is distributed in the proper proportions between the two divisions of industry, and no crisis results, or it is not properly distributed, thus making a crisis inevitable. Underconsumption has nothing to do with what happens in either case, according to Tugan-Baranowsky, because the expansion of the means of production in department I is not dependent upon what happens in department II, where the means of consumption are produced; the producers of department I create a market for each other, while the expanded production of means of consumption in department II remains there. Consequently, since the two departments are independent of each other, underconsumption is impossible, and the cause of crises must be found elsewhere.

[4] Tugan-Baranowsky, *Les Crises industrielles en Angleterre*, pp. 202 ff.

capitalistic countries actually do expand. In seeking an answer to the latter question Marx's followers were forced onto somewhat new ground.

In developing the new theory, the neo-Marxists departed rather radically from what was found in the pages of *Capital*. Marx, it will be recalled, regarded the precapitalist, or colonial, period as one in which exploitation of backward peoples or undeveloped territories was based on sheer brute force. Then came the period of industrial capitalism, in which (as the neo-Marxists saw more clearly than Marx) the export of consumers' goods was incapable of producing imperialistic exploitation, because the capitalists as yet had no means by which they could force the exchange of goods containing a low percentage of exploited labor for goods containing a higher percentage. Instead of treating backward peoples as coolies or slaves, the industrial capitalists regarded them as potential users of such consumer goods as textiles and hardware and accordingly encouraged the activity of missionaries and civilizing missions of all kinds. Thus the export of consumer goods, as long as their sales were not tied in with the export of capital, was entirely nonimperialistic. All this changed when, in the nineteenth century, the export of capital became the predominate form of export and supplied the capitalists with the means by which the exchange of goods with a low labor content for those with a higher labor content could be forced because the capitalists were now in a position to exercise the power of ownership over both domestic and foreign products. This is what many of Marx's followers came to regard as the new imperialism, in which capitalistic technique, ownership, and organizing genius were combined with "force" on a more refined level than in the colonial period, when brute force alone was used.

## KARL KAUTSKY AND THE FIGHT AGAINST IMPERIALISM

Karl Kautsky is not a great figure in the development of the theory of imperialism, but in several respects he is an important one, if only because at times he was a foil for others. Born in 1845 (he died in 1938), Kautsky could look back to personal association with Marx and Engels, to whom he professed the closest discipleship, and he enjoyed over a long period the reputation of being the most faithful and the ablest "theoretician" of Marxian thought. As editor of *Die Neue Zeit,* which he founded in 1883 (the year of Marx's death) and over which he presided until his dismissal in 1917, Kautsky was in a position of great influence both intellectually and politically. Between his own prolific writings and the enormous amount of material which came to his editorial desk from contributors there was a constant cross-fertilization of ideas.

From the beginning of his career Kautsky was a stanch believer in the underconsumption theory of crises, and in his earlier writings he helped greatly to strengthen the Marxian idea that chronic underconsumption must lead to chronic depression and force the masses to adopt socialism. In a review of Tugan-Baranowsky's book on industrial crises in England,[5] Kautsky severely criticized the fledgling heresy that capitalism can go on accumulating and producing without regard to consumption provided the proper proportions are maintained between producers' goods industries and consumers' goods industries. Regardless of the fact that capitalists behave as if the end of production is production, they cannot thwart the social fact that the end is consumption. Kautsky was equally critical of the revisionist views of Bernstein,[6] which laid emphasis on the belief that capitalism had demonstrated its ability to keep its house in order, avoid collapse, and provide an increase in general welfare as it increased production.

Scarcely realizing the subtle change that was overtaking socialist theory, Kautsky gradually swung to the revisionist point of view. He not only became less critical of the disproportionality thesis [7] but also finally came round to the view that capitalism might so plan and order its existence as to avoid indefinitely the dire predictions of the breakdown theorists. Capitalism, in other words, was becoming a supercapitalism, as implied in the statement, for which Kautsky himself was responsible, that it was capable of creating and

[5] Kautsky, "Krisentheorien," *Die neue Zeit,* XX² (1901–2), 110–18, 133–43; see especially pp. 117, 140–41.

[6] Kautsky, *Bernstein und das Sozialdemokratische Programm,* pp. 45, 166. Cf. Sweezy, *The Theory of Capitalist Development,* pp. 194–95.

[7] In a review of Rudolf Hilferding's *Finanzkapital* (see below, p. 163), Kautsky did not attack Hilferding as he had criticized Tugan-Baranowsky, for defending the proportionality thesis, but praised Hilferding's book *in toto.* See "Finanzkapital und Krisen," *Die neue Zeit,* XXIX¹ (1911), 764–72, 797–804, 838–46, 874–83.

maintaining a "superimperialism." [8] Indeed, Kautsky's changing views on capitalism were so much a part of his changing views on imperialism that it is difficult to determine which came first. There seems little doubt, however, that his belief in the possibility of a superimperialism came from his willingness to believe that a united capitalism might avoid a repetition of the first World War and preserve the peace.

By nature Kautsky was an idealist and pacifist rather than a man of action and political leadership. He was utterly uncompromising in his hatred of militarism and colonialism long before it became the fashion to lump these two concepts together and call them "imperialism." He waged an unrelenting fight against Edward Bernstein and the revisionists and against even the slightest word or deed that appeared to represent a compromise with capitalism. Easily the most dangerous compromise of which Kautsky could conceive in his earlier writings was the prospect that Social Democratic parties in the various countries, and the Socialist International itself, would adopt a "colonial policy." In their national and international congresses the socialists of the Second International began, about 1900, to speculate as to what they would do with colonies should the Social Democrats come into power in countries already possessing colonies. Those more to the right proclaimed that in such an event it was their duty to take the colonies under their protection, treat them better than they had ever been treated under capitalist domination, and prepare them as rapidly as possible for independence. Although willing to take a sympathetic interest in the welfare of colonial people, Kautsky was unalterably opposed to the slightest suggestion that socialism could have a colonial policy, so imbued was he with the idea that "colonialism," with its association of violent conquest and forceful domination, had always been and must remain the symbol of oppression.[9]

---

[8] See below, p. 157.

[9] The most acute stage of this controversy was reached at the Stuttgart Congress of the Second International in 1907. For contemporary accounts see: Bernstein, "Die Kolonialfrage und der Klassenkampf," *Sozialistische Monatshefte*, XIII (December, 1907), 988–96; Calwer, "Kolonialpolitik und Sozialdemokratie," *Sozialistische Monatshefte*, XIII (March, 1907), 192–200; and Schippel, "Kolonialpolitik," *Sozialistische Monatshefte*, XIV (January 9, 1908), 3–10. A good general account is found in Hovde, "Socialistic Theories of Imperialism Prior to the Great War," *Journal of Political Economy*, XXXVI (October, 1928), 569–91.

The earliest manifestation of Kautsky's interest in imperialism is to be found in numerous articles on colonial questions which he published in the eighties and the nineties.[10] It was not until several years later, however, that Kautsky began to attach theoretical significance to these articles. When it was first questioned at the time of the first World War to whom should go the honor of having first formulated a socialist theory of imperialism, Kautsky harked back to these early contributions as proof of his own claim to consideration. This was after other writers had popularized the importance of the role of "finance capitalism" in the rise of the new imperialism, but there was just enough of this same idea in Kautsky's articles on "Aeltere und neuere Kolonialpolitik" to justify, in his own mind, the honor of priority. Actually, compared with Hobson, who was developing his theory at about the same time, Kautsky merely played with the idea. But it must be put down to his credit that he saw and called attention to the way in which "high finance" was beginning to exert an influence over the state which old-fashioned industrial capitalism in the free-trade era had never dreamed of and that it was particularly successful in pressing for the acquisition of colonies, or stricter control of existing ones, as new and more profitable fields of investment for surplus capital.

In his earlier writings Kautsky did not call this phenomenon imperialism, nor did he say explicitly that industrial capitalism was giving way to financial capitalism. He was impressed by the same struggle for colonies and by the same Boer War that had stirred Hobson in England; it is even possible that Kautsky got some ideas from Hobson's *Imperialism* (1902), as he had been influenced by other English writers.[11] In any case, he began to lay more and more stress on the idea that capitalism became protectionist, militaristic,

---

[10] In later years Kautsky liked particularly to refer to his articles on "Aeltere und neuere Kolonialpolitik," *Die Neue Zeit*, XVI (1897–98), 769–81, 801–16, as evidence of his claim to having been the first socialist to see and explain the nature of imperialism. Prior to this, during the eighties and nineties, Kautsky had published a number of articles in *Die neue Zeit* describing conditions and rivalries in Egypt, India, Africa, and the Far East, but they contained nothing of theoretical significance.

[11] Kautsky's wife points out that he was profoundly influenced by Buckle. Rosa Luxemburg, *Letters to Karl and Luise Kautsky, from 1896 to 1918*, ed. by Luise Kautsky and tr. from the German by Louis P. Lochner, p. 233. I have found no direct evidence that Hobson also influenced Kautsky, but the latter could hardly have failed to see and be impressed by Hobson's *Imperialism* and other writings.

and imperialistic as the financial interests began to seek outlets for producers' rather than consumers' goods, and changed over from short-run marketing interests to long-term investment interests.[12] But other socialists had made similar contributions to the theory of imperialism at about the same time, and, like Kautsky, they have not been backward in claiming the honor of priority.[13]

Before 1914 Kautsky had used the term "imperialism" relatively little, and when he finally adopted it he continued to insist that it was merely another term for colonialism. He defined imperialism as the product of "highly developed" industrial capitalism and held that it consists "in the striving of every industrial nation to annex larger and larger *agrarian* regions, irrespective of what nations inhabit them." [14]

Irked by Lenin's criticism (which will be considered more fully in a later section) that he was a back number in regarding imperialism as the product of "industrial capitalism" [15] after Hilferding [16] had shown that it was a product of "financial capitalism," Kautsky responded that obviously "highly developed" industrial capitalism meant the same thing as financial capitalism. In addition, Lenin denounced the definition as one-sided and incomplete because Kautsky described imperialism as the annexation of "agrarian" regions by industrial nations, whereas actually imperialism strives to annex industrialized regions as well. Kautsky's reply to this criticism shows his determination to keep the term synonymous

12 See, for example, Kautsky's *The Class Struggle;* especially pp. 43–47, 101–2, 202–4; and his *The Road to Power.*

13 For example, Heinrich Cunow, who replaced Kautsky as editor of *Die neue Zeit* in 1917. Cunow in one respect had a somewhat stronger claim to priority than Kautsky, inasmuch as he could point to the fact that in 1900, in *Die neue Zeit,* he had actually used both the terms "finance capital" and "imperialism" in conjunction. Cunow made his claim in "Was ist Imperialismus?", *Die neue Zeit,* XXXIII (1915), 199–200, and referred to his article "Handelsvertrags- und imperialistische Expansionspolitik," *Die neue Zeit,* XVIII² (1900), 207–15, 234–42. See especially p. 239.

14 Kautsky, "Der Imperialismus," *Die neue Zeit,* XXXII² (1914), 909. As quoted in Lenin, *Imperialism, the Highest Stage of Capitalism,* p. 82. Kautsky had expressed a similar idea in 1901 ("Krisentheorien," *Die neue Zeit,* XX² [1901–2], 80), in reviewing Tugan-Baranowsky's book, *Studien zur Theorie und Geschichte der Handelskrisen in England* (1901). In his review Kautsky denied Tugan-Baranowsky's theory that crises are avoidable under capitalism, and in answer restated the Marxian thesis that because the accumulation of capital increases at a more rapid rate than consumption in a given capitalist country, that country must seek additional outlets in noncapitalist areas outside its domain. Even this ends in crisis, however, and will eventually culminate in chronic depression.

15 See below; p. 185.                      16 See below, pp. 164–69.

with colonialism. While he had no intention of excluding such non-agrarian activities as investments in railroads, mines, and other capitalistic enterprises, he insisted that the real prizes sought by capitalist investors were the relatively undeveloped or agrarian regions, not highly developed or capitalistic areas. Thus, he argued, it would not do to make the term "imperialism" cover a field of activity as broad as capitalism itself (including such phenomena as cartels, trusts, protective tariffs, and financial control), because that would merely lead to the tautology that capitalism is the cause of capitalism.[17]

The climax of Kautsky's apostasy from "pure Marxism," however, was a direct outgrowth of his recoil from the horrors of the first World War and his fears that a triumphant communism would prolong the spirit of revenge and conflict. During the long years of his intellectual leadership of the left-wing Marxists, Kautsky had believed in and preached the doctrine of revolutionary socialism. When the war had convinced him that he was, after all, an ardent pacifist, he sought an escape from his dilemma by asserting that socialism can be a revolutionary movement without being a revolution-making movement in the war-and-bloodshed sense, and on this ground he denounced the Bolshevists and their revolution in Russia.[18] This caused him to lose all the influence he had ever had with this group. Since he was also unwilling to support the war merely for the sake of a German victory, he found himself equally at odds with the vast majority of the German Social Democrats, who supported the war in the hope that their party would be in a better position to take over the government after the war if they maintained a positive and patriotic attitude of support while hostilities lasted. To take a negative and obstructionist stand, they believed, would discredit them in the eyes of the people and would win them the approbrium of having been responsible for defeat should the war end disastrously for Germany. Thus, in the eyes of the Social Democrats, Kautsky was a defeatist, and in the eyes of Lenin and the Communists a "renegade" to pure Marxism, a revisionist, and a pacifist.[19] As a direct result of his failure

[17] "Zwei Schriften zum Umlernen," *Die neue Zeit*, XXXIII[2] (1915), 107, 110, 111.
[18] See Kautsky's *Terrorism and Communism*.
[19] See, for example, Trotsky, *Dictatorship vs. Democracy*, 91 ff. Trotsky attacks Kautsky for attempting to prove that Marx did not favor terrorism. He also denounces

to conform to the party program, Kautsky was removed in 1917 from the editorship of *Die Neue Zeit* and replaced by Heinrich Cunow.

Kautsky's pacifism was the immediate issue, but back of this conviction lay a heresy that was even more alarming to his former associates. On the surface it looked as if Kautsky the great anti-imperialist had become a convert to imperialism. But in his own mind it was a question of choosing the lesser of two great evils, of preferring to see the world dominated for a while longer by capitalist powers, united for their self-preservation in a kind of "super-imperialism" to preserve peace, rather than what he feared even more, a reign of chaos and revolution which would destroy the hope of socialism as well as capitalism. As he saw it now, peaceful order was the only atmosphere in which socialists could continue to work towards their ideal by peaceful change. He even went so far as to say that the idea that imperialism is the only driving force back of war had been exaggerated. The fact that the World War broke out at a time when imperialistic issues were at their ebb seemed to him proof that imperialism had little to do with the war; and furthermore, such expansionist policies as were then in evidence, particularly in Russia, were pre-imperialist and pre-capitalist in origin [20]—in other words, they were atavistic.

Strange doctrine, coming from an old-time Marxist, but this was not all. In 1915 Kautsky asks "whether it is possible that the present imperialist policy might be supplanted by a new ultra-imperialist policy, which would introduce the joint exploitation of the world by an internationally combined finance capital in place of the mutual rivalries of national finance capitals? Such a new phase of capitalism is at any rate conceivable. Is it realizable? Sufficient evidence is not yet available to enable us to answer this question." [21]

---

him as an "Austrian forgery of Marxism" and says that the Austro-Marxists, Bauer, Renner, Hilferding, Max Adler, and Friedrich Adler were characterized by their fear of revolution and a lack of will and zeal for action. For Lenin's criticism of these men see below, pp. 183–84.

[20] *Nationalstaat, imperialistischer Staat und Staatenbund*, p. 64.

[21] "Zwei Schriften zum Umlernen," *Die neue Zeit*, XXXIII[2] (1915), 144. As quoted in Lenin, *Imperialism*, p. 106. Lenin implies that Kautsky got his idea of "ultra-imperialism," or "super-imperialism," from Hobson; at any rate, says Lenin (*Imperialism*, pp. 107–10), the theory is absolutely irreconcilable with Marxism, because it

Despite his willingness to concede that capitalism might thus consolidate to maintain peace, Kautsky had not the slightest intention of adopting a compromising attitude towards imperialism. Socialism was still the great ideal, but war was a greater enemy than imperialism; imperialism, especially "ultraimperialism," might enable capitalists to exploit the workers more severely than ever (as Kautsky had maintained in 1914),[22] but war could only brutalize and kill them.

## IMPERIALISM AS THE POLICY OF "FINANCE CAPITALISM"

The first great and original contributions to the socialist literature on imperialism came from the Marxists of the right, that is, from those who believed in evolutionary rather than revolutionary socialism and were reconciled to living with capitalism, even perhaps compromising with it a little. They were not convinced that the collapse of capitalism from innate necessity was inevitable, but they had faith that the workers, with proper educational guidance, would learn that through peaceful and parliamentary means the socialist commonwealth could be established.

On the positive side there seemed to be enough observable capitalist practices to explain imperialism without the labor-cost theory of value and related doctrines. Monopoly was developing on a grand scale, as Marx had predicted, and was becoming international through the medium of the great cartels. At the same time there was an intensification of "economic nationalism," with its high protective tariffs, which clearly had only a short way to go into "economic imperialism," with tariff walls around a wider area. Above all, these socialists were impressed by the rising power of the great banks. Industrial capitalism appeared to be giving way not only to "monopoly capitalism" but also to "finance capitalism." The two were joining forces to produce capitalist imperialism.

The first step in the development of the thesis that imperialism is not an inescapable stage of capitalist development, but only a policy of expansion, is found in the reasoning that capitalism, al-

---

glosses over the most basic contradictions of imperialism, his own view being that capitalism is incapable of having a policy of any kind.

[22] Kautsky, "Der Imperialismus," *Die neue Zeit*, XXXII[2] (1914), 921.

though it can and must expand, has a choice between inward expansion, such as the older economists had in mind when they talked of intensive cultivation, and outward or extensive expansion. It was also conceivable, of course, that the two kinds of expansion might be followed simultaneously. The conclusion follows that there is no inherent reason why capitalism could not, if it wanted to, settle down within a given area and stay there, utilizing the market within its national confines without going outside to look for markets. In short, production could be capitalistic without being imperialistic.

As we saw in Chapter VI the roots of this idea, so far as socialists were concerned, go back to that part of Marx's analysis wherein he considered the necessary conditions of balanced production under any economic system, including capitalism. Although no one related this idea to the theory of imperialism until long after Marx's death, the thesis that capitalism can expand indefinitely within a closed system is clearly implied in Marx's demonstration that the two great economic divisions (I, which produces means of production, and II, which produces means of consumption) can remain in equilibrium provided the proper proportions of investment in labor and investment in machines is maintained between them.

A definitely socialistic theory of imperialism based on this conception of capitalism began to develop between 1900 and 1910, and the finished result was largely the work of the Vienna school of socialists, notably of Otto Bauer and Rudolph Hilferding. Regarding themselves as strictly orthodox, they had much influence on radicals such as Lenin, but at the same time they shared numerous points of view with the revisionists. Their original concern was to bring Marxian principles into line with new developments, especially the growth of monopoly. They were impressed in particular by the role of the great banking institutions in the organization of cartels, trusts, holding companies, and mergers and with the relation of these developments to protectionism and the export of capital. Their theory of imperialism was a by-product of their theoretical and historical incursions into the nature of the new capitalism. Unlike Hobson, who started with imperialism and traced its roots back to high finance, the Austrian socialists began with the developments in the field of "finance capitalism" and then projected their new ideas into the field of international relations. *Imperialismus* suited them perfectly as a descriptive term for the ideas which they wanted to convey.

Though always more or less vague as a concept, imperialism served very well to combine two powerful contemporary movements—the growth of nationalism and the changing methods of capitalism. It was Otto Bauer who did most to investigate and explain the relationship between nationalism and imperialism,[23] while Hilferding made his greatest contributions on the economic side. Bauer was impressed by two phenomena—the enormous hold which the spirit of nationalism had on all elements of the population and the economic advantages possessed by large states over those possessed by small states. Both phenomena were of very recent development. During the day of economic liberalism, when the spirit of nationalism was weak and economic interdependence was the great ideal, the size of a state made no difference. With the rise of protectionism and economic nationalism, however, it did make a difference. Capitalist nations soon discovered that they had lost the economic advantages of being part of a larger whole, but instead of going back to free trade in order to recover the old advantages, the tendency was for each state to become as large as possible itself.

The ideal of a large composite state under the domination of a single power having replaced the old liberal system of independent nations united economically under free trade, it became necessary for a capitalist power to retain exclusive control over its own *Wirtschaftsgebiet* by high protective tariffs and to organize its industries into powerful monopolies and cartels in order to maintain a high domestic price level, the latter being best accomplished under the leadership and control of the large banks. A nation so equipped can take the initiative—even to the point of aggressiveness—in doing things which were impossible, or at least unheard of, under liberalism. The nation—or its capitalists—can dump surpluses abroad whenever it is apparent that selling them at home will spoil the market and disturb the price structure; it can export capital when that procedure appears to be more profitable than exporting goods. It can import whatever will be of the greatest ad-

---

[23] Bauer, *Die Nationalitätenfrage und die Sozialdemokratie.*

vantage to a capitalist society, especially for the building up of strong military and imperialistic power, which is done at the expense of cheaper foodstuffs and other imports which would be primarily of benefit to the workers. The whole economy, in fact, is visualized as being run more and more at the expense of labor, and yet, curiously enough, many workers are beguiled into believing that it is all to their advantage. Bauer, of course, warns against this subtle danger, but he also warns against the mistake of thinking that the solution lies in a return to the old liberal free-trade system which the capitalists had abandoned. Nationalism is too deeply rooted in human nature to be eradicated in favor of cosmopolitanism, and the only question is whether it shall be perverted into the economic nationalism of the capitalists or made a vehicle for the realization of socialist ideals.

Bauer also had some new ideas regarding the economic aspects of imperialism, although the fundamental idea was Marx's old hypothesis, which had been reformulated by Tugan-Baranowsky, that capitalism can keep on expanding indefinitely in equilibrium provided certain correct proportions are maintained within the economy. The chief problem, as always, is to find continuous outlets for surplus value. Marx, it will be recalled, found the outlet (under rigidly assumed hypothetical conditions) in newly mined gold; Bauer finds it, so to speak, in newly mined people: all that capitalism requires for healthful expansion is a steadily expanding population.[24] On this point he differs from Marx.[25] He assumes that the working population increases at the rate of 5 percent per annum, that variable capital (the investment in labor) increases at the same rate, and that constant capital (the investment in machinery, materials, etc.) increases at double this rate, or at 10 percent; the rate of surplus value remains constant at 100 percent. This means that the organic composition of capital rises. Bauer concludes that

[24] Bauer developed this point later in "Die Akkumulation des Kapitals," *Die neue Zeit*, XXXI[1] (1913), 831–38, 862–74, in answer to Rosa Luxemburg's theory (see below, pp. 169 ff.).

[25] In *Capital*, I, chap. xxv, secs. 3–4, Marx contends that increasing population, instead of creating a demand for more products, merely supplies new sources of surplus value and capital accumulation for the capitalists; surplus population, or the industrial reserve army, is also a product of accumulation. In short, the laboring element of a growing population grows poorer as the capitalists become richer at their expense. The extent to which their capacity to produce can be exploited, not the number and needs of the workers, is the point of departure for capitalist production.

unless something happens to upset the equilibrium of capitalist production and consumption, such as a too-rapid increase of population or a too-slow increase of accumulation, capitalism can expand indefinitely without the occurrence of crises.[26] To prove it he constructs some equations and proceeds to manipulate them for a period covering four years and discovers that, as predicted, the system does not break down. But he did not manipulate them over enough years for the defects of his assumption to show up. For the sake of his theory it was well that he stopped, for eventually it would have become obvious that a source which increases only at the rate of 5 percent (in this case surplus value) is bound to run dry if it is pumped at the rate of 10 percent (in this case by taking out constant capital). Indeed, another Marxist, Henryk Grossmann, not for the purpose of exposing Bauer, but with the object of using Bauer's *schema* to illustrate his own point, kept on pumping the equations until the well ran dry and there was no more surplus value for the personal consumption of the capitalists, let alone for the expansion of production.[27] Although actually Bauer's equations broke down, Grossmann took this as proof that capitalism must break down.

Since Bauer failed to arrive at the same conclusion because he neglected to push his analysis far enough, he was left free to point out that capitalism finds expansion desirable because foreign trade is relatively more profitable to a capitalist country than purely domestic trade. It will be recalled that Marx regarded foreign trade as one of the methods of counteracting the falling rate of profit by cheapening the elements of constant capital (raw materials, etc.,) which are imported, but Bauer reasoned from a different premise. Foreign trade, he argued, is profitable to the highly developed capitalist countries because they have a higher organic composition of capital (that is, more capital equipment relative to labor), and

[26] It is true that Marx says or implies substantially the same thing in various places. In the early stages of capitalism, he says, the rising composition of capital (i. e., the shift from labor to labor-saving machinery) took place very slowly, and the demand for labor kept pace with accumulation, and crises could not occur (*Capital*, I, 694). But under advanced capitalism, according to Marx, the possibility of maintaining equilibrium by maintaining a proper balance between the various branches of production was nil because of the uneven race between the factors on which balance depends. (See above, Chapter VI).

[27] Grossmann, *Das Akkumulations- und Zusammenbruchsgesetz des kapitalistischen Systems*, p. 178. See below, pp. 182–83.

therefore, since profits are distributed or equalized, according to the amount of capital used, the highly industrialized countries attract to themselves a larger share of the surplus value than corresponds to the quantity of labor congealed in it. This means that surplus value is appropriated not only from the workers at home but from those in the less advanced countries.[28]

Bauer's theory that capitalist expansion is a matter of policy, not of absolute necessity, despite its pretension of being an answer to capitalist apologies for imperialism, was regarded by the radical Marxists as nothing more than a cheap revisionist apology for capitalism. In trying to show how capitalism could remain in equilibrium within a large political area without resorting to foreign trade and capital export he was not so much guilty of supplying the enemy with ammunition—for capitalists were doubtless unconvinced by his reasoning—as he was of replacing the old sharp socialist broadsword of capital accumulation and falling profit rates by an array of new weapons—cartels, protective tariffs, and capital export.

Rudolph Hilferding's *Finanzkapital* [29] is one of the most original and convincing pieces of work on imperialism ever written, on the Continent comparable in influence with Hobson's *Imperialism* among English and American readers. It was frankly Marxian, but

[28] Bauer, *Die Nationalitätenfrage und die Sozialdemokratie*, pp. 246–47. See also Sweezy, *The Theory of Capitalist Development*, pp. 290–92. Sweezy points out that it is contrary to Marx to assume that the equalization of profit rates between countries (or for that matter between monopolized industries within the same country) comes about through trade alone. Equalization is possible only if *capital* is exported from low-profit countries (usually those which are highly developed) to higher-profit countries; capital flows out because the profit rate is higher than at home, and the profits, in flowing back, tend to raise the domestic level of profits.

[29] Hilferding, *Das Finanzkapital*. Except for minor changes, Hilferding points out, this book was completed in 1906. It is the third volume in the Marx-Studien, of which Otto Bauer's *Die Nationalitätenfrage und die Sozialdemokratie* was the second. The reprint here used bears the date 1923. Hilferding rose to political prominence under the German Republic and for a time was Finance Minister of Germany. The term "finance-capital" is a Germanism, used only to a limited extent by English and American writers, except those who have been influenced by neo-Marxism or who regard it as a useful addition to the language in which modern capitalism must be described. See, however, Edwards, *The Evolution of Finance Capitalism;* after having used the term in the title of his book, he abandons it in the text for the equivalent term "security capitalism," which he defines as "the economic system which is financed through the conversion of the saving of investors into security investment," the banks being the middle-men between the savers and the users of capital (p. 2). The term "security capitalism" (*Effekten-Kapitalismus*), he says, was first used by Robert Liefmann in *Beteiligungs- und Finanzierungs-Gesellschaften.*

not too Marxian in the sense of being dogmatically and bel-
ligerently radical. Though Hilferding was professedly orthodox,
his acceptance of the Tugan-Baranowsky thesis that capitalism can,
theoretically at least, remain in equilibrium, provided certain conditions are observed, identified him with the general viewpoint of
the revisionists. His conclusion that imperialism is a policy of
capitalism, not capitalism itself in a certain stage of development, definitely aligned him against the breakdown theorists, who
thought that capitalism must collapse from its own inner contradictions and be overthrown (more or less violently, according to
one's views on evolution *versus* revolution) by the conscious and
deliberate acts of the proletariat.

Hilferding's central concept is "finance capital," around which
he develops the role of the banks, their relation to monopoly,
monopoly's relation to protectionism, and the part played by all
these forces in producing imperialism and the inevitable war. In
accepting the thesis that capitalist equilibrium is a matter of proportionality, Hilferding naturally took the position that crises are
not inevitable and that imperialism is not an absolute necessity
for the continued existence of capitalism. The new power in the
world is high finance. Quite obviously, to Hilferding, it is powerful
enough to do almost anything it chooses, and it is a highly significant contrast with what is usually regarded as strict Marxism that
it can choose a policy of imperialism, for this implies that imperialism is not an inevitable stage of capitalist development.

Few words have been more annoying to the radical Marxists than
this word "policy," and it is a never-ending source of astonishment
to them that a person otherwise as sane and orthodox as Hilferding
could ever have accepted the idea that imperialism is or can be a
policy. The tendency is to place the blame largely on Tugan-
Baranowsky. It is easy enough, of course (as we shall see in connection with the views of Rosa Luxemburg), to exonerate Marx on
the ground that the idea of capitalistic self-containment was a
hypothetical sideshow with him, not the center of attraction.
Nevertheless, Hilferding, like Tugan-Baranowsky, attached great
theoretical importance to the proportionality thesis. To Hilferding,
therefore, must go the chief responsibility for introducing the idea

into socialist literature, and along with it the idea that the question of crises can be disposed of mainly by engaging in a little discourse on the reasons for disproportionality.[30]

After explaining how capitalism can remain in equilibrium provided the proper proportions are maintained between the production-goods and the consumption-goods branches of industry,[31] Hilferding goes on to explain that such perfection is unattainable under capitalism because the only general regulator and stabilizer of capitalist production is a price mechanism which is itself easily and unavoidably thrown out of balance and into chaos.[32] Therefore, by centering attention on the price mechanism and on the financiers who stand at the controls of the monetary and banking structure, Hilferding had at his command a new and powerful analytical approach to the vagaries of capitalism.

The opening wedge to the revolution which converted free trade and laissez faire capitalism from the peaceable ways of industrialism to the imperialistic outlook of finance capital and the bankers, according to Hilferding, was the accumulation of capital and its centralization in the modern business corporation. The social significance of corporate financing was the separation of ownership from management, thus forcing the first break with industrial capitalism by supplanting a system of responsible manager-ownership with a system in which investors not only might scatter their risks in a diversified security market [33] but also scatter and weaken their responsibility and control. This was the beginning of the great *rentier* class which is interested only in dividends. Inevitably management went from their hands into the hands of the directors of the corporations, and the old-fashioned industrial capitalist with an eye to profit is transformed into a moneylender with an eye to a safe return in the form of interest. This created the promoter's opportunity to make money by organizing companies and selling shares, and in turn became the banker's opportunity to market securities and assume the role of the promoter. The final upshot is

[30] Cf. Sweezy, *The Theory of Capitalist Development*, pp. 159–60.

[31] *Finanzkapital*, pp. 304–18.

[32] *Ibid.*, pp. 318 ff.; the subject of crises in relation to "finance capital" is discussed pp. 297–374.

[33] *Ibid.*, p. 112.

the complete domination of industry by finance, "finance-capital" being, as Hilferding defines it, "capital controlled by the banks and utilized by the industrialists." [34]

It is in the field of banking and finance rather than in the field of production, therefore, that the factors of disequilibrium and disproportionality first began to operate. Hilferding accepts Marx's basic idea that the rate of profit must continually tend to fall, but he does not accept the idea that this is disastrous to all capitalists alike. In the first place capitalists are no longer all alike, as they once were when the industrial capitalist dominated the scene. In the old days the typical capitalist owned shares in a corporation, for which he received, or hoped to receive, profits; with the rise of corporate financing and banker control of industry the typical capitalist lends money to the bank at a fixed rate of interest. Lending money to the banks and from the banks to industry on perfect security, in other words, has become the more profitable branch of the capitalist process and is made all the more profitable to the bankers owing to their power to create credit on the basis of fractional reserves and to control the industries which they promote and finance.[35] In other words, Hilferding believes that the circulation process has come to dominate the production process, thus reversing the position taken by Marx, who maintained that production is dominant despite his strong suggestions that banking and credit play an important role in disequilibrium. Hilferding also believed that the cartel movement means the substitution of monopoly agreements for the price mechanism to such an extent that prices are rapidly losing their meaning and function in the distribution process.

Marx visualized the coming of monopoly as a sheer process by which big capitalist producers swallow smaller ones, but Hilferd-

---

[34] *Ibid.*, p. 283; see also p. 301. Many economists about this time were beginning to comment on the power over industry exercised by German banks. Alfred Marshall, in his *Industry and Trade*, remarks that "the rise of some German industrialists to a high place in the ranks of finance has gone together with an ever closer interweaving of broad financial counsels in the control of particular industrial interests" (p. 566). In Germany "banks are alert and forward in associating themselves with the strongest industrial enterprises" (p. 567). In the United States the outstanding financial leaders have had their origin "more especially in industry" (p. 566); and American industrialists "control finance, perhaps as much as they are controlled by it" (p. 566). Britain, Marshall believes, stands somewhere between Germany and the United States with respect to industrial organization and control.

[35] *Finanzkapital*, pp. 102, 107–10.

ing's analysis greatly refines this brutal procedure. It is the great banks who do the swallowing, but with an innate nicety and aplomb that makes the victims believe that they are being done a favor. Finance capitalism, unlike the old industrial capitalism, says Hilferding, does not want freedom, but domination; its whole ideology is one of power [36]—but power gained and exercised in subtle ways that are alien to brute force. Having gone to the trouble of organizing corporations, getting seats on their boards of directors, and being careful to create interlocking directorates—all for the sake of profit—no bank is going to be so foolish as to permit its creatures to fall to fighting among themselves to the detriment of profits.

Though Hilferding's economic analysis of the cartel movement [37] leaves much to be desired, it is in many respects a remarkable piece of work, considering its essentially pioneering penetration of a new field. It was a far better analysis than the conventional Marxism of its time and even went beyond that of contemporary orthodox economists, who had done little more than continue to deal in the old analysis of the fixation of monopoly price. As Hilferding pictures it, the cartels are enormously profitable because of their power to keep prices at a higher level than would be possible under competition. They attract capital away from the less favorably situated uncartelized industries, take trade away from them by superior organization, better staying power in the war of competition, and unscrupulous methods of competition, thus forcing independent concerns to take cover in the cartel organization. It was good Marxism, of course, to play up the role of monopoly in the concentration of wealth by picturing how the huge cartel profits flow into the banks.[38] It was also in line with Marxism to insist that investment opportunities shrink as concentration proceeds because the cartelization process reduces and stabilizes production instead of permitting it to expand and because of the timidity of capital to move towards what remains of the uncartelized industrial opportunities. Instead of controlling and stabilizing the economy in such a way as to prevent crises, cartels merely shift the full weight of the crisis to the uncartelized industries,[39] thus forcing them into the cartel scheme of control.

[36] *Ibid.*, p. 426.  
[37] *Ibid.*, chap. xv (pp. 285–96).  
[38] *Ibid.*, pp. 294–95.  
[39] *Ibid.*, p. 374.

The imperialistic phase of finance capitalism in Hilferding's analysis arises directly out of the export of capital. The role of the cartel in capital export, however, is secondary. Monopolies of this sort do not force the export of capital; they merely serve as the agent of a tendency that is inherent in the capitalist world when finance reaches the position of dominance over industry. Unlike Otto Bauer, who took it for granted that surplus value is transferred in international trade through the mere exchange of products, which sets in motion the process of equalizing the rate of profit,[40] Hilferding insists that only the export of capital can effect such a transfer, and then only if ownership of the capital remains in the exporting country.[41] In somewhat the same way that financiers within a country create surplus value by supplying capital to the individuals whom they control, capitalist countries reap profit from the countries to which they supply capital. Annexation—the final imperialistic touch—is a natural outcome of this process. In contrast with the free-trade era of industrial capitalism, when goods were exchanged for goods and exclusive territorial control was unnecessary, finance capital demands protective tariffs as the means of monopolizing the domestic market [42] and the complete domination of backward or colonial areas in order to maintain exclusive control of the source of profits. And if this policy meets resistance, finance capital is strong enough to induce the state to support its claims by force.[43] For a time the great banking houses and international cartels may succeed in maintaining a precarious economic stability [44] and the semblance of peace and may even appear to control the world, but sooner or later the truce is broken and the underlying conflict of national interest emerges in the form of economic warfare, which eventually degenerates into military hostilities.[45] In the great sweep of events the movement is from industrial capitalism to finance capitalism, from free trade to protectionism, from

---

[40] See above, p. 163n.                    [41] *Finanzkapital*, p. 395.
[42] *Ibid.*, pp. 384–86, 389.              [43] *Ibid.*, pp. 401, 406.
[44] When this stage is reached, says Hilferding (*ibid.*, p. 296), money can be dispensed with, because the great central monopoly of industry and finance can make a purely arbitrary distribution of products without bothering with the price mechanism. In any case, owing to the great complexity of the economic system, the price mechanism as a stabilizing factor for capitalist production can no longer perform its function and becomes useless before complete cartelization takes place. (*Ibid.*, pp. 318–19.) This accounts for the necessity of purely arbitrary control by the cartels.
[45] *Ibid.*, pp. 392 ff.

the export of consumer goods to the export of capital, from an unstable free enterprise to the rigidities of monopoly, and from a peaceful policy of live-and-let-live to imperialism and war.

What could appear more logical? No wonder Hilferding's book was hailed as the greatest contribution to socialist thought since Marx, and as the first attempt by a socialist (Hobson's priority could never be overlooked even by those who denounced him as a bourgeois apologist) to analyze in detail the relation of capitalism to imperialism. But there were dissenters from this view in the socialist ranks, and in addition the possibility of dissent from those outside the socialist circle who remained unconvinced that such ancient and powerful institutions as militarism and imperialism could suddenly, in the modern world, be interpreted as the exclusive product of economic development.

## "BACK TO MARX": ROSA LUXEMBURG AND THE THEORY OF CAPITAL ACCUMULATION

In a book [46] that marked another epoch in socialist thought, Rosa Luxemburg, in 1913, tried to revive the waning underconsumption theory of crises and reformulate Marx in such a way as to leave no doubt that he, too, was an underconsumptionist. Thus, she sought to counteract the doctrine that capitalism can expand indefinitely without showing signs of collapse provided the proper proportions are maintained within and between the two great divisions which supply production goods and consumption goods. Having proved to her own satisfaction that because these proportions cannot be maintained capitalism must collapse, she concluded that capitalism must necessarily follow an imperialistic policy without any choice in the matter such as is suggested by those who had come to regard imperialism as a policy which capitalism adopts merely because it chooses to do so.

Luxemburg was greatly disturbed by the growing tendency

[46] Rosa Luxemburg, *Die Akkumulation des Kapitals; ein Beitrag zur ökonomischen Erklärung des Imperialismus* (Vereinigung Internationaler Verlags-Anstalten, Berlin, 1921; first published in 1913). Later, while in prison, Rosa Luxemburg wrote a summary of her earlier work and an answer to her critics under the title *Die Akkumulation des Kapitals oder was die Epigonen aus der Marxschen Theorie gemacht haben. Eine Antikritik* (Frankes Verlag, Leipzig, 1921), hereinafter referred to as *Antikritik*. A good résumé of Luxemburg's views is to be found in Laurat, *L'Accumulation du capital d'après Rosa Luxembourg*.

among socialists to accept this point of view, and she wanted to return to the fundamentals of Marxism. But the road back was difficult. Not only had she to dispose of Tugan-Baranowsky and all the others, beginning with Say and Ricardo, who had popularized the idea of a self-contained capitalism, and of professed Marxists, such as Bauer and Hilferding, who had perpetuated the doctrine; she had even to correct Marx himself and his attempted demonstration of the same thesis. It is one of the most interesting episodes in socialist literature to see how Luxemburg leaped these hurdles and especially how she tried to make a true Marxist out of Marx.

In the first place, she restated a proposition on which she thought all Marxists could agree. It had become common doctrine that under expanded (enlarged or capitalistic) production constant capital is used up by the capitalists in replacing worn-out capital; that variable capital received by the wage earners is spent by them for consumption goods; and that surplus value, or what is left over and above the relatively small part spent by the capitalists on their own consumption requirements, must be accumulated.[47] But the crucial question, then as always, was where the buyers were to come from to take this surplus off the market. In other words, where was the source of effective demand? At every stage of her analysis Luxemburg raises this question,[48] only to discard every known answer until she reaches her own.

It will be recalled that Marx had set up a hypothesis in which he assumed capitalism to be world-wide,[49] and in connection with this one-world idea of capitalism he appeared to reach the conclusion that such a closed system can function indefinitely in equilibrium; in other words, that surplus value can always find a market. This in turn had given comfort to those of his followers who had reasoned that no single capitalist country was absolutely compelled to go outside—that is, into imperialist expansion—in order to keep on functioning. It was in line with the old idea of Say and others in the classical tradition of economic thought who had held general overproduction to be impossible. And it was the essence of Tugan-Baranowsky's theory which had made such an impression in some socialist circles.

[47] *Die Akkumulation des Kapitals*, pp. 114–15.
[48] As, for example, *ibid.*, pp. 105, 110, 114, 115, 131, 132; *Antikritik*, pp. 16, 17.
[49] See above, p. 132.

How anyone could conceive of a capitalist society not constantly in need of outward expansion was to Luxemburg the great mystery. Equally puzzling was how anyone could think that Marx ever really entertained such an idea. There was no questioning his exact words, but what was their context, and what of the ocean of other words in which Marx talks about the necessity of capitalist accumulation and markets for surplus value? To all this Luxemburg had a ready answer—and in general a sound one, so far as her interpretation of Marx is concerned. The soundness of her own or Marx's answer to the question of effective demand is another question. At any rate, at the outset Luxemburg is especially eager to distinguish clearly once and for all between the economics of simple reproduction and that of enlarged, or capitalist, production. In the former the problem of surplus value and capital accumulation never arises, because by definition simple reproduction means that all surplus value is consumed by the capitalists themselves. Under capitalist production it is the lack of capitalist consumption of the surplus which creates the problem of capital accumulation and what to do with it.

Although Marx dealt endlessly with these two concepts of production, he often confused them, failing to make it clear when he was talking about the one and when he had the other in mind. Consequently a careless reader might get the impression from *Capital* that a closed system of capitalist production can function in a self-contained manner and keep on going like a merry-go-round, when actually Marx means only that a closed system of simple (nonexpanding, noncapitalist) production can operate in this fashion. So argues Luxemburg. She is certain that he never intended anyone to take literally or as a final judgment the idea thrown out hypothetically in Volume I of *Capital* that capitalism, either as one world or as a single country, can continue to function in equilibrium as a self-contained entity.[50] It was Marx's intention, she claims, to make it clear in Volumes II and III of *Capital* that the capitalist class as a whole cannot absorb the surplus which their constant investment and reinvestment creates. But Engels, not understanding the tentative and incomplete character of Marx's hypothesis, failed to take this into consideration in preparing

[50] Luxemburg discusses Marx's one-world hypothesis in *Die Akkumulation des Kapitals*, pp. 108–9, and in *Antikritik*, p. 18.

Marx's notes for publication in the two posthumous volumes of his work.[51]

By this process of reasoning Luxemburg was able to dismiss Marx's one-world hypothesis and all other similar ideas as merely part of a general methodological device for bringing out the fundamental laws and contradictions of capital accumulation and its part in capitalist development.[52] Whether true or not in this case, it has been the fate of many another economist to have his methodological simplification of a problem taken to be, not a hypothesis, but a picture of reality. In fact a good part of Luxemburg's book is devoted to the creation of a straw man of her own in order to show that it is impossible for her, or for Marx or anyone else, to make a going concern even theoretically out of a merry-go-round conception in which capitalists merely continue to accumulate capital for the sake of accumulation.[53] To her it was as clear as day that this was no picture of the real world, for in reality labor literally cannot consume the surplus of capitalist production because it lacks purchasing power, while the capitalist class could not even if it had the physical capacity to do so, because it has to accumulate—to save and invest—in order to fulfill its function as the profit-seeking and profit-taking part of the system.

Being an uncompromising underconsumption theorist herself, Luxemburg naturally could see nothing but underconsumption in Marx's theory. She admits that Marx seemed at times to reject the underconsumption theory of crises in favor of the idea that crises are involved with the falling tendency of the rate of profit, but she insists that it was only when he was considering simple reproduction that he rejected the underconsumption hypothesis. She was convinced that in the vital part of his analysis, where Marx was concerned with enlarged production, he believed underconsumption to be the cause of capitalism's distress. At the same time, she was not satisfied with the old Marxian answer that surplus value is merely "accumulated." Though acceptable to Luxemburg as a general statement, it failed to explain where the demand is to come from to take it off the market. For obviously capitalists are not go-

[51] See Die Akkumulation des Kapitals, p. 140; Antikritik, pp. 23–25.

[52] Die Akkumulation des Kapitals, pp. 301 ff.; see also Antikritik, pp. 46, 105 ff.

[53] This point is made repeatedly by Luxemburg. See particularly Die Akkumulation des Kapitals, pp. 104–5, and Antikritik, p. 17.

ing to continue to produce a surplus year after year, using it only to construct more means of production to create more means of consumption, unless there is some prospect of finding a market. Yet belief in this senseless merry-go-round is what a strict adherence to Marx's assumption of a closed capitalist economy requires.

Most regrettable of all to Luxemburg was the fact that Marx became side-tracked in a long and fruitless attempt to explain "where the money comes from" to purchase surplus goods. This in turn prevented him from considering "where the consumers come from." Thus, he (or rather, Engels) was led to the conclusion in Volume II of *Capital* that newly mined gold is capable of supplying the deficiency of effective demand. On the other hand, had he concerned himself exclusively with the question of consumption, he would at least have concluded that consumers of surplus value are not found in the closed system of capitalists and workers. Furthermore, this would have provided a firm basis for the underconsumption theory of capitalist crises and for the further and final thought that it is underconsumption at home which requires capitalists to seek a remedy in new consumers outside the home system.

Since Luxemburg regarded the source of the money as irrelevant, she naturally regarded Marx's discussion of gold mines as a source of purchasing power as entirely irrelevant.[54] Similarly, she could have no patience with Marx's discussion of hoarding and dishoarding, credit, the banking system, the velocity of circulation of money, and the various economies in the use of circulating media resorted to by capitalists in supplying additional purchasing power for enlarged production.[55]

In getting back to the fundamentals of Marx, or to what he would have said had he lived to finish his work, Luxemburg felt it necessary to clear up a great deal of accumulated undergrowth which other writers had produced in perpetuating the basic error regarding the self-sufficiency of a closed capitalist economy. Tugan-Baranowsky was, of course, a major object of attack,[56] but since he was not a Marxist in any case, Luxemburg had no reservations in disposing of his idea that the production of the means of production can remain independent of consumption provided the proper pro-

[54] See *Die Akkumulation des Kapitals*, pp. 72, 75, 112, 126–27, 136, 299; and *Antikritik*, p. 33.

[55] *Antikritik*, pp. 130–37.  [56] *Die Akkumulation des Kapitals*, pp. 280–95.

portions are maintained within and between the production-goods and consumption-goods branches of the economy.

Bauer and Hilferding, from Luxemburg's point of view, had been led into the same error and, while posing as Marxists, they were really closer to heretics such as Tugan-Baranowsky than to Marx. To make matters even worse, they had tried to develop a theory of capitalist imperialism on this heresy.[57] Since they had shut themselves off from the possibility of finding the basis of imperialism in the simple fact of underconsumption and believed that capitalism need not follow an imperialist policy from the sheer necessity which underconsumption imposes, and yet were obliged to find an explanation of the capitalist imperialism which was all around them, they were required, as Luxemburg saw it, to indulge in some very bizarre and unnecessary mental gymnastics. Why should capitalism despite the lack of necessity for doing so, nevertheless resort to imperialism? To Luxemburg the heretical answer that it had something to do with the relative attractiveness of outlying territories was no substitute for the Marxian idea, found in the underconsumption theory, that such things take place because of absolute necessity, not because someone chooses a certain policy from among alternatives.

Furthermore, Luxemburg regarded it as a perversion of Marxism and of obvious reality to force the separation of economics from politics, or policy, which could only lead, as it had led Bauer and Hilferding, into superficial speculation about nationalism, protectionism, cartels, finance capital, and the like, when the real need is to see that all these phenomena are only reflections of the accumulation of capital and of the resulting crises of underconsumption. To Rosa Luxemburg this was a most serious matter, not academic hairsplitting. Bauer and Hilferding and the Austrian socialists were weakening in their revolutionary zeal and swinging away from the bitter concepts of capitalist breakdown and violent revolution towards the despised position of the revisionists; they were "frightened pacifists," who were undermining the workers' zeal for revolt by teaching—or in effect teaching—that imperialism is nothing to be afraid of and that everybody can share in the benefits of the productive powers of capitalism.

[57] It was not in *Die Akkumulation des Kapitals,* but in the much later *Antikritik* that Luxemburg went into detailed criticism of Bauer and Hilferding, especially Bauer.

Taking surplus value as her starting-point and underconsumption as her answer to why capitalism must seek markets outside its own confines, Luxemburg had little to do except to define what she meant by "capitalist" and "noncapitalist" areas, or milieus. In place of Marx's closed system, Luxemburg presents what she regards as a realistic picture of capitalism and its "actual surroundings." By its actual surroundings she meant not solely the noncapitalistic colonial or so-called backward areas lying on the periphery of a purely capitalistic system, which are usually regarded as the only fields of imperialist operation; she also included the little islands of noncapitalist enterprise, such as are found in agricultural and handicraft industries, which persist in what is mistakenly regarded as a society composed exclusively of capitalists and wage earners.[58] In other words, there are noncapitalist areas both at the extensive and at the intensive margin of capitalist production, and it is these areas which are the object of capitalist exploitation and give rise to the phenomenon of imperialism.

Capitalism may appear to expand within the closed system envisaged by Bauer and Hilferding, but actually, from Luxemburg's point of view, it is not a closed system of capitalists and workers, but a society—outwardly capitalistic—which still contains enough unexploited noncapitalist elements to account for the expansion which is observed. Neither an increase of population, nor "third persons," nor foreign trade can account for capitalist expansion.[59] It can be accounted for only in terms of the exploitation of persons outside the circle of capitalists and those who already belong to the proletarian class.[60] Expansion can be understood only in terms of a return to primitive accumulation. Imperialism thus is not a matter of national boundaries, for the line of demarcation between what is capitalistic and what is not, and between what is imperialistic and what is not, is to Luxemburg an economic, not a political, question. Capitalism has always evinced a readiness to use resources

[58] *Antikritik*, pp. 7–20.

[59] Historically, according to Luxemburg's analysis, capitalists undertook to dispose of their surplus to the nonproductive elements at home, such as doctors, lawyers, teachers, and others; and they also seek export markets, only to discover that for the country as a whole exports must be paid for by imports of equal value, thus producing no net change. Neither method pushes the capitalist process beyond the stage of simple reproduction.

[60] *Antikritik*, pp. 105–10.

regardless of their origin and to sell in markets regardless of their character. For example, it used cotton produced by American slaves under noncapitalist conditions, while today the peasants of Germany constitute an "external" market for German capitalism; and from the capitalist point of view most of the trade between countries such as Germany and England is "internal." [61] Nor, according to Luxemburg, is imperialism a matter of finance capital, international finance, protective tariffs, and all the other elements which Bauer and Hilferding mistook for fundamental causes. These elements play a purely superficial role—finance as an episode in capitalism's search for markets; [62] tariffs as symptoms of the helplessness of weak countries against the power of international capital. The only crucial factor is the accumulation of capital, for as soon as the noncapitalist fields of exploitation dry up, accumulation will dry up too, and capitalism will be at a dead end. Nothing else is vitally important. No matter how important tariffs and finance appear to be, they are mere symptoms of the dearth of accumulation. But the results are unmistakable; in the final, desperate stages of the disappearance of their markets capitalists will be driven into disastrous competition, first in the internal noncapitalist markets, and finally in the external markets. It is at this stage that the world becomes engulfed in world-wide depressions, imperialistic wars, and revolutions. Long before the world is completely absorbed in the capitalist system, however, class antagonisms and economic and political anarchy will precipitate the rebellion of the international proletariat.[63] For although she believed in the breakdown theory of capitalism, Luxemburg belonged to the school of thought which has confidence in the zeal and ability of the masses to revolt before the final natural collapse occurs.

So absorbed was Rosa Luxemburg in the brilliance of her new discovery that she was entirely incapable of seeing how ridiculous it is to ask "for whom" production takes place in a closed system, where she insists production becomes a meaningless merry-go-round, and then to think that she has found a solution in the equally obvious merry-go-round of selling surplus products to noncapitalists. For if the goods are disposed of—as they must be—in return

---

[61] *Die Akkumulation des Kapitals*, p. 338.          [62] *Ibid.*, pp. 394–423.
[63] *Die Akkumulation des Kapitals*, pp. 338–39, 445; *Antikritik*, pp. 20–21, 115.

for goods of equal value, nothing has happened that was not already taking place within the so-called closed system.[64] Back of this blind spot in her analysis is the persistent failure of theorists like herself to see that expanded production is capable of throwing purchasing power into the hands of the workers as well as into the hands of the capitalists, enabling them to absorb what would otherwise be an unsalable surplus.

Marx was confused here, too, but at least he worked towards an economically consistent explanation of effective demand. Neither Marx nor Luxemburg, however, was able to see any other answer to the problem, as it exists under capitalism, than that demand must come fortuitously from the outside, as a sort of manna from Heaven. Marx found the answer in newly mined gold, and Bauer found it in population increase, while Luxemburg visualized it as coming from noncapitalist milieus. But whereas Rosa Luxemburg let the matter rest at this point, Marx threw out suggestions in arriving at his conclusion (which was hypothetical and tentative) which indicate an awareness of the possibility of another and more satisfactory solution. He realized that if all savings were immediately invested there would be no problem of lag in the production process and therefore no crisis so far as this process is concerned. Since savings are not immediately invested, and since there is a lag, the problem is to bridge the gap. Thus visualized, the problem is monetary rather than economic, but it is a monetary problem which quickly reduces to the following questions: Why do men hoard? How, by maintaining a sound monetary and banking system, might hoarding ("liquidity preference") be reduced to a nondangerous minimum? How, even though hoarding is great enough to create a serious problem, can its effects be mitigated by the creation of credit? By excluding credit, which was the only promising clue Marx had in this connection, he threw the problem of effective demand back where it had been at first—the unfilled gap. Rosa Luxemburg, however, never got near the point reached by Marx; there is no hint in her writings that it is a gap that can be filled by capitalist methods, but only the curious conclusion that capitalism must be saved—or its evil day postponed—by extra-capitalist means.

[64] Such a theory also, of course, deprived its author of any reasonable explanation of crises under capitalism, for if capitalism can keep on relieving itself of the surpluses which are supposed to cause crises, there can be no such weakness in the system.

## LATER DEVELOPMENTS: LENIN AND SOME OTHERS

Despite the impression one gets from the literature that there are as many socialist theories of imperialism as there are socialist theorists, there are in fact but two main lines of thought—that typified by Hilferding's theory, with its emphasis on the relative economic attractiveness of undeveloped and highly developed areas of the earth and its reduction of capitalist expansion to a matter of policy, and that made famous by Rosa Luxemburg, with its emphasis on the absolute necessity of capitalism to expand, which makes imperialism an inescapable stage of capitalist development. The rest of the vast literature on the subject by socialists revolves more or less around these two points of view, which reflect widely different conceptions of the nature of capitalism and the workers' attitude towards revolution.

Although the "stage" and "policy" doctrines of imperialism have split socialist thought into these two schools, in general socialists are unanimous in their belief that capitalism somehow produces modern imperialism and that socialism would immediately put an end to both. The idea that there could be a "totalitarianism" powerful enough to enslave capitalism, override the hopes of socialism, and make imperialism seem like a relatively mild form of aggression occurred to no one until the first World War and the rise of a communist dictatorship in Russia and fascism in Italy and Germany demonstrated its possibilities. Kautsky and others who spoke of "superimperialism" continued to think in terms of an enlarged form of capitalist imperialism, but there were a few who were beginning to see that here was a phenomenon that was broader and more inclusive than the capitalist motive for profit, that it included the militarist's motive for power, that it was reflected in politics and diplomacy, and that even the workers shared in it. Was it possible that there could be such a thing as socialist imperialism?

Kautsky no doubt sensed the danger in opposing a socialist colonial policy, and there were always charges from left-wing socialists that the so-called "centrists" and "rightists" in the Social Democratic party were essentially imperialists; there was also more or less general acknowledgment that the workers were attracted by imperialist foreign policies. It was generally assumed, however, that the imperialist impulse was lacking in the workers. They might be attracted to imperialism as a policy initiated by the capitalists, but, it was felt, they would not naturally initiate it themselves. But the ease with which the rank-and-file socialist workers were led into a war which everybody on their side regarded as imperialistic and wholly capitalistic, planted the seed of doubt. Socialist imperialism was not unthinkable and might even become a reality.

The outstanding socialist to voice this new worry was an Austrian, Karl Renner, who came to the conclusion that the imperialist impulse is no longer an exclusively capitalist phenomenon.[65] To begin with, perhaps it was, but as capitalism turns into an all-powerful financial system and not only exploits peoples' lives but also capitalizes on their nationalistic and patriotic feelings, it finds support among the rank and file not only for imperialist activities in peacetime but also for military and naval expenditures and finally for war itself. This constitutes what others have called *Volksimperialismus,* or what Renner fears must be called a kind of "socialist imperialism." At any rate, all the hopes that the leaders of Social Democracy had of preventing war by a wholesale refusal of their followers to fight or to support any "capitalistic" war that might break out were completely dashed by the rush of socialists to the colors in all the warring countries of 1914–18. Renner was writing in 1918, but he was describing what was to happen even more alarmingly after the war was over—the march of the rank and file into the ranks of Italian fascism and German National Socialism. Here, indeed, was to be found the triumph of the imperialist impulse.

Aside from Renner, whose views obviously run completely beyond the bounds of traditional socialist theorizing, no other socialist since the beginning of the first World War has departed much from one or the other of the two divergent patterns of speculation laid down by Hilferding and Rosa Luxemburg. Both had their ardent followers, but it was their critics—especially, friendly critics who aimed to be helpful rather than destructive—who brought the two major doctrines to their present form.

---

[65] Renner, *Marxismus, Krieg und Internationale.* See especially pp. 86–94, 134–41, 154–58, 210–25, 323 ff. See also below, p. 235.

Hilferding's theory of finance capital as the key to an understanding of imperialism has been criticized in various ways for
being too narrow or too much concerned with a transitional form
of imperialist policy. Lenin, who certainly had no time for the
policy doctrine,[66] nevertheless gives Hilferding credit for pointing
out the role of finance capital as the new technique of capitalist
expansion. He criticizes Hilferding for failure to emphasize the
"parasitic" character of imperialism, meaning that financial interests are not the only ones to gain from imperialism, but that the
virus of expansionist prosperity also spreads to the workers.[67]

An almost opposite criticism of Hilferding is that he was wrong in
ascribing to the banks a permanently dominant position over the
industrialists, whereas this is but a transitional relationship which
will be reversed as soon as the industrial combination movement
has reached a stage of monopoly.[68] The reasoning here is that while
the banks were in a strategic position as long as their chief business
was based on the issuance of new securities and their chief function
was to take the leadership in the combination movement, they
have largely lost this power to the large monopolistic corporations,
which are now in a position to finance their own operations without depending on the market for new securities and therefore without the old dependence on the banks. Hilferding undoubtedly over-
stressed the role of the banks, not only as regards the presumed
permanency of their position, but also as regards the assumption
that they exercised their control and took the leadership in expansionist policies in the rest of the world as clearly as they did in certain Continental countries. At any rate, he was criticized for failure
to note that in England (which is always cited as the classic home of

---

[66] Lenin, *Imperialism, the Highest Stage of Capitalism*, pp. 90 ff.

[67] This was a point strongly suggested by Hobson (see above, p. 102); and it
was the same idea which led Renner to the conclusion that out of this situation "socialist imperialism" might develop.

[68] Sweezy, *The Theory of Capitalist Development*, pp. 260, 266–67. Still another idea
suggested by dissatisfaction with Hilferding's thesis is that, inasmuch as the financiers
constitute a relatively small part of the capitalist group, it might be possible for the
remaining capitalist interests, such as the industrialists, merchants, and savings banks
(as distinct from banks of issue), and even the workers, to join forces against the big
bankers and thus, for a time at least, be able to run the capitalistic system without
imperialism. See Duret, *Le Marxisme et les crises*, p. 35; see also Primus (*pseud.*),
*L'Imperialisme et la décadence capitaliste*.

imperialism) it was actually the industrialists and exporters of consumer goods and the protectionists who had been clamoring for imperialism, while the financial interests, supported by the free-trade elements, were on the opposite side.[69]

Rosa Luxemburg's theory of imperialism has undoubtedly been criticized and defended—and in turn amended—more vehemently than anything ever written on the subject. Supporters of the Bauer-Hilferding school of thought charge her with having made a great to-do about nothing in her reformulation of the theory of capital accumulation, although admitting that she here disclosed one of the possible roots of imperialism, without, however, telling the whole story.[70] Bukharin called her argument a "sophism," a "gross and absurd tautology, bordering on the naïve," because she asked "for whom" production takes place and at the same time denied that the capitalists themselves are the buyers of the surplus value embodied in the new capital goods.[71] "Speaking generally," he declared, "enlarged capitalist production is fully possible, even without the so-called 'third persons' (i. e., for example, the peasants)." [72] His own formulation of the problem led him to the conclusion that although in the end the contradiction between the growth of the productive forces of capitalism and its economic structure is bound to result in crises, which will grow more and more severe until the "final explosion" occurs, the system has dangerously powerful

[69] Hashagen, "Marxismus und Imperialismus," *Jahrbücher für Nationalökonomie und Statistik*, CXIII (July 1919), 205, cites this as the view of Kapelusz (*Die neue Zeit*, 1897); but he also refers to Bernstein's observation that while Hilferding's theory was of little value as applied to England, nevertheless, it was impossible to separate the financial and industrial interests in analyzing the expansionist policy of that country. On the Continent, however, the relation between financial capitalism and imperialism is more apparent. Hashagen himself criticizes the Bauer-Hilferding theory because it is too narrow to fit all modern cases of imperialism and fits none of the older forms. He also points out (p. 206) that Mehring regarded imperialism as a sign of weakness and decay and that anti-imperialist rather than pro-imperialist sentiment is characteristic of the most highly developed stage of capitalism.

[70] Cf. *ibid.*, and Luxemburg's *Antikritik*, in which she reviews in detail the criticisms of her critics, especially Bauer, and recapitulates her own arguments. See also Laurat, *L'Accumulation du capital d'après Rosa Luxembourg*, pp. 133–61 (résumé of Luxemburg's *Antikritik*), and pp. 163–93 (controversies since the death of Rosa Luxemburg).

[71] Bukharin, *Der Imperialismus und die Akkumulation des Kapitals*, pp. 17, 18.

[72] Bukharin and others, *Marxism and Modern Thought*, p. 62. See also Bukharin, *Imperialism and World Economy*, especially chaps. ix and xii.

capacity to expand for a considerable period of time. Therefore he professed to believe that the collapse of capitalism was not imminent and that it would not be obliged in the near future to resort to imperialism.

Fritz Sternberg agrees with Luxemburg that Marx neglected the influence of noncapitalist areas, and he accepts her general thesis that such areas are essential to an explanation of imperialism. But whereas Luxemburg regarded them as necessary for the disposal of *all* surplus value above that required for simple reproduction, Sternberg maintains that such outside markets are not necessary for the disposal of *consumption* goods, except such unsold balances as always exist. Unless it is admitted, he argues, that consumption goods can be absorbed by the capitalist society that produces them, the existence of relatively high wages in imperialistic countries cannot be explained. By way of supporting this thesis, Sternberg declares that Marx's formula itself proves only that the unsold balance of consumption goods must be sold outside the capitalist circle and that all surplus value except this balance finds buyers in the two classes which compose that society. It is this unsold balance alone, according to Sternberg, which causes pressure for imperialism.[73]

Henryk Grossmann may be mentioned as a Marxist of real originality who has continued the controversy regarding the nature of capitalism and imperialism—a writer who at once bears a family resemblance to Tugan-Baranowsky at one extreme, Rosa Luxemburg at the other, and Otto Bauer between them. He is in agreement with Rosa Luxemburg that capitalism cannot remain indefinitely in equilibrium, and is therefore on her side in opposing the views of Tugan-Baranowsky, Bauer, and Hilferding. In other words, Grossmann believes that capitalism must break down, but instead of associating this catastrophe with too much surplus value, which was Luxemburg's thesis, he uses Otto Bauer's reproduction scheme, as we have already noted,[74] to show that ultimately capitalism must break down not from a surplus, but from a lack of

---

[73] Sternberg, *Der Imperialismus;* see especially, pp. 101, 103, 117–18. For a review of Sternberg's book see Henryk Grossmann, "Eine neue Theorie über Imperialismus und die soziale Revolution," *Archiv für die Geschichte des Sozialismus und der Arbeiterbewegung,* XIII (1928), 141–92. Sternberg's theory is also discussed by Laurat, *L'accumulation du capital d'après Rosa Luxembourg,* pp. 94, 183–84, and by Duret, *Le Marxisme et les crises,* pp. 59 ff.

[74] See above, p. 162.

surplus value. While Rosa Luxemburg concentrated on the problem of how surplus value is realized (the problem of effective demand), and concluded that realization is impossible except by recourse to "outside" markets, Grossmann sounds like Tugan-Baranowsky on this point, since he denies that there is a realization problem.

Naturally, if capitalists are plagued by a lack of surplus value they are not confronted by the problem of how to realize it, and neither is the theorist who conjures surplus value out of existence. This, of course, calls for an explanation of imperialism in terms of something other than overaccumulation and recourse to noncapitalist areas of the world economy. Yet Hilferding's theory of imperialism as a policy of finance capital is not acceptable to Grossmann. He regards this as a passing phase of capitalist development and places his emphasis on the tendency of capitalist nations, like individual capitalists, to jockey for monopolistic position.[75] They annex territory in order to keep other nations from annexing it, and in exploiting it they follow the same monopolistic practices that are used at home. In this respect, at least, Grossmann is in agreement with Lenin.

Lenin's views on imperialism belong to the field of criticism and exposition rather than among the original contributions of writers such as Bauer, Hilferding, and Luxemburg. Indeed, he frankly owes much to Hilferding. Because of the fame of its author and the fact that it has been translated into so many languages, Lenin's *Imperialism* has had an influence second to no other work on the same subject, except perhaps Hobson's *Imperialism*. Lenin's book is an attempt to set the disciples of Marx right on the proper theoretical and tactical attitude to take towards the question of imperialism, and to this end Lenin makes Kautsky the chief foil for his remarks. The word for the heterodoxy which he is attacking is "Kautskyism," against which he places what his own disciples call "Leninism."[76] He leaves no doubt concerning his attitude towards

---

[75] Grossmann, *Das Akkumulations- und Zusammenbruchsgesetz des kapitalistischen Systems*, pp. 450 ff., 572–79. Cf. Sweezy, *The Theory of Capitalist Development*, pp. 268n, 303n.

[76] Stalin (*Leninism*, II, 43–44) remarks that Lenin added no new principles to Marxism and rejected none of the old. He defines *Leninism* as "Marxism of the epoch of imperialism and proletarian revolution," in which Lenin developed the question of "monopolistic capitalism—of imperialism as the new phase of capitalism." As stated

"the leaders of the Second International (Otto Bauer and Co. in Austria, Ramsay MacDonald and others in England, Albert Thomas in France, etc., etc.,) and a multitude of Socialists, reformists, pacifists, bourgeois democrats and priests." He is equally caustic towards "Hilferding, ex-'Marxist,' now a comrade-in-arms of Kautsky, [who] has taken a step backward compared with the *frankly* pacifist and reformist Englishman, Hobson, on this question." [77]

If there is any hero in Lenin's *Imperialism* it is Hobson. Pacifist and free trader though he was, Hobson anticipated the professional "theoreticians" of Marxism on nearly every important point connected with the theory of imperialism. According to Lenin, Hobson not only established the political meaning of imperialism as well as Kautsky did but also saw the fundamental economic causes much better; [78] he foresaw the danger that a federation of great powers might intensify the evils of imperialism, while Kautsky talked of the peaceful possibilities of "ultra-imperialism," [79] and he backed up his theory with facts. Despite Hobson's bourgeois point of view, we gather from Lenin that he was in these respects a better Marxist than some of the professed socialists, but because of his bias in favor of a reformed capitalism he was naïve enough to protest that imperialism was not inevitable and that it might be overcome by raising the consuming power of the workers.

But if Hobson was somewhat of a hero in spite of being a non-Marxist, Kautsky is the villain of Lenin's little book because, from Lenin's point of view, he became a non-Marxist. He merely echoed Hobson in protesting against the inevitability of imperialism and in emphasizing the need to raise the consuming capacity of the

in the "Explanatory Notes" which accompany the translation of Lenin's *Imperialism* (p. 118), "Leninism grew on the theoretical base of Marxism in the epoch of imperialism, and Lenin's teaching of proletarian revolution and dictatorship in each of its propositions rests on that understanding of Marxism which is unfolded in this book of Lenin. The Leninist teaching of imperialism lies at the foundation of the program of the All Union Communist Party as well as the program of the Communist International as a whole." Lenin himself did not hesitate to declare Marx incomplete: "In no sense do we regard the Marxist theory as something complete and unassailable," he says. "On the contrary, we are convinced that this theory is only the corner-stone of that science which socialists must advance in all directions if they do not wish to fall behind life."—A statement made by Lenin in 1913 as reported by Max Eastman (editor), in Marx, *Capital, the Communist Manifesto and Other Writings*, p. xix.

[77] Lenin, *Imperialism*, pp. 12–13.          [78] *Ibid.*, pp. 83, 92–94.
[79] *Ibid.*, pp. 87, 106.

workers, says Lenin, and he persisted in talking about imperialism being a product of industrial capitalism when it is plainly a product of financial capitalism and monopoly, and he regarded imperialism as a policy, whereas actually it is a stage of capitalism.[80]

Although Lenin criticizes Kautsky for his belief in "ultraimperialism," he himself uses a somewhat similar expression when he speaks of "supermonopoly," meaning the world-wide expansion of cartels, syndicates, and trusts, which divide the world between them. However, it is not the form of the capitalist struggle which is important in these supermonopolies, as implied in Kautsky's view that superimperialism may be a peaceful form, says Lenin, but the fact that they are merely another expression of the class struggle—a means which capitalism is forced to adopt in order to maintain profits.[81] To Lenin, in brief, imperialism is "the monopoly stage of capitalism," or "capitalism in that stage of development in which the domination of monopolies and finance capital has taken shape; in which the export of capital has acquired pronounced importance; in which the division of the world by the international trusts has begun, and in which the partition of all the territory of the earth by the greatest capitalist countries has been completed."[82]

Echoing Hilferding, Kautsky, and others who had long been summing up the situation in the same words, Lenin relates how imperialism emerged historically as a product of "capitalism in general," but soon became the expression of the more highly concentrated and aggressive finance capitalism. From interest solely in exporting goods it shifted to a devouring appetite for the economic and political advantages of exporting capital. This at last brings the conflict to a new, more bitter, and decisive stage, which can be resolved only by force, but a force so destructive to all the participants that the world of capitalist powers and empires will soon be in a state of collapse.[83] Then the final and complete victory of socialism will emerge from the revolutionary *coup de grâce* which it will be in a position to apply.

Lenin did not believe that capitalism would collapse automatically and that socialism could be depended upon to rise spontaneously from its ruins. Strong and energetic leadership was neces-

[80] *Ibid.*, pp. 82, 101.   [81] *Ibid.*, pp. 62, 68.   [82] *Ibid.*, pp. 80–81.
[83] Cf. *ibid.*, pp. 43, 57, 80–81, 88–89.

sary, and Lenin was not one to shrink from the call. Kautsky had turned out to be no leader at all, and his pacifism and his conversion to the idea that imperialism might bring peace was to Lenin nothing short of treachery to the whole socialist cause. In this light Lenin's advocacy of the leadership principle, which meant dictatorship in the revolutionary and formative period of socialization, can be easily understood.[84] In contrast with Rosa Luxemburg and others he desired a very narrow and exclusive membership in the Communist party, believing this to be the only means of organizing the proletariat for the task of overthrowing capitalism and of organizing the socialist state for the accomplishment of its peaceful aims. Dictatorship, not democracy, in other words, was the first stage through which socialism must pass if it were to succeed.

The break between Lenin and Trotsky was over a similar issue, Lenin believing that communism was possible of realization in a single country, even in a country such as Russia, which had not passed through the capitalistic stage, providing revolution could be successfully organized and a dictatorship imposed, while Trotsky held that socialism was impossible of realization in any country taken alone, because capitalism had first to run its course in all countries before the revolution could be permanent and successful. Thus, capitalism must develop into imperialism, and imperialism must become a world-wide superimperialism of capitalist powers; in other words, capitalism must fulfill its historic mission of creating a unified world economy, independent of national

[84] Cf. Sidney Hook, *Towards the Understanding of Karl Marx,* especially pp. 60–63. According to Hook (p. 60) the work of Luxemburg and Lenin marked the beginning of the Marxian reformation. Both took the position that Marx and Engels were to be read in the light of the original spirit of their work and were not to be taken literally in every respect—which to Luxemburg and Lenin meant being "orthodox" in a formula-ridden and pedantic way.

Yet on other issues, as Hook points out (p. 61) Luxemburg and Lenin were far from seeing alike. Lenin, in rejecting the theory of the spontaneity of capitalist breakdown, advocated a strong socialist organization to combat capitalism and was opposed to the sort of compromise and evolutionary tactics represented by Bernstein and Kautsky. In short, he believed in strong leadership and revolution. Luxemburg, on the other hand, wanted a more democratic socialist organization, which she believed would reflect the views of the masses outside the party. She was opposed to any worker-peasant alliance under a revolutionary dictatorship; the revolution, she believed, would come spontaneously once the home market became exhausted and the imperialist powers began the partition of the world. Thus—to those who take the opposite stand—Luxemburg was merely misled in thinking that in an era of monopoly capitalism national wars had become impossible.

boundaries, before the revolution and socialism can be successful in any country. At least, this is Lenin's interpretation of Trotsky's views in the Explanatory Notes to his *Imperialism*, which add that "Trotsky's denial of the victory of socialism in one country had its basis in the anti-Leninist, Kautskyian, reformist conception of imperialism." Bukharin (who was eventually tried and sentenced to death as a "Trotskyite" wrecker) believed that a universal world trust of capitalist powers is possible, because there is no limit to the process of cartelization, and that under such unification crises of overproduction could be avoided. He also came to believe that a single capitalist state could organize itself into a great trust which would have similar results with respect to crises.[85]

Whatever the socialists and the communists may think of each other's theories of imperialism or of the nature of capitalism itself, they are generally united in their contempt for the views of the "bourgeois" political and economic theorists and historians. These people, say the socialists, in fact have views and prejudices rather than scientific theories; having been nurtured in and favored by the capitalist system, they are apologists for capitalism and all its works. Nor are they given the least credit for understanding the true nature of capitalism or of its most notorious works, imperialism and war. The orthodox economist may talk about "economic" imperialism and even condemn it, but always with the implication that it is a problem capable of solution by correcting some particular and unnecessary aspect of capitalism that produces it. They may even deny that capitalism has anything to do with the phenomenon of imperialism, arguing that imperialism is much older than capitalism and therefore a force capable of being explained on grounds other than the economic factors involved. The socialist, therefore, is not obliged to find fault with the details of the theories set forth by nonsocialists, as he feels obliged to do in criticizing the theories of his fellow socialists. The only need is for a general explanation of the perversions of the nonsocialist theorist.

A characteristic answer to the broad view that imperialism is a very old and a very general phenomenon is to say that this idea is "unscientific," which comes down to saying that only modern imperialism can be explained scientifically in the same way that capi-

[85] See Lenin, *Imperialism*, Explanatory Notes, pp. 119–20.

talism can be explained; it is Marx's "science" as opposed to utopian wishful thinking. Thus, Pavlovitch dismisses as unscientific the "philosophical" theory of the essence of imperialism [86] as set forth by Seilliere [87]—the idea that throughout life, in nature as well as among men, there is a constant struggle which can be called imperialism: a striving for survival, of species against species, race against race, nation against nation, group against group, and class against class—even of proletarians against capitalists. Pavlovitch does not deny that these struggles exist, for indeed they are the very basis of Marxian doctrine; but he does deny that the term "imperialism," or even the word "domination," describes all these phenomena, least of all the struggle of the proletarians against the capitalists.

Likewise, Pavlovitch dismisses as unscientific the theory of imperialism expounded by the historical school, because from this point of view "imperialism exists at all stages of human development: from the moment that human society was formed, imperialist policy commenced." [88] Although the ancient empires of Greece and Rome were undeniably based on economic grounds and represented definite class interests of a "robber character," this was not imperialism in the proper sense, because it admitted noneconomic phenomena as factors. Capitalist imperialism, on the other hand, is determined solely by economic factors.[89] These economic factors, in other words, explain everything that happens today. They did not exist before capitalism and therefore cannot be used to explain precapitalist events.

[86] Pavlovitch, *The Foundations of Imperialist Policy*, pp. 9–18.
[87] Seillière, *Introduction à la philosophie de l'imperialisme*. See below, p. 236.
[88] Pavlovitch, *The Foundations of Imperialist Policy*, p. 19.
[89] *Ibid.*, pp. 23–26.

# VIII ·

## CAPITALISM AND
## SOCIALISM IN A NEW
## PERSPECTIVE

NEITHER of the two main socialist theories of imperialism—
that capitalism chooses imperialism as a policy, and that
capitalism has imperialism thrust upon it as a necessary condition
of its struggle for existence—can be dismissed as the product of an
unreasonable anticapitalist bias. Whether the theorists were successful in their earnest attempts to explain the relation between
capitalism and political manifestations is another matter.

Many critics of Marxism have seen the fallacy of the labor-cost
theory of value and the weakness in such concepts as underconsumption and the falling tendency of the rate of profit, and have gone to
great pains to expose the fallacy of assuming, as the socialists do, that
there is an insoluble contradiction between "production for profit"
and "production for use" and that economic competition and competition in the war-and-conquest sense are identical. It is not enough
to discredit these old stock doctrines of socialism and to conclude
that thereby it is possible to discredit the socialist theory of capitalist imperialism. Even socialists have found it possible to discard
some or all these doctrines and still believe that the nature of capitalism is such as to make imperialism and war inevitable. And some
nonsocialists, unencumbered by most of these doctrinal stage props,
have reached similar conclusions. At the same time, it is essential to a
theory of capitalist imperialism to believe that somehow economic
competition between nations for territory and resources is basically
war-like and imperialistic; that overproduction, in some sense or
other, drives nations to seek outside markets; and that bankers, or
finance-capitalists, are powerful enough to make protective tariffs,

monopolies, international cartels, and international loans the effective agents of an aggressive foreign policy.

Sooner or later students of the problem must face the basic issue of whether an aggressive foreign policy is the agent or the master of capitalism. Is imperialism an independent force reflecting the sheer desire of men for power, which merely uses for its own ends whatever economic system happens to be at hand? Or is there after all something to the contention that capitalism itself represents the active force and produces a power complex which must be expressed in terms of imperialistic activity? If the latter, then we may stop right here, conceding that the socialists have the answer, with no further responsibility on our part except to decide whether we want to accept the reasoning of Hilferding, or Luxemburg, or someone between these two extremes. If, on the other hand, we are willing to pursue the other point of view and examine the possibility that the power complex known as "imperialism" can be and has been the dominant force in world politics, then we may be able to see not only capitalism but also socialism in a new perspective. For if imperialism—or the power complex for which imperialism, militarism, or some other word is the synonym—can capture and use capitalism and make this kind of system look like its master, it is not inconceivable that it can capture socialism or any other kind of collectivist economic system and impose upon them its own pattern of behavior.

It is not a complete answer to the socialist contention that capitalism is the creator and master of modern imperialism to show that free enterprise, properly conceived and run, is neither actually nor theoretically dependent upon an aggressive foreign policy. So long as free enterprise is not lived up to in practice and capitalism is encumbered by monopolies and trade barriers, the critic can always maintain that such encumbrances are inherent in the system and that it is nonsense to try to imagine a private enterprise economy without them. In rejecting this point of view and presenting in its place the conditions of economic stability in a free society, we can do no more than answer the socialists on the level of argument of their own choosing, namely, the economic level. There still remains the question: Given an economic system, either capitalistic or socialistic, which can solve the economic problem of effective demand and self-contained equilibrium, are political forces still powerful enough to dominate such a system and make it imperialistic? Finally, there is the quite different question (which we shall discuss in the following chapter) of the economic interpretation of history itself—whether the economic motive or some other motive is the ultimate determinant of human behavior.

## THE NEED FOR A TYPE OF CONTROL
## CONSISTENT WITH FREE ENTERPRISE

The nearest any socialist reasoning comes to absolving capitalism of responsibility for making imperialism inevitable is, of course, that which regards imperialism as a policy. Industrial capitalism, or the capitalism of free competition between the producers of consumer goods, is entirely absolved. This amounts to saying that one can imagine a fictitious form of capitalism (something akin to the concept of a "pure economy" in orthodox economic literature), entirely removed from the modern world of reality, which is capable of solving its inner problem of equilibrium without recourse to forced expansion.

The kind of capitalism which is not absolved of responsibility for imperialism, according to Hilferding's reasoning for example, is what he calls "finance capitalism," or the kind of banker-dominated capitalism which succeeded the brief reign of industrial capitalism. Finance capitalism is visualized as adopting an imperialistic policy because it is profitable to the financiers, and of employing new techniques for suppressing the old-fashioned, nonimperialistic, free competition of industrial capitalists. This is not regarded as capitalist planning in the sense that industrialists collaborate to maintain equilibrium between the producers of consumers' goods and the producers of capital goods. It is planning of another sort, involving only financiers who are interested, not in establishing correct proportions between producers' and consumers' goods, but in reaping monopoly profits. Competing industrial capitalists, according to this view, had no incentive to get together and plan a balanced system of production, because each individual capitalist stood to profit most from following independently a policy of adopting labor-saving devices, which only aggravate, instead of ameliorating, the problem of disequilibrium in the capitalist system as a whole.

The concentration of industry might be furthered through what Marx had called the act of big capitalists swallowing little capitalists, but this was a relatively slow process compared with the technique developed by powerful banks of forcing competing units of an industry into great holding companies. Since this development in turn aggravates, instead of ameliorating, the tendency to overproduce, the banks are led into fostering a highly aggressive export policy. By making foreign loans and then requiring that the proceeds be spent for the products of their own industrial empires, finance capitalists are able to obtain the most advantageous terms for their exports. In addition, they seek protection from foreign competition through high tariffs and international cartel agreements.

The conclusion that this kind of capitalism follows an imperialist policy comes as close to making sense as anyone could desire, once the basic assumptions are admitted. The argument does not say that competitive capitalism or the free enterprise of the classical economists produces imperialism; in fact, it carefully excludes such a theoretical possibility. Yet it just as plainly says that the competitive system of free enterprise is powerless to resist the movement towards the kind of monopoly capitalism or finance capitalism which does favor and create the imperialistic movement.

To the socialists this means that the only remedy for imperialism is the socialization of the means of production. Here, again, logic as well as history seems to be on their side. If the state, in the interest of society as a whole, can plan production to the end of solving the problem of effective demand, that is, the problem of equilibrium or correct proportionality, there no longer would exist recalcitrant individual capitalists to balk at over-all planning, no aggressive finance capitalists taking it upon themselves to organize great holding companies, and no absolute surpluses in need of foreign markets. Under such a regime there could be no imperialism.

The only kind of reasoning that can meet the socialist logic on the ground thus marked out must start with a challenge to the idea that socialization of the means of production can alone solve the problem presented to society by the vagaries of capitalism. Quite naturally, neither Marx nor any of his followers have ever been in-

terested in trying to discover a type of social control consistent with
free enterprise. Having reached the conclusion that capitalism can
have no plan and that no plan can be devised to control it except
socialization of the means of production, at which point it ceases
to function as free enterprise capitalism and becomes socialism, the
socialists have merely hit upon a scheme consistent with the view
that in the field of production, and here alone, social control can
be effectively applied.

Historically, it may be too late to overcome this conviction. So
much has happened which seems to verify the need for Marx's
special brand of social control, and it has in fact been so widely
adopted or partially adopted, that any plea for turning back to free
enterprise appears indeed to be benighted counsel. To suggest what
steps might long ago have been taken to stave off the need for Marx's
solution is probably even more futile. Nevertheless, theoretical
integrity demands that we at least sketch the outlines of the case
for a type of social control consistent with and not antagonistic to
the system of free enterprise.

Much as we may regret the fact that Marx sold the world on the
idea that social control of the means of production is the only way
out of the dilemma of capitalism, at least we must give him credit
for having seen so clearly that the modern, highly complex economy
cannot be permitted to operate on a purely laissez faire basis, but
must be controlled. It is not his assertion of the need for social control, therefore, with which we can take exception, but only the
dogmatism with which the socialization of production is advanced
as the only solution.

The alternative to social control of production is not laissez
faire, but social control of the monetary aspects of the economic
process. Mild and insignificant as this brief statement must appear
—as if one were offering a lame man a frail reed instead of a crutch
—it is no less revolutionary in its implications than Marx's solution. But where the socialization of production is revolutionary
from the viewpoint of private enterprise, the proposal for social
control of the monetary system is a revolt from Marxism itself.

Yet what has the matter of choosing between production and
the monetary system as the object of control to do with the theory
of imperialism? For the socialist point of view, curiously enough,

imperialism is the product of a weak and degenerate capitalism. It is evident that there could have been no theory of capitalist imperialism had capitalism not shown those weaknesses which Marx singled out in building up his case for social control, and which to his followers appeared to call for imperialism as an antidote. It seems equally clear that had Marx and other critics of capitalism been able to see that proper social control of the monetary system could have made capitalism strong and given it greater internal cohesion, they would never have found it necessary to regard the lack of social control of production as at once the signal for capitalism's demise and the birth of socialism. To say that capitalism could have been saved by the application of controls consistent with free enterprise is to say that it could have been saved from the charges that it inevitably follows an imperialistic policy. Furthermore, it may be said that a properly controlled and strong capitalism would have been more resistent to the blandishments of imperialism. After all, our great modern social problem is to produce an economic system as resistant as possible to this particular kind of blight, in much the same way that scientists have tried to develop blight-resisting wheat. The main difficulty is that control of the economic system is not an economic problem, but a political one. Economists may point the way, but it must be left to the realm of political action to establish the means.

The reason Marx could see no alternative to the socialization of production was that he inherited the view of the classical economists that the process of production constitutes the heart of the economic problem and that the phenomenon of exchange, with its elaborate price mechanism, is merely a superficial reflection of what goes on in the field of production. From the point of view of Marx and his followers, it is always production which gets out of joint, production which lacks proportionality, production which is responsible for overproduction and underconsumption, and production, therefore, which needs to be controlled—controlled, that is, in order to make it serve the ends of consumption instead of the aim of the capitalist, which is profits. Hence the new slogan, "production for use," came to be the common property of all reformers who wanted to outlaw "production for profit."

Those who are content to answer this argument with the assertion (true as it is) that production for profit need not be inconsistent with production for use miss the point and the force of the claims for social control of the economic system. Those who place the whole emphasis on the social control of production assume, with equal onesidedness, that there is nothing else worth considering.

The modern economy is highly complex, and its processes confusingly roundabout, and from this condition stems a great deal of the conviction that it ought to be planned and rationalized in order to keep it from flying to pieces. Yet the fact that production is bewilderingly complex and roundabout does not in itself cause maladjustment between supply and demand or between producers' and consumers' goods. Given a free economy, that is, one free of barriers to trade and obstacles to price flexibility, the operation of the price mechanism can adjust the flow and use of the factors of production in such a way that the tendency towards equilibrium is always at work. But if the production process is not accompanied by a monetary and credit system which is consistent with its own roundaboutness, and if nothing is done to establish a system of monetary and credit control consistent with free enterprise, there is no alternative to chaos in the whole economic system except the social control of production.

Competition in the field of production is basic to the free enterprise economy, while competition in the creation of the circulating media which is complementary to this process is in dangerous, if not fatal, conflict with competitive production. Yet we actually witness the spectacle of vigorous competition in the field of credit creation, where state monopoly belongs, and an increasing degree of monopoly in the production field, which is the proper place—in a free society—for competition. And the presence of monopoly in the latter sphere is not unrelated to the practice of permitting competition in the creation of that money substitute we call credit. No nation would tolerate for one moment the creation of money by private individuals. This is a prerogative universally reserved for the sovereign state, and counterfeiters, which is what private enterprisers in this field are called, are ruthlessly suppressed. Yet everywhere the same sovereign power which denies to private individuals the right to create money takes immense pride in the fact that it can give these same private individuals, provided they are organized into a bank, the right to create credit.

The fact that the competitive creation of bank credit has been permitted in countries where the competitive creation of goods is to a large degree lacking has made it clear, at least to some economists, that herein lies the key to the "boom and bust" agonies through which such an economy periodically goes. If their analysis is correct, the solution obviously lies in establishing a program of social control over the creation of bank credit which will take this power out of the hands of competing banks and place it in the hands of a public monetary authority. This does not mean the "socialization" of banking, in the sense that people think of the socialization of industries, as the advocates of this scheme of reform have made clear.[1]

As an antidote to Marxism—because it is an antidote to that particular weakness of capitalism which Marx regarded as incurable, namely, its lack of social control—this approach to the problem offers something new and unique.[2] It offers a positive program of control, thus supplementing the so-called "negative" controls, such as antitrust and antitariff legislation, which thus far have been the liberals' chief hope of preserving free enterprise. It places the blame for inflation and overexpansion of industry on the com-

---

[1] Much has been written during the last fifteen years by economists who advocate 100 percent reserves as the basic element in a centralized control of bank credit. Some writers, particularly Simons, have from the first emphasized the relation between the social control of bank credit and the problem of stabilizing, and indeed preserving, the free-enterprise economy. See especially Simons, *A Positive Program for Laissez-Faire;* "Rules versus Authorities in Monetary Policy," *Journal of Political Economy,* XLIV (February, 1936), 1–30, and "Hansen on Fiscal Policy," *Journal of Political Economy,* L (April, 1942), 161–96; Fisher, *100% Money.*

This scheme is not posed as a remedy for those economic fluctuations in business which are caused by factors other than lack of credit control, but it does assume that lack of the latter is the major cause of general economic instability and crises. Those who stress the monetary aspects of instability and who still believe that 100 percent bank reserves and centralized control of credit creation would not solve the problem of crises may believe that the desired stability can be realized by centering control on other factors. Our present concern is not so much to say where social control can best be applied as to stress the point that it must be compatible with free enterprise if the objective is to maintain free enterprise. Those who believe that the trouble, and therefore the need for control, lies preponderately on the side of production, have still to show how their remedy can prevent socialization in the Marxian sense.

[2] It is also an alternative to Keynsian economics and offers a positive program for capitalism, while Keynes and his followers still think in terms of central planning and controls which are much more akin to Marxism than to economic liberalism.

petitive creation of purchasing power and singles out this phenomenon as the "loose screw" in the economic system. There is no
"Marxism" in this approach; yet, ironically, there was more than
a little of this same approach in Marx—not in those parts of his
works which are today recognizable as socialist doctrine, but in the
parts in which he considered aspects of capitalism other than the
economics of production.

In Chapter VI it was pointed out how Marx had struggled to
find the answer to the way in which capitalism was able to solve
the problem of effective demand. Historically, as Marx saw it, the
constant influx of newly mined gold had kept capitalism from running out of purchasing power and accounted for its ability to maintain a much higher degree of equilibrium than otherwise would
have been possible. He was dealing here, not with the question of
capitalism's weaknesses and its inevitable decline into socialism,
but with its strength, and in doing this he appears more as the devil's
advocate than as prosecutor. In many respects he came nearer to
finding the answer to capitalism's problem than did the contemporary "bourgeois economists," whom he accused of being
merely the apologists of capitalism.

The fact that Marx allowed himself to find something favorable
to the strength of capitalism on the monetary side opened the possibility that here, rather than in the field of production, was to be
found the key to the application of social control. Furthermore, the
fact that he understood the devastating effect of unregulated bank
credit on the capitalist economy led him a step nearer to this conclusion. At the same time, he was elsewhere too deeply committed
to the conviction that the real causes of capitalism's breakdown are
to be found in the anarchy of capitalist production to see any possibility in the socialization, or social control, of the monetary and
credit factors. He regarded newly mined gold as merely a historical
accident, for which capitalism could claim no credit. As for the institutions of banking and credit, Marx regarded them as capitalist
inventions completely in harmony with the capitalistic exploitation
of labor in the field of production. He considered them the worst
features, the most devastating instruments, in the whole capitalist
process of getting something for nothing. In spite of this, however,
he thought that the monetary and credit aspects of capitalism, or the

"circulation process," could be ignored, and he repeatedly insisted on ruling out credit in that part of his analysis which terminated with newly mined gold as the great equilibrator of supply and demand. This sort of abstraction, however, was not original with Marx. It was the commonly accepted notion of his time that the whole money-credit system—indeed, the price mechanism itself—can be ignored in economic analysis, in no way related, except as a convenience, to the fundamental business of production. All the economist had to do, it was believed, was to look behind the veil of money and prices into the real world of production and barter in order to discover the secrets of the economic process.

Thus, Marx saw both the stabilizing effect of a proper, though accidental, relation of money to production and the damaging effect of unregulated credit, which can only imply that he was on the way to seeing that a proper—and deliberate, not accidental—control of credit might provide the key to the stability of capitalism. In other words, he moved a long way in the direction of recognizing that production, after all, is not the whole story. Instead of being harsh in his indictment of credit as being merely a capitalist trick (an indictment which could have been applied equally to the willingness of capitalism to depend upon newly mined gold, as far as the theory is concerned), Marx might have regarded it, instead of production, as the proper object of social control. As it was, he succeeded only in concluding in favor of an alternative type of control, which is incompatible with free enterprise. Yet the irony remains that he came so near to finding reasons for not being a socialist; much nearer, in fact, than those economists who were unable to suggest any alternative to the socialization of production except laissez faire.

## THE SENSE IN WHICH CAPITALISM CAN BECOME IMPERIALISTIC

The main conclusion to be drawn from the foregoing commentary on the essential characteristics of an ideally controlled capitalism, so far as the question of imperialism is concerned, is that private ownership of the means of production need never in itself create difficulties of the sort which can give critics an opportunity to say that imperialism must be resorted to if the difficulties are to be overcome. It is possible, of course, to reach the same conclusion without invoking some such ideal type of social control as was discussed above, simply because it is by no means conclusive that capitalism, even without such control, has been obliged to pursue the imperialistic policies of which it is accused. Without such control, capitalism is in danger of reaching an impasse which calls for ending the system of private enterprise by socializing the means of production, and it is in the process of reaching this point that it engages in those practices which the critics have called not only imperialistic, but necessary. The defenders of free enterprise can no longer hope to sound convincing by arguing that capitalism can be made to work simply by erecting a few "no monopoly" and "no trade barrier" signs and arresting the violators. The problem runs deeper than this and calls for positive action in the form of a large dose of preventive medicine.

Marx was not the only one who had a glimmering of the fact that capitalism might function as a self-contained mechanism; Hilferding, too, in specifically developing a theory of imperialism (something which Marx never attempted) made clear the theoretical possibility that capitalism is not forced by necessity to be imperialistic. Obviously, the reason for such a position lies in the fact that capitalism itself, despite ups and downs, panics, crises, and depressions, has demonstrated its capacity to solve the problem of effective demand. This ability has been at times greatly weakened by the terrific dislocations and burdens of war and by throttling political interference, but the tendency towards equilibrium continues to assert itself as long as the odds are not too much against it. Despite its planlessness, private enterprise is a system which can be complex without being chaotic and orderly without being ordered. The key to this inner cohesiveness is, of course, the price mechanism, with its huge index of cost-price relationships and its calculus of profit and loss. The ways in which this planless system operates— or can operate—to establish economic values, to effectuate the exchange of goods, to produce some semblance of balance between consumption and investment, and to allocate the factors of production to their most economical use while distributing the products and services of industry according to their respective contributions has been made clear enough in the literature of economics to need no repetition here.

At the same time, there is not sufficient consideration in the literature, or at least not enough that is adequately and pointedly presented, concerning either the conditions under which this system can be made to work better or the steps by which it can be brought to utter ruin. Social control of the monetary side of the system has already been suggested as a way to make the system work better, in the belief that such betterment as this sort of reform might bring would remove the last vestige of the criticism that capitalism must adopt imperialism as a way out of its difficulties. On the other hand, any compilation of indictments concerning the actual steps in the process of capitalism's decline into helpless chaos, where it cannot be orderly without being ordered, only serves to increase faith in the idea that the socialists are right.

It can be admitted that the socialists are right in thinking that the breakdown or destruction of capitalism would be followed by the socialization of production, without accepting the Marxian argument as to how or why the process would take place. We can dispense with such Marxian concepts as the labor-cost theory of value, the rising composition of capital, the falling tendency of the rate of profit, the underconsumption theory of crises, and other familiar socialist doctrines, and still account for the degeneration of capitalism. Even if capitalism were subject to no degenerative tendencies, but remained entirely stable, it could be destroyed and the means of production socialized if it had enemies powerful enough to overthrow it. So neither the decline nor the final fate of capitalism need have anything to do with the "economic necessities" which Marx thought he could see at work. The real enemies of free enterprise are much more likely to be what the socialists regard as the necessities of imperialism than something cancerous lurking within the economic system itself. These enemies can be variously identified as the desire for power, the desire for monopoly, the desire for protection and special privilege, and even as ignorance of economic laws, but in some guise or other these same attitudes can be enemies of socialism. They can destroy any economic system despite the fact that no inner working of the system drives them to it.

Monopoly and protectionism symbolize the chief types of barrier that confront the system of free competition and free trade, and neither derives from anything that can be called "economic necessity" in the working of the free-enterprise system. They can, however, be very largely understood and explained in the light of the instability—itself not an economic necessity—in the operation of capitalism. Both monopoly and protectionism represent an attempt of business men to find security in a world of economic instability, and both in a sense are to be regarded as measures of frustration and desperation rather than as the antisocial behavior of aggressive men.[3] What they are trying to do in their limited way to solve their own depression problems reflects what needs to be done on a broad social scale, because a great social problem is involved, namely, the problem of preventing general depression. If monopolists and protectionists were merely behaving as enemies of a really free economy, it would be clear that social action should be taken against them; as it is, it is much clearer that the initial action needs to be taken against the kind of economy which actually exists and which encourages countermeasures of self-preservation.

When, on the other hand, business men profess their stanch adherence to the principles of free enterprise and the capitalistic system and then try to defend monopoly and protectionism, that is another matter. Here they are not in the role of frustrated victims of economic instability who are doing their best to find security measures of their own devising. Rather, they are victims of that species of reasoning which makes reform of the economic system seem so unattainable, and the socialization of production appear to be, after all, the only final solution.

The protectionist provides the most clear-cut demonstration of the working of this defeatist process, but he is only the leading species of a large genus. The trust, cartel, and labor movements to a greater or less degree share the responsibility for perpetuating

[3] For a defense of monopoly under these circumstances, which at the same time is a strong attack on the underlying conditions which breed monopoly, see Boulding, "In Defense of Monopoly," *Quarterly Journal of Economics*, LIX (August, 1945), 524–42.

this attitude. The spectacle of professed believers in capitalism leading the procession towards collectivism, not from the necessity about which Marx preached, but from much less defensible reasons, is a more sorry spectacle than if it were inevitable.

Once tariffs are adopted to protect the producers of a nation from foreign competition, there is no logical place for the principle to stop, short of being applied, in the form of some kind of relief measure or other, to every section of the country—not measures of relief or protection against foreigners, but of section against section, group against group, and even neighborhood against neighborhood. If it is logical and right for manufacturers who must compete with imports to be made the recipients of relief, it cannot be denied to other groups. Producers who are on an export basis, as are large sections of American farmers, sooner or later see the logic of demanding protection in other forms, such as subsidies which establish floors for the prices of their products. Barriers to interstate trade, another American phenomenon, are in response to the same reasoning. Also, are those campaigns to "Buy in New England" or "Buy in Massachusetts," which were fostered a few years ago—campaigns which did not stop at state borders, but inspired such slogans as "Trade in Somerville" and "Buy at your Neighborhood Store." The demand for wage differentials, price differentials, or some other advantage by one section of the country against another belongs to the same protectionist mentality.

The danger to free enterprise in the tendency for economic groups to seek and obtain help in this fashion—literally to be put on relief—may not be very apparent when only a limited group is specially favored. When carried to its logical conclusion, however, protectionism calls for economic planning on a scale as broad as the economy itself. An economy shot through with price-supporting and wage-supporting measures and with price and wage differentials must be subjected to still further planning to correlate the complex diversity of interests. The wholesale interference with the price mechanism blunts its capacity to allocate resources according to their most economical uses, so that machinery must be set up to determine the requirements of the various groups competing for the factors of production. The stultifying effect of all this on private investment in turn calls for government financing. At every turn, government finds itself called upon to plan, co-ordinate, and regulate industry, and eventually to run it with no pretense of trying to maintain private enterprise. The final result may not look much like Marx's dream of social control of the economic system by the proletariat, but at least it is collectivism. It is ordered enterprise as distinct from free enterprise, and the dictatorship which such a system calls for, whether it be called "fascist" or "communist," is the end product of a logic which runs "from protectionism through planned economy to dictatorship." [4]

The totalitarian form of government and dictatorship in a country are but the national equivalent of that brand of "internationalism" called imperialism. Although protectionism, as the symbol of exclusive nationalism, may appear to be the opposite of the outward thrust associated with imperialism, it belongs essentially to the same pattern of thought and behavior. Superficially, protectionism looks like a sort of imperialism-in-reverse, but this "hidebound" kind of imperialism is perfectly consistent with the "outbound" type. Both are symbols of exclusiveness, lack of mutuality, and power. Both are expressions of competition in the war-and-conquest sense, not of the kind of economic competition which operates in a framework of cost-price relationships, which in turn, by setting metes and bounds to competition, make it fundamentally co-operative. The mind that thinks in terms of the protectionist symbol is equally at home in the imperialist symbol. It never appears inconsistent to such a mind to press strongly for export markets and foreign investments while insisting on heavy restrictions on imports, however inconsistent such diverse policies must appear according to even the most elementary economic reasoning. Both policies represent a retreat from true internationalism. Economically, they represent a retreat from the free pricing mechanism, which is the

---

[4] "The leadership of the State in economic affairs which advocates of Planned Economy want to establish, is . . . necessarily connected with a bewildering mass of governmental interferences of a steadily cumulative nature. The arbitrariness, the mistakes and the inevitable contradictions of such policy will, as daily experience shows, only strengthen the demand for a more rational coordination of the different measures and, therefore, for unified leadership. For this reason Planned Economy will always tend to develop into Dictatorship."—Gustav Cassel, *From Protectionism through Planned Economy to Dictatorship,* Cobden Memorial Lecture, London, 1934. Reprinted in *International Conciliation,* No. 303 (October, 1934), pp. 307–25; the quotation is from p. 323.

basic condition of a free enterprise economy within the nation and of free trade between nations, into a situation which calls for—and even may welcome—that species of ordered enterprise known as "planning."

The word "retreat," which best describes these two movements, does not belong in the vocabulary of economics or in that of free-enterprise capitalism. It is a military expression. Just as an army in retreat, in order to save itself from complete rout, calls for far sterner measures of control and regimentation than are required for the advance, so the retreat from the advance into true economic internationalism is the signal for hasty reorganization and stern commands in order to prevent collapse of the economy into utter chaos. The planless economy of free enterprise has never had to develop a technique of retreat; consequently, in this kind of system there are no planners and leaders to assume such a responsibility. Only when it has been defeated by the forces of separatism, which literally represent the principle of "divide and rule," must such a system be saved by leaders and techniques entirely foreign to it. To change the simile a little, it is taken into receivership in the court of bankruptcy. Whatever the simile, it is "taken in."

Looking back to the events and logic which turn free enterprise into monopoly and free trade into imperialism, what economic necessity can be discovered to explain the phenomenon?

It is true, of course, that so-called "economic" reasons are used to explain why capitalists prefer monopoly to free competition, and protection to free trade; and the reasons are just as good for explaining why labor prefers unions to a free labor market. In both cases it is the "profit motive," which is one aspect of that most pervasive and fundamental of all economic laws, namely, that all men may be assumed to prefer more rather than less of this world's goods.

Unless there are certain well-defined rules of the game of competition which are lived up to or enforced, and unless there is an over-all system of social control designed to prevent that insecurity in the economy which itself encourages business men and labor to apply their own limited and independent schemes of social control, this all-pervasive economic motive may operate so as to result in dangerous threats to the general welfare. There is nothing incompatible between production for profit and production for use in a free economy, but there is in an economy in which monopoly thwarts and limits the operation of the profit motive. Production for profit is one thing; limiting production for the sake of profit is quite another.

The failure of organized society, through the agency of government, to provide and enforce rules of the game for free enterprise in business (as it has provided rules for free enterprise in politics, which we recognize as a constitution for democracy), and the failure of society to devise a positive system of control consistent with free enterprise, places a major share of the blame for the breakdown of capitalism on what, for lack of a better name, we call politics.

Since neither business nor political organizations have shown any great disposition to bring about reform of the economic system on the lines indicated, some critics—characteristically, the Marxian socialists—have explained the lack of positive action on the assumption that capitalists want no such reforms and, because they dominate politics, see to it that none are forthcoming. A case might be made for blaming this arid state of affairs on ignorance—especially ignorance of economic laws, which becomes so apparent when one considers the number of economic fallacies which pass for economic truths. Or, what amounts to the same thing, the failure might be explained on the hypothesis that people are still dominated by the old behavior pattern of force and power, which calls for no knowledge of economic laws, but operates only on the knowledge that economic resources can be used to further the ends of power.

To say that the profit-motive in a certain stage of economic development called capitalism operates in such a way as to destroy the system, and that capitalism in a certain stage of its own development produces imperialism in an attempt to prolong its life, is intended to mean only that the economic motive in modern times operates through a set of capital-labor relationships which at long last promise to kill the motive by putting an end to the class through which the motive operates. The socialist theory does not intend for a moment to imply that precapitalist imperialism operated without an economic motive; it is only in the age of capitalism that the motive finally promises to disappear in the wholesale scheme of socializing the private property on which the profit system depends. This way of looking at the matter would seem to leave no loophole for the critic who would try to throw doubt on the theory of capitalist imperialism by pointing out that, after all, imperialism as a going concern is vastly older than capitalism and might still be regarded as the master instead of the slave of capitalism.

Whether one believes in the socialist argument or not depends entirely on whether or not one accepts the dictum that the profit motive, working through private property in the means of production in a free-enterprise economy, must inevitably create antitheses in the system (to use Marx's expression) which at once doom capitalism and force it in self-defense to adopt imperialist forms of expansion. If one does not accept this view, then the way is open for the entirely opposite conclusion that modern imperialism still has the power and authority, because of its continued hold on people's minds, to use the economic system—any economic system —for its own ageless purposes. Only in the sense that it is thus used by imperialism can capitalism be regarded as "imperialistic."

## THE SENSE IN WHICH SOCIALISM CAN BECOME IMPERIALISTIC

When Karl Renner lectured his socialist colleagues on the theme that socialism might become imperialistic in much the same way that capitalism had become imperialistic, he opened the way to the theory that both types of economic system can become the victims of forces greater than themselves. The bolshevist revolution in Russia had ushered in a totalitarian regime, and it was not difficult to sense the danger that "socialist imperialism" might develop in any country if socialists, once in power, should discard democratic principles and run the state with a dictatorial hand. Not that socialists who feared such an outcome were ready to admit that imperialism is inherent in socialism—no socialist could say that. Yet it was almost inevitable that someone, surfeited with the socialist argument that capitalism causes imperialism, should stand the socialist theory of imperialism on its head and try to prove that it is socialism, not capitalism, which has a natural affinity to imperialism. No one has undertaken this task more vigorously or more ably than Ludwig von Mises.[5]

To Mises the sense in which socialism can become—or actually is—imperialistic is to be found in two main propositions; first, that socialism is bound to become totalitarian, in spite of its pretensions of fealty to democratic principles, because it is incapable of operating on the basis of economic calculation, which constitutes the primary element of economic freedom and therefore of all freedom; second, that socialism, like imperialism, is incapable of grasping the economic principles and policies on which, under capitalism, the world tends to become unified. Both socialism and imperialism create division where unity should be and are forced into the logical position of using force to attain the unity which, after all, both regard as essential for the preservation of the systems they represent.

Belief that socialism cannot avoid imperialism arises primarily from Mises' conviction that socialism cannot possibly work as an economic mechanism. If it succeeds at all, it must do so by non-economic or political methods, which he identifies with the methods of imperialism. The economic problem under any system is that of utilizing limited resources in such a way as to maximize the satisfaction of human wants. Under capitalism, free enterprise, operating under conditions of a free labor market and free consumers' choice, works towards this end through the medium of the price system. The question is whether socialism can retain the price mechanism, or the system of money, markets, and economic calculation, and at the same time permit the continuation of a free labor market and free consumers' choice.

Mises is convinced that socialism cannot succeed in these respects because it cannot maintain a market in which free pricing takes place. The very essence of socialism is the repression of the entrepreneurial function and the profit motive, and when the profit motive and profit calculation disappear the market ceases to exit; at least it ceases to have any meaning. "Where there is no market there is no price system, and where there is no price system there can be no economic calculation." [6] Since the market is the focal

[5] Mises, *Socialism, an Economic and Sociological Analysis;* tr. from the German by J. Kahane.
[6] *Ibid.*, p. 131.

point of the capitalist system it is the very essence of capitalism. Only under capitalism, therefore, is it possible; it cannot be "artificially" imitated under socialism.[7] Socialism's need to succeed despite this deficiency, once it has been launched, forces it to adopt totalitarianism, which is synonymous with imperialism, militarism, and the rule of naked power. It represents the triumph of force over reason and is at the opposite pole from capitalism, which represents the triumph of rationality over force. Mises' description of the way in which imperialism leads to war must, in view of his indictment of socialism, explain also how socialism leads in the same direction.

History [says Mises] is a struggle between two principles, the peaceful principle, which advances the development of trade, and the militarist-imperialist principle, which interprets human society not as a friendly division of labour but as the forcible repression of some of its members by others. The imperialistic principle continually regains the upper hand. The liberal principle cannot maintain itself against it until the inclination for peaceful labour inherent in the masses shall have struggled through to full recognition of its own importance as a principle of social evolution. Wherever the imperialistic principle is in force peace can only be local and temporary: it never lasts longer than the facts which created it. The mental atmosphere with which Imperialism surrounds itself is little suited to the promotion of the growth of the division of labour within state frontiers; it practically prohibits the extension of the division of labour beyond the political-military barriers which separate the states. The division of labour needs liberty and peace. Only when its modern liberal thought of the eighteenth century had supplied a philosophy of peace and social collaboration was the basis laid for the astonishing development of the economic civilization of that age—an age branded by the latest imperialistic and socialistic doctrines as the age of crass materialism, egotism and capitalism.[8]

By professing to work towards one goal while actually working towards another the socialists perpetrate a fraud on their followers and beguile the whole world with their talk of peace. The imperialists, although equally culpable for their lack of economic sense, are at least in no position to fool anyone as to their general philosophy and intentions. The imperialists, as Mises points out, act on the firm conviction that a nation actually should possess its own sources of raw materials, its own ships and ports, and all its own means of

[7] *Ibid.*, p. 138.                          [8] *Ibid.*, p. 302.

production and that only those nations benefit which have physical control over them. By failing to understand that the division of labor and exchange makes such possession unnecessary and by carrying the idea of national ownership as far as they do, the imperialists find themselves logically on the same road as the socialists, who also believe in national ownership. But whereas the socialists have worked towards a closed economic system, coterminous with national boundaries, the imperialists, by their very emphasis on colonies, have not been able to stop here.[9] Despite their profession of internationalism, the socialists would be faced with the practical necessity of making their system work first of all in a world only partially socialistic. In order to prevent their plan from being interfered with and disrupted by outside forces, they would have to be highly nationalistic. Under capitalism and free trade it is as easy to invest abroad as at home, but a socialist state could not conceivably own means of production in other nations.[10] It could not be frankly international in either the capitalist or the imperialist sense, but it can be totalitarian. At some crucial point the totalitarian nation will not hesitate to overstep its boundaries.

Simply by fostering the single idea that conflict is inevitable between nations and that any given nation must therefore protect itself against the forces of international rivalry by acquiring as many resources as it can lay claim to, the imperialists ignore the conflict of interests within the nation which the socialists have taken so much pains to single out. As a liberal, Mises can only insist that neither international nor intra-national conflict need exist—or at least that it can be peaceably resolved—under free enterprise and free trade, because competition takes place and economic rivalries work themselves out through economic calculation and the price mechanism. Without these mediums, competition has no way to express itself except by recourse to violence.[11] Imperialism fosters violence by going to the opposite extreme of fostering tariffs, prohibitions of imports, premiums on exports, and similar types of control

[9] *Ibid.*, pp. 49-50.
[10] *Ibid.*, p. 235. As suggested by Bonn, *The Crumbling of Empire*, pp. 35, 36, 37. Bonn points out that, even though the collectivist profit-motive is at present lacking in Soviet Russia, the power-motive (the desire to rule men by force) is very much in evidence and that imperialist policies will be pursued whenever the leaders deem it advisable.
[11] Mises, *Socialism*, p. 323.

over trade. It goes farther and places limitations on emigration and imigration, with increasing emphasis on race hatred and the struggle for existence: "Modern Imperialism especially relies on the catchwords coined by popular science out of Darwinism." [12] When all these efforts have failed, when imperialists have not completely succeeded in discrediting liberalism by trying to prove that it serves only certain classes and that the kind of peace which it maintains is a peace of suppression and exploitation, then the imperialist policy of resorting to violent tactics emerges. "The *ultimo ratio* of imperialism is . . . war. Beside war, all other weapons that it may use appear merely insufficient auxiliaries." [13]

In his blanket indictment of socialism along with imperialism, Mises undoubtedly states the case too strongly for many economists who are otherwise of his general persuasion. To say that economic calculation is impossible under collectivism is to deny what is at least theoretically possible, as is shown conclusively enough by economists who have made a fresh appraisal of this problem. To the present writer it seems clear that Mises would have greatly strengthened his argument had he admitted this theoretical possibility. He would still have been free to add that politically there is little or no likelihood that economic calculation will ever be realized in practice under socialism and that totalitarianism is the result of socialism's failure—or society's failure—to solve the political problem. He would thus open the way also to the conclusion that capitalism, even granting its opposition to imperialism "in theory," can actually become the victim of imperialism in the same way that socialism can be victimized.

It would be much more reasonable to take the position that socialism is by nature totalitarian and imperialistic, were it not demonstrable that a collectivist economy can be economically rational. The question of whether socialism can preserve such democratic institutions as free consumers' choice and a free labor market and whether it can be made to operate through a price mechanism, is primarily a political problem. Until very recently socialists gave little or no attention to this question, while the critics of socialism, such as Mises, took the position that socialism would mean economic and political authoritarianism. The new approach to this

[12] *Ibid.*, p. 317.                                    [13] *Ibid.*, p. 228.

problem makes it clear that it is entirely feasible under collectivism —that is, under the common ownership of the means of production—for the central authorities to set up an accounting system', indexes, and other mechanical aids which would enable the price system to operate efficiently on the basis of economic calculation. The economists who have worked out the ingenious blue-prints of the economic processes in a socialist commonwealth,[14] or have at least insisted upon the possibilities of economic calculation under socialism, have also given socialism the benefit of the doubt on the question of liberty by including within the framework of their analysis the assumption of democracy in the form of free consumers' choice and a free labor market. It by no means follows that they all agree that socialism actually will ever succeed in preserving economic and political freedom. Some—Taylor, for example [15]— merely indicate how production might be guided in a socialist state, assuming that the state is determined to let it be guided through the calculus of free pricing. Others apparently assume that socialism will maintain the essential freedoms merely because it is demonstrable that it can successfully employ economic calculation, and are inclined to think that this is a sufficient answer to Mises.[16]

There is no more reason to think that the problem of imperialism has been solved simply because it is demonstrable theoretically

[14] See, for example, the essays by Pierson and Barone in Hayek, ed., *Collectivist Economic Planning;* Pigou, *Socialism versus Capitalism;* Hall, *The Economic System in a Socialist State;* Taylor, "The Guidance of Production in a Socialist State," *American Economic Review,* XIX (March, 1929), 1–8; Lange, "On the Economic Theory of Socialism," *Review of Economic Studies,* Vol. IV: October, 1936, pp. 53–71, and February, 1937, pp. 123–42. (The articles by Taylor and Lange were republished under the title *On the Economic Theory of Socialism,* Benjamin E. Lippincott, ed.); Dickinson, "Price Formation in a Socialist Community," *Economic Journal,* XLIII (June, 1933), 237–50; Dickinson, *Economics of Socialism;* Frank H. Knight, "The Place of Marginal Economics in a Collectivist System," *American Economic Review,* Supplement, XXVI (March, 1936), 255–66; Frank H. Knight, "Two Economists on Socialism" (review of the books of Pigou and Hall, listed above), *Journal of Political Economy,* XLVI (April, 1938), 241–50.

[15] Taylor, "The Guidance of Production in a Socialist State," *American Economic Review,* XIX (March, 1929), 1–8.

[16] Dickinson, in his article "Price Formation in a Socialist Community," *Economic Journal,* XLIII (June, 1933), 237–50, opens his remarks by pointing out that in the early days of the socialist movement the chief argument used against it was the Malthusian bogy. More recently (until Soviet Russia proved otherwise), says Dickinson, socialism was attacked for lack of incentive. Lastly has come the argument of Mises and others (which the author sets out to refute) that socialism is incapable of solving purely economic problems.

that socialism can behave rationally in economic matters than to think that it can be solved because capitalism demonstrates the same ability. There is every reason to believe that the spirit of rationality in economic matters is the chief hope of overcoming the economic irrationality of power politics. The present imperfections of capitalism indicate how far it is still necessary to go before we can have a better economic system based on free enterprise, to say nothing of a better world based on economic rationalism. It can be expected, therefore, that many things would happen to prevent economic calculation from guiding production in a socialist state, thus making it seem expedient for such a state to resort to totalitarian methods.

There are numberless ways in which consumers and workers can become chiselers and saboteurs of the plans and controls required to maintain economic calculation, and many points at which the managers of the system can fail. In a world dominated by power politics there is bound to be constant threat from this source to any rational economic system. Therefore, if repeated experiences in trying to run a socialist society with the price mechanism of free enterprise should fail to measure up to expectations because of a breakdown in the functioning of consumer choice and a free labor market or a breakdown in management, or because threats from outside the system call for a combative reaction, there is nothing left to do except to discard the whole elaborate machinery of rational economic calculation and depend entirely on ordering and forbidding from beginning to end.

Simply by abolishing all opportunities for individuals to have personal economic problems—which can have meaning only if people have personal choice as to what they will do or what they will consume—a police state could then go directly and vigorously about its business without any pretense of being democratic or of being guided by the dictates of the market. It could solve the unemployment problem by dictating where the workers shall work and at what remuneration, and it could provide for social security and insurance against the personal risks inherent in old age and sickness. There would be no business cycles, such as plague the capitalist economy. Individuals who might try to thwart the will of the state would certainly be suppressed as chiselers, saboteurs, and wreckers. The economic content of such a system would be relatively simple, but its political or control side would be extremely complex, in contrast with the free-enterprise economy, in which order in the midst of complexity on the economic side calls for no elaborate system of political control. Where free enterprise is confronted with the problem of how to deal with a relatively small number of monopolists, the collectivist state has the far greater problem of dealing with the large mass of individuals who in some way or other try to compete. The problems of trying to enforce prohibition when large numbers of individuals undertake to "make their own" and of trying to enforce price controls in the face of evasion and "chiseling" (which becomes another word for competition whenever attempts are made to create monopoly) indicate the sort of difficulties confronting a collectivist society. Turning such a society into a police state is the logical final step.

Whether a collectivist economy can save itself from the clutches of the police is not entirely dependent upon its ability to solve the economic problem democratically. Both socialism and capitalism can maintain the essentials of freedom if they are backed by a strong enough will and intelligence. But at the crucial point where totalitarianism and imperialism become a threat to a rational economic system, the collectivist state has certain great weaknesses, from the democratic point of view, which the free-enterprise system does not have, namely, its high degree of centralization and its enormous sensitivity and touchiness to the kind of criticism and rebuff that can easily set off a war. Such a state has too military a character to be safely trusted with the institutions of democracy. It may too easily be taken over by a power-intoxicated and trigger-happy group, led by a dictator. The issue for both capitalism and socialism is not their rationality from the economic point of view, but the power menace to which both are exposed.

It would be possible, but hardly necessary, in order to support the argument, to illustrate in other ways how both capitalism and socialism could become increasingly tied in with and controlled by the forces of power. The possibilities and some of the actualities are too obvious to escape the attention of anyone who will take the trouble to look about him. From the point of view of the lessons these tendencies have to teach, it becomes increasingly clear that neither capitalism nor socialism, as economic systems, are imperialistic or warlike and that neither creates a way of life that is of this character. Both can be instruments of welfare, or both can be instruments of power.

This does not mean that capitalism would work perfectly if only the power problem were solved or that socialism as now visualized would need no further perfecting in a world free from imperialism, nationalism, and militarism. The same state of human perfection which the proponents of each of these economic systems assume to be necessary for the perfect working of the other would make either work perfectly. For capitalism this would certainly require a far more intelligent handling and enforcement of those principles vaguely referred to as the "rules of the game of free enterprise" and a great deal more attention to the monetary side of the economic process.

Our next problem, therefore, is to understand the relation between economic systems and political aims and purposes. The Marxists have characteristically placed their faith in changing the economic system; let us now see what is to be said for approaching the problem the other way around.

# IX ·

## IMPERIALISM AND WAR AS
## POLITICAL PHENOMENA

REJECTION of the theory that capitalism operates so as to cause imperialism and war does not mean that the economic interpretation of history has been disposed of. The economic motive transcends economic systems, and the idea that it is one of the factors leading to conflict must be examined on its own merits.

Economists generally have been more critical of the economic interpretation of historical events than have other social scientists, but it is by no means always clear on what grounds they base their criticism or why they reject such concepts as "economic imperialism." Sometimes rejection of these ideas springs from their general disagreement with Marxist economic reasoning. On the other hand, some of the most unsparing critics of Marxism find it entirely agreeable to concede something to Marx's economic interpretation.[1] The easiest way out of this difficult debate is to criticize the economic interpretation, not because it has no truth in it, but because it is not what it sometimes is implied to be, the whole truth.[2] It is commonly stated that the economic interpretation is sound as far as it goes, but that there are also other factors, such as religion, the love of adventure, military behavior, and other social behavior

[1] Thus, for example: "But though the Marxist interpretation of history is, in its broad outlines, true, it has also ambiguities and limitations which are of considerable importance with reference both to the understanding of present society and to the practical tasks of social reorganisation."—Parkes, *Marxism; an Autopsy*, p. 157.

[2] The following is perhaps a typical statement: "We understand, then, by the theory of economic interpretation of history, not that all history is to be explained in economic terms alone, but that the chief considerations in human progress are the social considerations, and that the important factor in social change is the economic factor. Economic interpretation of history means, not that the economic relations exert an exclusive influence, but that they exert a preponderant influence in shaping the progress of society." Seligman, *The Economic Interpretation of History*, p. 67.

patterns inherited from past ages which must be given due weight
in the hierarchy of causes.

Sometimes it appears to be a sufficient answer to the economic
interpretation to say merely that economists find no supporting
evidence for it in theory or in history. The authors of a recent study
of war say exactly this, without giving any reasons:

Believing that wars arise mainly from non-economic factors, they [the
authors] have been stimulated to investigate the contrary opinions of
historians, publicists, and Marxists. Among the "economic forces" often
said by these writers to cause war are "capitalism," "imperialism," the
"international arms trade," and "international finance." Most economists have found that economic theory and historical evidence give little
support to these assertions.[3]

While the closing statement is probably true, there are some
economists who take strong exception to it. A reviewer of the book
from which the quotation is taken is of the opinion that few economists would agree with this view; he even doubts that the authors
of the study believe that wars arise mainly, as they say, from noneconomic factors, since in various instances they ascribe a good deal
of weight to economic factors.[4]

These statements indicate the existence of considerable disagreement among those who use such terms as "economic" and "economic factors" as to what the terms really mean, or what their relation to other factors is. Indeed, they are rarely defined by those
who use them, as if their meaning is so obvious as to require no
definition. On the contrary, these are such extremely difficult concepts to popularize that it is always safer to leave them alone—a
rule which we now proceed to violate.

## LIMITATIONS OF THE ECONOMIC
## INTERPRETATION

The economic interpretation of history is a philosophy which
undertakes to explain events in terms of the efforts of man to attain
ends by means which are dictated by the economic motive. It has
nothing to do with capitalism or any other type of economic order
except as these systems serve as channels through which the mo-

[3] Wright, ed., *A Study of War*, 2 vols., p. 710; see also pp. 284–85.
[4] Harris [A Review of Wright, ed., *A Study of War*], *American Economic Review*,
XXXIII (June, 1943), 417.

tive operates. In all ages men have struggled for the material means of satisfying their basic wants. In much of the modern world these means are obtained through the mechanism of the capitalist mode of production, and the men who actually run the system are driven by the profit motive, which becomes associated under capitalism with the institution of private property in the means of production. As the socialists appear to see it, the desire for profit becomes a sort of detached segment of the general economic motive which attaches itself to capitalism. Certain consequences of the operation of the profit economy presage the breakdown of the system, and to save themselves from ruin the capitalists, backed by the state, resort to practices and policies which result in expansion, conflicting interests, and war.

The destruction of the capitalist system does not destroy the economic motive, but according to socialist logic it does end the existence of the profit motive as a detached segment of the general economic motive. The workers also have an economic motive in their struggle to gain control of the economic system, and their victory over the profit motive means that at last the motive is in the right hands, where, presumably, it can no longer drive men to conflict. Henceforth, since socialism is presumed to bring an era of peace, the operation of the economic motive can have no power to drive men or their system into acts of violence. It is only in a non-socialized world, therefore, that the economic motive can be regarded as the key to conflict; and since the whole presocialist era left this motive free to work its terrible consequences, the economic interpretation is only a method of revealing and explaining historical events.

Reduced to its simplest terms, the economic interpretation of conflict visualizes a person, or a nation, desiring some object, such as territory, goods, or raw materials. It thus assumes to have set up at one stroke the economic motive and the economic end. Since clearly there have been both a desire for things which other people possess and wars for these same things, the conclusion that such wars were caused by the economic motive seems as simple as putting two and two together.

The more obvious amendment of this facile reasoning begins with the question whether the desire for such things as territory, goods, or raw materials necessarily calls for the use of brute force to obtain them. Even Marx saw in capitalism a more refined method than brute force of realizing objectives of this sort, but he did not absolve capitalism of the guilt of sometimes resorting to war to gain its objectives when things were unobtainable by the simple act of trade or purchase. Territory and resources belonging to others clearly had to be taken by force if they were to be possessed at all, and it was this phenomenon of going to war for territory and resources which constituted the heart of the neo-Marxian theory of imperialism. Granting this amendment of the theory, the economic interpretation of conflict appears to remain substantially intact. If one can believe that the economic motive is the most basic and powerful of all human motives and that it means what it appears to mean, namely, the desire for specific things of value, there remains nothing further to quibble over.

It seems almost a pity, therefore, to raise the next question: Does the desire for any concrete thing or service of value constitute the economic motive, and is the given objective to be regarded as the economic end? To suggest a negative answer to this question seems to violate the basic meaning of economics, and in fact it does deny the commonsense view that the desire for specific things constitutes the central data of economic reasoning. Yet if economics is to be regarded as a science it is necessary to go beyond the mere ethical valuation contained in the myriad "I wants" of human beings to a complete restatement of the nature of the economic motive and the end to which it is directed.

Such a restatement makes it clear that the economic motive can never be associated with concrete ends, that is, identified with the desire for any particular or specific object.[5] It is basic to any science that the data with which it deals shall remain fixed, or constant. Without such data, analysis and prediction are impossible. The desire for concrete things such as bread and wheat, oil and oil fields, iron and iron mines, or territory does not fulfill the scientific requirement, because of the instability of such data. Not all men want

[5] Frank H. Knight has done more than any other economist to clarify the issues between economics and ethics. See his "Ethics and the Economic Interpretation," *Quarterly Journal of Economics*, XXXVI (May, 1922), 454–81; and "Bertrand Russell on Power," *Ethics*, XLIX (April, 1939), 253–85.

these particular things or any one particular thing, and those who do want them do not have the same intensity of desire. Whether anything is desired and the degree of desire are matters of choice between alternatives, which depends upon the exercise of value judgments. Such rejecting and choosing belong to the field of ethics, not economics. It is the nature of ethics to deal with values which change, just as it is the nature of science to deal with data which possess the hard quality of constancy. Even if all goods were free, so that there would be no economic problem involved in obtaining them and therefore no economic motive, the ethical problem of choosing between alternative goods would remain. The economic motive, therefore, emerges with the fact of scarcity and the need to economize, not with the ethical problem of choosing between alternatives.

The only thing which men desire which meets the rigid but essential test of scientific reasoning is "wealth." It can be assumed for scientific purposes that all men want to have more rather than less of this world's goods, and that they will work (economize, in one way or another) to maximize their wealth in general. This sort of behavior does not operate within the field of choice; it is a reliable feature of human conduct. Only when the general economic objective is realized are men free to exercise their ethical bent to make choices. The fact that some men engage in farming and others in manufacturing is itself a matter of no consequence, but the fact that each can be presumed to use appropriate means to produce wheat or automobiles is basic to economic reasoning. The fact that one produces wheat and the other automobiles is likewise of no consequence, but the fact that they produce "value" is basic. Economics is concerned with the creation of value, not particular things, and the economic motive is directed to the creation of value, not particular things.

An economic motive, therefore, is not directed towards some specific end, and there are no ultimate ends which can be called economic. The creation of wealth out of scarce resources constitutes the heart of the economic problem, but the problem of selecting specific objectives on which to expend this wealth constitutes not an economic problem, but an ethical one. The producer of wealth, as producer, is impelled by a purely economic motive, but as a consumer his motives are noneconomic, or ethical.[6]

A little reflection on the special nature of stealing enables us to make the essential distinction between economic and noneconomic activity. Thieves admittedly have the same motive as honest people in desiring an object, and if the motive and the object are the only elements involved there is no difference between stealing something and working for it by the sweat of one's brow. Yet there is a difference between the two kinds of activity, and it centers on the meaning of the word "economic." If there is no difference between stealing and getting a thing through economic activity—a difference which is not found in the nature of either the motive or the object—the term "to economize" becomes an absurdity and a separate science of economics is impossible. Economics can be rescued from this pitfall only by insisting upon a definition of activity which distinguishes between the creation of value and the creation of specific things and between the desire for wealth-in-general and the desire for particular forms of wealth. Thieves do not, by the very definition of their activity, create wealth, and they cannot steal anything as abstract as wealth-in-general. Other men are distinguished from thieves by the fact that they obtain command over a particular good by first producing wealth. In fact the very act of producing wealth implies that any object the producer desires and which his command over wealth will buy is his. Resources which already exist, which have value because they are scarce, and yet are initially there for the taking, cannot be regarded as mere loot simply because someone appropriates them. By nature they are free goods to begin with, and in a society of free goods, or with respect to any good that is free, there can be no difference between thieves and honest men. Theft becomes possible only as a result of scarcity, which is the origin of ownership, or private property, not as a result of the desire for things. Economic activity, on the other hand, emerges in the creation of command over property by the act of utilizing scarce resources.

The activity of warfare, when directed towards the acquisition of things, is subject to the same sort of logical treatment as the

---

[6] For an excellent discussion of the meaning of economic causation see the appendix to Robbins, *The Economic Causes of War*.

activity of stealing, with one possible exception. Although warfare itself is not an economic process, it might conceivably be waged in the interest of the economic process. For example, a nation might go to war in order to break down barriers created by another nation for the purpose of preventing the former from having access to the scarce resources in the latter's possession which are regarded by the attacking nation as essential for the creation of its own wealth. Similarly, a nation might have an economic motive in using its police force to break down internal barriers or impediments to the productive process. As such, the war machine is to be regarded as a kind of nutcracker deliberately created to do a job which cannot be done by economic or political machinery.

Before we can be justified in writing such a war off as economic, we must be sure that the general motive of assisting the productive process was the effective reason for resorting to war, not merely an afterthought or a plausible excuse. The desire of a nation to obtain such concrete things as oil fields or iron mines cannot be regarded as an economic motive, and war to obtain such specific objects cannot be regarded as based on economic causes. In such cases it would not be a question of breaking down barriers to obtaining oil or iron, but only of getting possession of their sources. The fact that the nation owning these sources wants to retain control of them naturally constitutes a barrier to some other nation's acquisition of them, though it need not constitute a barrier to the sale of oil and iron to other nations or their nationals. But the desire of another nation to possess these resources and the act of going to war to obtain them constitute neither an economic motive nor an act of economic warfare; the desire has the nature of an ethical valuation, and the act the nature of plain theft. No economic content is observable in the whole affair.

This does not by any means prevent our saying that nations desire oil fields and iron mines and that they go to war to obtain them. It only precludes our saying that the reason for going to war—even assuming this to be the only reason—is economic. If wars actually could be regarded as economic, we might get some comfort from such a fact, for at least it would be clear that the motive had a rational basis, aimed at the desirable end of removing impediments to general economic welfare. But if people had sense enough to confine their motives for warfare to purely economic considerations, it is axiomatic that they would know how to avoid wars entirely.

This way of defining economics and the insistence of the economist that economic motives, ends, and means are distinct from ethical values are not dialectics invented for the purpose of cheating the economic interpreter of history out of his old stock in trade. They are simply ways of avoiding certain logical difficulties inherent in regarding the desire for concrete things as the essence of the economic motive. Actually this way of handling the problem does greatly limit the sense in which it is appropriate to speak of the economic causes of war and practically puts the economic interpretation out of business. Even if we leave intact the idea that the desire for concrete things constitutes the economic motive, it still remains true that the economic interpretation of war in these terms appears pale and anemic compared with the powerful forces, mostly political, which operate in the world, and which none but the most resolute economic interpreter can pretend to regard as bound up with a desire for this world's material goods. Desire for power and the inclination to use violence as a means open the way to an understanding of the nature of imperialism and war which makes any other interpretation seem almost utterly insignificant.

## THE CONFUSION OF ECONOMIC POWER WITH "NAKED POWER" AND OF ECONOMIC WITH NONECONOMIC COMPETITION

Out of the failure to distinguish between the proper fields of economics and ethics comes a confusion not only of "economic" with "noneconomic" on the abstract level, but between economics and politics, between economic power and "naked power," and between economic and noneconomic competition. Thus Bertrand Russell, in holding that economic power is synonymous with naked power, in the sense of being arbitrary and one-sided, involving the absence of acquiescence on the part of the person or group upon whom economic power is exercised, reaches the conclusion that "Economics as a separate science is unrealistic, and misleading if taken as a guide in practice. It is one element—a very important element, it is true—in a wider study, the science of power." [7]

From Russell's point of view military and economic power are "realistically" indistinguishable. According to his theory "economics" is merely "another word for politics" (to use an aphorism common to those who hold this position); it leaves no room—and is sometimes deliberately intended to leave no room—for a separate science of economics. By assuming that economics is concerned with the fleeting and changeable motives involved in value judgments, which belong to the field of ethics, this point of view implicitly assumes that there are no economic ends as such.[8] The idea that the end of economic activity is the general one of creating wealth—which is the generalized form of all valuable things and services—is either overlooked or deliberately discarded. In its place economic activity becomes merely "one element . . . in the science of power"; that is, a means of acquiring control over the things and services which are useful to those who seek power. Thus, economic power becomes identified with naked power, and economic activity is made to appear a major explanation of such expressions of naked power as imperialism and war.

Failure to distinguish between economic competition and rivalry in the war-and-conquest sense is another corollary of the failure to make a distinction between the field of economics and the realm of ethics, or between fitting means to ends (which involves constant shuffling of resources which compete with each other) and comparing, adjusting, or reconciling one end with another (which involves a clash of opinion and perhaps a clash of arms over the things that men live and die for, as distinct from what they live and die with).

It has long been a commonplace of the textbooks that economic competition is "fundamentally co-operative," the fundamental element being the conditions under which competition takes place, not the conditions under which co-operation takes place when competitors join hands in an act of brotherly good will, which is the essence of monopoly. It is more accurate, of course, to say that economic competition is fundamentally interdependent, in the

---

[7] Russell, *Power; a new social analysis*, p. 135.

[8] An answer to Russell's thesis is found in Frank H. Knight, "Bertrand Russell on Power," *Ethics*, XLIX (April, 1939), 253–85.

same sense that international trade makes nations interdependent. The basic concept is the division of labor, from which springs exchange and the price mechanism. It is through this mechanism that economic adjustment, or competition, takes place, and it is free competition only in the sense that individuals have an equal opportunity to use this medium. It becomes unfree, or monopolistic, only when individuals are allowed to go outside the price mechanism, that is, to engage in extracurricular activities, as far as this mechanism is concerned, in order to evade or to avoid its sanctions. Within the limits set by this mechanism, competition is indirect and impersonal, and competitive rivals are kept within bounds. Only when competition is carried on outside these limits does it become direct, personal, cutthroat, and dangerous. To permit the kind of activity and the kind of machination that build up monopolies is to permit "extracurricular" activities of this nature, and imperialism and war belong in the same category. But the fact that such activities are expressions of extreme rivalry and conflict no more entitles them to be called economic than it entitles highway robbery to that designation. All such behavior is strictly excluded when we speak of economic competition.

In order to visualize a society in which there is no co-operation we have only to imagine one in which there is no competition, where each man is a self-contained minuscule monopoly, producing what he consumes and consuming what he produces. Here there would be no "production for profit," but only "production for use"; no division of labor or exchange, and no price mechanism or rule of the game of competition to prevent such a rugged individualist from doing as he pleases. Assume that it pleases him to try to "expand" and that he lives in a world of limited resources, where he can expand only at the expense of someone else in a similar state of self-sufficiency and self-containment, but with an urge to acquire more. Obviously the ensuing competition will be resolved by force—and may the better man win. Both cannot win, and so one must gain what the other loses. Each tries to expand at the other's expense, and since the expansion is not of the kind that operates within a reciprocating mechanism of give and take, with limits beyond which they cannot go, they must go on until one or the other is exterminated.

Competition that is not based upon the reciprocal character of the division of labor and exchange and is not kept within bounds by the price mechanism is precisely the sort of rivalry that is associated with imperialism and war. But imperialism and war require their own kind of group action, or co-operation, for it is inconceivable that every man should undertake to be his own warrior and imperialist. Even in war division of labor is recognized as the basis for organized co-operation; Marx, in fact, believed that division of labor first took place for the purposes of warfare.

It is hardly necessary to add that division of labor for war purposes is not governed by a price mechanism, but only by purely arbitrary ordering. A social group organized and co-operating in the interests of imperialism and war obviously has no idea of co-operating with the enemy. All it can do is to compete on the terms of force, not on economic terms. It may make material or economic gains from such an enterprise, and this may well be the professed motive. The only point is that war is a method of gaining an end that centuries of industry and trade have shown can be gained by peaceful means.

It is out of the rejection of the economic interpretation that the search for other explanations begins; rejection of the capitalistic theory of imperialism and war merely absolves capitalism without suggesting an alternative explanation on the same superficial level of mechanistic relationships. Therefore, what one is impelled to look for is some sort of noneconomic, as distinct from a noncapitalistic, explanation of the persistence of these forces. At this point the distinction between the field of economics and that of ethics contributes directly to what now becomes obvious—the necessity of identifying the noneconomic forces, whatever they are, with the field of ethical judgments.

The first general observation resulting from an identification of noneconomic with ethical, so far as our present quest is concerned, is that the problem of imperialism and war—their causes and remedies—must be worked out in the area of human values. This means that as long as people continue to want the things and to support the behavior patterns and institutions which cause imperialism and war they can expect no other results. This is axiomatic. People get what they pay for in this field as in the market place.

What are these values? There are several eligible candidates for consideration, all of which quickly reduce to what people want, or at least to what their behavior, which must be presumed to harbor motives, obtains for them. To say that "the principal cause of war is war," or that "war is an end in itself," or that imperialism is an "atavism," or that nationalism is to blame—all these ways of stating the issue lead at once into the field of human values.

## IMPERIALISM, MILITARISM, AND OTHER COEVAL TERMS

The view that imperialism and war are to be explained as general phenomena in terms of themselves, as kindred self-generating institutions, and indeed as atavisms, is of recent development and has resulted largely from the criticism leveled against the economic interpretation by economists themselves. This point of view is clearly stated in Hawtrey's flat assertion that "the principal cause of war is war itself"[9] and in Pigou's assertion that "the desire for domination for its own sake, apart from any economic advantages it may confer, is a real and effective motive for action"; to which he adds that the explosive force of war "has little to do with economics." [10] Wars, like business cycles, may be self-generating:

> One with another, soul with soul,
> They kindle fire from fire.[11]

But to say that the principal cause of war is war, while a penetrating observation in its way, does not get us very far unless it leads to the conclusion, which is implicit in the statement, that this vicious circle can only be broken by means which are the opposite of war. From this point of view a "war to end wars" becomes a completely ridiculous approach to the problem. The principal

[9] Hawtrey, *Economic Aspects of Sovereignty*, p. 105. Hawtrey does not, of course, rest his case with this aphorism. His point is that the vicious circle of war can be broken only by the establishment of international law and order. As for the causes of war, Hawtrey makes no attempt to distinguish between the economic and political. "The distinction between economic and political causes," he says, "is an unreal one. Every conflict is one of power and power depends on resources" (*ibid.*, p. 120). This would seem to confuse the "economic causes" of war with its economic aspects, or its causes of whatever nature with the means of conducting it.

[10] Pigou, *The Political Economy of War*, pp. 19–20.

[11] Rossetti, "Advent," from *The Poetical Works of Christina Georgina Rossetti*, p. 202, quoted in Pigou, *Industrial Fluctuations*, p. 79.

cause of war is also the principal cause of all conflict. In Plato's words, war is "derived from causes which are also the causes of almost all the evils in States, private as well as public." [12]

Nevertheless, such statements as these of Hawtrey and Pigou turn our attention in the right direction. However much we may wish to identify imperialism and war with the absence of international government in our own day, something must be made of the idea that war can be an end in itself, and a false end at that. From this point of view the pursuit of any policy which aims at the aggrandizement of national power, whether it be called nationalism, mercantilism, imperialism, or militarism, constitutes a false end; not merely an end which one rejects because it is not in accordance with his own sense of values, but an end impossible of attainment by all men because it is exclusive rather than embracing, and against the common interest of mankind rather than a policy to which all men can subscribe. A policy which produces peace in the world therefore reflects a true end because peace is the universal end desired; a policy which produces war, on the other hand, reflects a false end.

Militarism and imperialism clearly constitute an identical pattern of thought and behavior. The relationship between them has often been remarked, but it has seldom been better described than by Alfred Vagts in his *History of Militarism*. Militarism and imperialism are here quite properly described as "coeval terms." They share the same tendency to extend dominion, but whereas imperialism seeks size, militarism seeks strength. "Where the one looks primarily for more territory, the other covets more men and more money. The two hardly ever exist by themselves."

This author distinguishes between "militarism" and "military," the former being an end in itself, the military way being a means to an end. He says:

Every war is fought, every army is maintained in a military way and in a militaristic way. The distinction is fundamental and fateful. The military way is marked by a primary concentration of men and materials on winning specific objectives of power with the utmost efficiency, that is, with the least expenditure of blood and treasure. It is limited in scope, confined to one function, and scientific in its essential qualities.

12 See above, p. 71.

Militarism, on the other hand, presents a vast array of customs, interests, prestige, actions and thought associated with armies and wars and yet transcending true military purpose. Indeed, militarism is so constituted that it may hamper and defeat the purposes of the military way. Its influence is unlimited in scope. It may permeate all society and become dominant over all industry and arts. Rejecting the scientific character of the military way, militarism displays the qualities of caste and cult, authority and belief.[13]

Furthermore:

Militarism is thus not the opposite of pacifism; its true counterpart is civilianism. Love of war, bellicosity, is the counterpart of the love of peace, pacifism; but militarism is more, and sometimes less, than the love of war. It covers every system of thinking and valuing and every complex of feelings which rank military institutions and ways above the ways of civilian life, carrying military mentality and modes of acting and decision into the civilian sphere.[14]

Substitute for "militarism" in the above passages the word "imperialism"—indeed throughout the book—and entitle it "A History of Imperialism," and little violence would be done to the author's objective of presenting a pattern of thinking and behavior which is the very opposite of "civilianism," free enterprise, or any other analogous concept. He is right in regarding these "coeval" institutions as covering every civilian thought, feeling, and mode of action and decision. Today, as in Roman times, it is a concept and a practice of absolutism—complete power over life and death. Although the life that it so completely covers is broader than economics, the conflict between militarism-imperialism and freedom is best portrayed in the economic branch of the "civilian sphere." It is all summed up (although the author of *A History of Militarism* never says it in so many words) in the economic and the non-economic (militaristic) concepts of competition. Finally, by associating militarism with the totalitarian state Vagts again places the emphasis where it belongs, on "totalitarian militarism" (the title of his last chapter), which is just as obviously "totalitarian imperialism."

However the terms "imperialism" and "militarism" may be defined, they are certainly the opposites of those elements of mutuality and tolerance in modern society which provide the basis

[13] Vagts, *A History of Militarism*, p. 11.          [14] *Ibid.*, p. 15.

for democracy and free enterprise. Imperialism and militarism are as old as history and represent behavior patterns which were formed when the human race was in a stage of savagery and barbarism; democracy and free enterprise are the products of modern thought and institutions, in which religious teachings, scientific education, the suppression of violence, and the development of law and order all had a decisive part.

## IMPERIALISM AS AN ATAVISM

Only since the first World War, thanks to the impetus which Professor Schumpeter gave to this line of reasoning,[15] has there been much recognition of the idea that imperialism is an atavistic force, ancient in inception, decadent and self-conscious in an age of rationalism, yet still powerful enough to lord it over its rival, the upstart capitalism. But this idea is not new. In some form, usually very primitive compared with Schumpeter's highly sophisticated thesis, men have long blurted out the common-sense idea that the power complex overrides the economic rationalism of men, especially the power complex of statesmen against the economic interests of little men. Montesquieu, two centuries ago, observed [16] that "Commerce is the cure for the most destructive prejudices"; that "Peace is the natural effect of trade"; and that "the spirit of trade produces in the mind of man a certain sense of exact justice, opposite, on the one hand, to robbery, and on the other to those moral virtues which forbid our always adhering rigidly to the rules of private interest, and suffer us to neglect this to the advantage of others. The total privation of trade, on the contrary, produces robbery."

This was an eighteenth-century way of saying that robbery ("imperialism") is the opposite of commerce ("capitalism") and happily an outmoded way of carrying on. Marx, too, had the idea that capitalism, although a new and refined type of exploitation, had replaced the colonial system and all the crude wickedness that went with it. Nor did he, any more than Montesquieu, think that the old system would ever again arise to contest the supremacy of modern

---

[15] Schumpeter, "Zur Soziologie der Imperialismen," *Archiv für Sozialwissenschaft und Sozialpolitik*, Vol. XLVI: December, 1918, pp. 1–39; June, 1919, pp. 275–310.
[16] See above, pp. 15–16.

industrialism. If he could have observed such a reconquest of power, he might well have regarded it as atavistic. And Hobson, despite his theory of economic imperialism, could still speak of conquest as a "forceful domination surviving in a nation from early centuries of animal struggle for existence." [17]

What Schumpeter did with this idea was to depict modern capitalism as an innocent victim of forces which the civilized world had long fancied to have been forever consigned to the nether regions. Imperialism as a policy and militarism as a machine for carrying it out are indeed among the most ancient of human behavior patterns and institutions. They developed in those dark ages of the past when man knew no other way to expand and to expend his surplus energy. Brute force had no competition until modern times from pacifism as a way of life, or from industrialism as a mode of enterprise based on mutuality and good will, or from democracy as a system of government. It had no opponents, practically speaking, to make it self-conscious and to put it on the defensive. The whole business of war and conquest was taken for granted, and in fact was the accepted way of life. Faced with no ideological opposition, the military and imperial authorities had no need of propaganda to capture the loyalty of their subjects. The system was taken for granted as much by the subject as by the master.

The institutions of imperialism and militarism became atavistic, to use Schumpeter's phrase, in the sense of being survivors in an age which could break away from the past and create new institutions and develop competing loyalties and patterns of behavior. They represented a reversion to type in a world that had developed a higher morality.[18] Schumpeter observes that the break came in the

---

[17] See above, p. 103.

[18] One of the characters in Jules Romains, *Verdun*, pp. 436–37, worked out the idea as follows: "There's a freemasonry of front-line fighters; they form a sort of order. . . . Taken by and large, you know, this feeling develops in od' ' ways, ways of which we're not really conscious. . . . It's something very deep down in human nature that's working up to the surface again. That's because the conditions that produced it long ago are recurring, are taking root and becoming permanent. What we're seeing now is the re-emergence of the warrior spirit in the bosom of society. I don't mean the spirit of the professional soldier. That's something comparatively recent; no, it's the warrior spirit as it existed centuries ago, the spirit of the man who fought from year's end to year's end while the others didn't . . . while the others cultivated their gardens, herded their cows, and looked after their children. The warrior knew all sorts of hardships which he kept at a distance from his neighbours, but in exchange for that he was spared the toil of every day and the cares of

Middle Ages, when military leaders for the first time felt called upon to rationalize and to justify their activities on moral grounds. Because of a feeling of insecurity they began to go on the defensive. Actually, their position was far from insecure, for the military profession reached its highest peak of perfection during this period, as exemplified in German knighthood and the creation of a definite military caste.

It is from this class that Schumpeter traces the perpetuation and spread of modern military virtues. The worship of power, pomp, and glory which characterized the military caste and was shared by all the nobility did not stop with these classes; they impressed the stamp of their moral code on every activity of the state and on every class of the population. Yet there was enough dissent to create a growing feeling of insecurity among the devotees of this ancient and powerful system and to make it increasingly necessary for them to cloak every act of aggression with the sanction of religion and morality, if not of reason.

The final climax in the development of opposition to this old combination of imperialism and militarism came with modern industrialism, the rise of which was not unrelated to the growth of parliamentary government and democracy. The spread of commerce, the development of banking and exchange, the growth of the factory system, and the greater and greater refinement in the division of labor, both nationally and internationally, created a world vastly different from the old—a world in which for the first time men could give free vent to their acquisitive proclivities through industry instead of squandering their surplus energy in destructive activities. By opening up new and greater opportunities for personal enrichment and power, capitalism attracted men of ability and ambition from military to business careers and from a way of life in which war was normal into a way of life in which it was a nuisance. Business became the normal state of affairs and war abnormal. The domination of the absolute state was no longer tolerated because men of business wanted freedom for their activities.

---

home. He had the right to be maintained and to be regarded with honour. The others, those who didn't do the fighting, had to make a shift to provide him with the necessaries of life. Such workaday problems were not for him. He looked down on the rest of the world—on women, craftsmen, peasants, all of whom seemed to him to live the lives of slaves."

Thus, in the more advanced industrial states the doctrines of laissez faire and free trade came to dominate the entire social structure. Gradually the bourgeois class, like the military class before it, brought all other classes under its influence, converting the workers themselves to a spirit of economic liberalism and philosophical radicalism. It ushered in an age of democracy, individualism, and rationalism. It provided an atmosphere of peace and became the natural breeding ground of peace movements, religious pacifism, and a determination to prevent, if possible, the recurrence of the scourge of war.

Though Schumpeter's thesis builds up to the hope that imperialism and war may eventually give way to more economical and rational behavior, the fact remains that they still are able to challenge the movement towards rationalism. They persist in the remnants of the military caste, in historic memories and military traditions, and in the minds of those who have not learned to think in terms of economic rationality, but still think in terms of exclusive rivalry. Although not at home in an age of industrialism and entirely inconsistent with it, the behavior pattern of militarism must still be reckoned as a great force. The first World War demonstrated its power to imbue whole nations with the idea of conquest by force of arms and demonstrated how powerful that force may be when backed up by modern technology and industry. But the war itself cannot be blamed on the existence of this economic power; it must be blamed on forces which are still powerful enough, on occasion, to impress the entire economy into their service.

The fact that imperialism is a very old institution and capitalism of very recent origin does not impress those who believe in the Marxian theory as reasonable proof that modern capitalism is not the effective cause of modern imperialism. It is impossible, they contend, to separate imperialistic and capitalistic motives, much less to show that the two institutions run counter to each other. Most critics would admit that the period of free-trade industrial capitalism was anti-imperialistic and pacifistic, but they would insist that this was but a brief interlude in the history of capitalistic development and was true only in one country, England, which had everything to gain from free trade during the period of British industrial supremacy. An appeal to English history is not an appeal to the history of the human race, and most of the world—even most Englishmen, once their industrial supremacy is challenged—believe in safeguarding their own national segments of capitalism by protective tariffs and the promotion of monopolistic privileges. This is advanced as proof that capitalism is not naturally liberal in policy, but is imperialistic.

In reply it can be just as forcefully argued—as Schumpeter argued—that protectionism and monopoly are themselves the products of the same behavior pattern that produced imperialism and that they would not rise spontaneously from the free atmosphere of a competitive economic system. It is certainly true that protective tariffs and monopolistic privileges long antedated modern capitalism, and that there was a tendency to cast them aside wherever free enterprise triumphed. They remained strong only in those countries (Germany being the outstanding case) where the feudal elements remained stronger than the spirit of free enterprise.[19] While the old ruling class of England was being converted into a community of business enterprisers and the rural and artisan classes were being absorbed by industrialism, something quite different was occurring in Germany. Neither the Junkers nor the peasants ever really came under the domination of capitalism, and the result was a Germany in which the old behavior patterns retained a position of superiority over the spirit of commerce and industry.

This contrast of cultures, between Anglo-Saxon countries, on the one hand, and most of the rest of the world, on the other, suggests other contrasts and differences. It is evident that German nationalism soon became more aggressive and far more explosive than British imperialism had ever been, and that German capitalism, though outwardly similar in appearance and organization to that of Great Britain, reflected the national aggressiveness of the state to an extent not matched by British imperial policy at its most imperialistic height, as in the case of the Boer War. But it is significant that British policy, instead of moving ahead on a liberal plane, became more and more like that of Germany under the enormous pressure of the first and the second World Wars. Capi-

---

[19] It is true, of course, that some countries have been imperialistic without being feudal in the European sense.

talism is no match for militarism, and in a world where power is accepted as a condition of national survival there is no choice but to make the economic system serve the ends of power. Like the "conquest of the United States by Spain" the conquest of capitalism by militarism was no mere aphorism. The persistent influence of an atavistic force such as militarism or imperialism is not confined within national boundaries, but spreads to every nation that has reason to fear the consequences of not adopting the same policy of power that threatens it, no matter how atavistic or primitive that policy may be in the light of ideals that are recognized as enlightened and civilized.

When such a policy is accepted as the only alternative, no holds are barred and economic warfare becomes as much a part of the system as military warfare. Tariffs and all other types of trade barrier, monopolies and all other types of trade control, pass for economic weapons, whereas in a world where such instruments are recognized as outmoded and undesirable remnants of a barbaric age they would pass for military, imperial, or political weapons. Obviously free enterprise has no use for such instruments of aggrandizement, and it is as much a contradiction in terms to speak of protective tariffs as instruments of free enterprise as to speak of militarism or imperialism as instruments of free enterprise.

While the atavistic theory of imperialism was intended as an answer to the Marxian interpretation, Schumpeter has been extremely generous to the older theory, both in his article of 1918–19 and in more recent writings. In particular he credits Bauer and Hilferding with a sincere and able attempt to explain modern imperialism in terms of trustified, or monopoly, capitalism, for, says Schumpeter, this theory conserves a unity of principle which has great attraction for every mind that has an analytical bent, and could be generalized to include post-war fascism.[20] Nevertheless, Schumpeter disagrees with the main thesis when he says that the export of capital into noncapitalistic areas is not to be regarded as a verification of the neo-Marxian theory of imperialism, which viewed this phenomenon as a flight of capital from shrinking rates of surplus value prevailing in an old capitalist country, in search of new opportunities for the exploitation of labor in semi-civilized

[20] Schumpeter, *Business Cycles*, II, 696n.

or uncivilized countries. "Of course," says Schumpeter, "there is nothing in this." [21] And as for the leadership of high finance in imperialism, as visualized by the socialists, the average banker's contribution (such as the formation of the steel cartel, for example), was subordinate, while the capitalist agglomerations of the period, with their mergers and financial sponsors, were not, as many believe, "the very incarnation of *Finanzkapitalismus* in the sense of R. Hilferding." [22]

More important, however, is Schumpeter's revision of his own original point of view regarding the source of the imperialistic motive. In 1918 he felt that despite all the forces making for war there still remains a deep and ineradicable community of interest among nations which even cartels and monopolies are unable to overcome and that only industrialists and financiers are the gainers by war. Sooner or later the masses will realize that their interests are being sacrificed and will refuse to endure it. While still adhering to the theory of the atavistic nature of imperialism as a hypothesis that best fits important cases, Schumpeter later came to the belief [23] that "social imperialism" as worked out by Karl Renner [24] is nearer the truth than either the Marxist view that imperialism is an outgrowth of the conditions of trustified capitalism or his own original view that it can be traced to the old militaristic aristocracies. Classes entirely unconnected with the old traditions, especially the lower middle classes, now appear to be the most important centers of imperialist feelings. Without committing himself definitely, Schumpeter feels that the problem must be approached—as Renner approached it—by recognizing that so-called rational ends are not what motivate human behavior, but rather that the fundamental volition arises from impulses which appear from the economic (rational) point of view to be nonrational or irrational.[25] If this is a common characteristic of practically all human behavior outside the economic sphere, the conclusion is unavoidable that the will to fight and to conquer may be found elsewhere than solely in the old professional military class. Thus, the way is opened to the recognition of a true imperialism of a people as a whole, that is, a

[21] *Business Cycles*, I, 432.     [22] *Ibid.*, p. 405n.     [23] *Business Cycles*, II, 696n.

[24] Renner, *Marxismus, Krieg und Internationale;* see also above, p. 179.

[25] This view was expressed by Professor Schumpeter in a letter to the present writer.

*Volksimperialismus* similar to that which Schumpeter had assumed existed only among ancient peoples.[26]

Once it is admitted that the expansionist or imperialistic impulse is as broad as life itself, logic would seem to indicate that we should say so in as few words as possible and let the matter rest. But even the outstanding person to take this point of view, Ernest Seillière, devoted four volumes to this particular philosophy of imperialism [27] and followed this huge work with an "introduction." [28] Seillière uses the word "imperialism" to mean, not the desire for conquest and domination possessed by powerful nations, but the instinctive impulse of every individual or group (including the lower animals and insects, even bees and ants) towards self-expression or domination. This instinctive thirst for power, practically synonymous with Nietzsche's "will to Power," becomes mystical when allied with a justifying principle or supernatural being, thus giving rise to the belief in "chosen people," a "superior race," the divine right of kings, or the idealization of the lower classes, whose "unspoiled instinctive goodness" is supposed to render them fit to govern.[29]

To say that imperialism is an atavistic force which has engulfed all classes and turned them from the road so hopefully marked out by nineteenth-century industrialism and liberalism is to say that a policy, or a political system, inconsistent with free enterprise in economic life, which we call capitalism, and with free enterprise in political affairs, which we call democracy, has gained the upper hand. Not only must there be a type of social control consistent

[26] It is interesting to note in this connection that similarly a German writer regards the post-war period as one of "popular" or *Volksimperialismus,* as distinct from the capitalistic imperialism which preceded it, and the feudal, or "elite," stage of imperialism which characterized the Middle Ages. Each stage is viewed as a widening of popular interest in expansion, with Russia, Japan, and Italy exemplifying the third stage. (In a few more years he could have added Germany to the list). Leadership in this new imperialism, as in former stages, rests in the hands of a select few, but because now the policy is avowedly carried on for the benefit and with the support of the masses, it has the popular backing which capitalist imperialism lacked and accordingly may be more successful.—Eckert, *Alter und neuer Imperialismus.*

[27] Seillière, *La Philosophie de l'impérialisme.*

[28] Seillière, *Introduction à la philosophie de l'impérialisme.*

[29] Spring, *The Vitalism of Count de Gobineau,* p. 5. Count Gobineau (1816–1882), about whom Seillière wrote extensively and more or less sympathetically, was a proponent of anti-intellectualism ("vitalism"), similar in his point of view to Rousseau and Nietzsche.

with free enterprise if the latter is to survive but also it is just as clear that the only type of political system capable of exercising such control is democracy. It is the political system of democracy as well as the economic system of free enterprise against which this atavistic force we call imperialism stands as enemy. It is not alone imperialism in the sense of forced territorial and trade expansion which free enterprise and democracy have to guard against; it is also that whole complex of monopolies and trade barriers which are permitted or encouraged by political considerations. Monopolies and trade barriers are not necessary, either in the Marxian sense of being economically inevitable, or in the political sense of being essential to national survival, and they are certainly not essential to free-enterprise capitalism—they are its deadly enemies. Any political system, therefore, which permits the growth of these forces is as atavistic in relation to free economic and political institutions as is imperialism; and in fact such a political system is to be identified with the same power complex that characterizes imperialism.

Thus, finally, we come nearer the point of this whole long discussion of the theories of imperialism, namely, that imperialism is a political phenomenon—a species of policy which opposes and seeks to destroy all free institutions, including democracy, as well as capitalism, and even especially seeks to turn nationalism from its original character as an expression of popular revolt against autocratic power and infuse it with the spirit of aggressiveness. Being itself a political form, nationalism is an easy victim of the power complex, and much more susceptible to it than is the economic system. Imperialism attacks the economic system through political channels, and the most obvious political channel is the nation-state. That the organization of peoples into regionally segregated political groups is the most potent cause of modern war is the one proposition which today claims the support of those who are unable to accept the Marxian theory that war is a product of capitalism.

## THE DILEMMA OF WORLD GOVERNMENT

Picture to yourself the great trusts and combinations of the early twentieth century, recall their practices in pursuit of market monopolies, magnify their power and their resources a hundredfold, remove from them all the restraint of law, put at their disposal the terrible engines of modern warfare with which to gain their ends, give them the ability to drive to their goals through calling upon sentiments of patriotism and national devotion, and you gain some conception of the menace which faces the world if economic nationalism runs its course unchecked.[30]

What is here called "economic nationalism" is seen reaching its culmination in "economic imperialism." Whether the process is called "economic nationalism" or "economic imperialism," in both cases powerful economic groups are visualized as controlling the state for their own profit and as leading the nation headlong into war if this is necessary to gain their ends. It is apparent, however, that economic nationalism has a much wider application than imperialism. It represents the sort of policy which any nation, small as well as large, can practice simply by erecting trade barriers and other arbitrary restrictions on the free flow of goods, capital, and persons and by permitting monopolies and cartels to have their way in the pursuit of profit. Although economic nationalism implies a policy of defense rather than offense, and of withdrawal from the world rather than participation in foreign commercial and political affairs, it is by nature unilateral rather than reciprocal, and shares with imperialism the same spirit of exclusiveness. As a cause of war, it can be visualized as going directly from some form of economic frustration to open conflict. The various barriers and restrictions placed on trade by a state, by making it difficult for the nations adversely affected to obtain raw materials and markets—so runs the argument—lead to resentment, conflict, and finally war. Another cause of war sometimes described as "economic" is the frustration of individuals caught in the throes of depression, unemployment and bankruptcy. They readily become disciples of leaders who blame the trouble on the policies of other nations—and incite the people to go to war as the solution.[31]

Such explanations as these, it will be noted, do not say that capitalism leads to imperialism and imperialism to war. The emphasis is on economic rather than capitalist and on war rather than imperialism. The desire of the frustrated nations to see the barriers removed can undoubtedly be called an economic motive; that economic motives played as great a role in the creation of the barriers

[30] Sayre, *America Must Act*, pp. 73–74.
[31] See, for example, Staley, "The Economic Side of Stable Peace," *Annals of the American Academy of Political and Social Science*, CCXL (July, 1915), 27–36.

is open to serious doubt in view of the powerful diplomatic, strategic, and other power motives which are always evident in such policies. How much economic content is in the behavior of individuals clamoring for war when frustrated by depression is also open to doubt. Although economic motives are unquestionably present in the desire to overcome the difficulties, the element of economic rationality is not so evident in the readiness—assuming there is a readiness—of people to resort to war as the remedy.

An explanation which sounds very much like the theory of economic nationalism differs, nevertheless, from the latter in stating directly the proposition that the seat of the trouble is political. By this is meant that the world is divided into politically independent nation-states which are potentially rivals and enemies and that the economic aspects contribute to belligerency only—or at least mainly—because they operate in a political framework which in itself is belligerent. The remedy, therefore, is to replace this kind of political system with some form of international government. This, of course, reverses the common socialist view that the political situation would take care of itself, being a product of the economic system, if first the economic system of capitalism were replaced by a co-operative economic order.

Viner, in one of his commentaries on the problem of the economic causes of war, starts "from the belief, hypothesis, or assumption that war is a natural product: of the organization of peoples into regionally segregated political groups—in the modern age, in the form of nation-states; of the awareness on the part of each of these groups of the existence of other groups; of the existence of contacts of various kinds between these groups; and of the emergence from these contacts of conflicts of interest." [32] In short, as Viner sees it, "war is essentially a political phenomenon, a way of dealing with disputes between groups. . . . Given the existence of nation-states, the factors which can contribute to war can be as varied as the activities, the hopes and fears, the passions and generosities and jealousies, of mankind." [33] Although war is essentially a political phenomenon, there are two possible economic

[32] Viner, "Peace as an Economic Problem," in *New Perspectives on Peace,* George B. de Huszar, editor, p. 85.
[33] *Ibid.,* p. 86.

causes of war: "first, the existence of conflicts of national economic interest and, second, the existence of economic conditions which operate to make countries willing to go to war in pursuit of interests which may or may not be themselves economic in character." [34] Under the first category Viner places the rivalry for export markets, for trade routes, and for access to essential commodities. Under the second classification, which covers internal economic conditions conducive to war, he mentions unemployment, depression, and inequalities in national standards of living, all of which, and more besides, may contribute directly or indirectly to conflict. But these are to be viewed, he concludes, only as contributing factors to general unrest and the arousing of international activities and jealousies of a warlike nature; they are effective, not from inherent necessity, but because they operate within a political framework which itself induces rather than curbs conflict. [35]

If the world's basic trouble is political—not economic, not capitalistic—in the sense that every nation-state acts in principle as if it potentially were a superstate, then there is much force in the argument that the remedy is to be found in a formula or technique for removing from nationalism, and therefore from internationalism, the superstructure of sovereign rights which prevents the rule of law from operating on a worldwide scale. There is nothing novel in this solution as an ideal. [36] How can it be realized? Such a reform cannot be forced without violating the democratic principles which it is sought to further. Therefore, can nations be persuaded to subordinate their sovereignty—their "states rights"—to a higher

[34] *Ibid.*, p. 101.                    [35] *Ibid.*, p. 110.

[36] No one has dealt with this problem more expertly or convincingly than Reves, *The Anatomy of Peace*. The thesis of the book is that "collective security without collective sovereignty is meaningless" (p. 210). National sovereignty, as distinct from world organization based on law, continues to be the road to war. "All the peace treaties ever signed, all the alliances ever concluded on this planet, the Covenant of the League of Nations, the United Nations Organization, the principles of collective security, are *identical* in their fundamental conception. They all arbitrarily divide the world into a number of sovereign social units, create a *status quo*, and try to prevent any changes in the established order except by unanimous consent, which makes no sense; or by force, which makes war." (p. 209) "The fundamental problem of regulating the relations between great powers without the permanent danger of major wars cannot be solved so long as absolute sovereign power continues to reside in the nation-states. Unless their sovereign institutions are integrated into higher institutions expressing directly the sovereignty of the community, unless the relations of their peoples are regulated by law, violent conflicts between national units are inevitable." (pp. 213–14)

conception which has as its only purpose the creation of something where nothing now exists? Can they be relied upon voluntarily to fill the vacuum of anarchy with law?

A world constituted of independent nation-states, each devoted to the principle of live and let live and each free from trade barriers and those attributes of sovereignty associated with huge military and naval establishments, would need no supergovernment. World supergovernment is called for only when each nation behaves as if it were a supergovernment. But a supergovernment sufficiently strong to challenge and control the separate powers is meaningless, that is, impossible, unless the powers consent. If two or more of them join forces to rule the rest of the world, there always remain their own uneasy relations with one another to keep the world in fear and turmoil.

Nationalism and sovereignty are inseparable, but it is also true that nationalism which has become deeply involved in the ideology of power is inseparable from the sovereignty of a world authority. In the process of surrendering to the cult of power, nationalism has lost its original democratic and liberal attributes. The problem of securing international order and peace is that of recapturing these attributes by ridding nationalism of its power complex. The first condition of achieving this end is to recognize that nationalism itself, like capitalism, has become the victim of those atavistic types of behavior and institutions which are associated with imperialism and militarism. Absolute sovereignty, or sovereignty with a power complex, is as atavistic as these other forces in a world that has become economically a unit. Indeed, absolute sovereignty is nothing more nor less than nationalism combined with and dominated by the spirit of imperialism and militarism.

The existence of such a system of world politics can only create a no-man's land where it is dangerous to go unarmed and, in the end, it is catastrophic because every nation actually enters it armed. It is here that imperialism flourishes and wars are bred, and it was in this vacuum that nationalism, under the influence of democracy and the freedom of international trade, originally gave promise of establishing the content of order based on law and not on the sovereign right to exercise the power of arms. In such a place it is perfectly safe to free colonies; but to drop them in the grab-bag of a no-man's land is only to risk seeing them gobbled up again. This is the answer of imperialism to such a state of affairs. The pretense of trying to solve the problem by setting up a "mandates system" over colonies is not an alternative which nations dominated by the spirit of imperialism will long recognize as realistic. Such a system is consistent with neither democracy on the one hand nor imperialism on the other.

There would seem to be no escape from the logic that eventually one powerful nation-state will have to rule the world. But this logic derives only from the present system of independent nation-states in which each acts on the principle that it is supreme. The only basic purpose in the grandiose schemes of world government which followed the first and second World Wars has been to prevent this logic from working itself out to its final conclusion. Experience with world organization has so far furnished little ground for optimism. Anything that resembles world organization, even if in reality it can be more exactly evaluated as a kind of "superimperialism" of the great powers, seems better than nothing. It will be recalled that Karl Kautsky [37] adopted this position after the first World War (and was upbraided by Lenin for doing so), but lived to see the complete breakdown of the system on the political and economic level alike.

In 1919 none of the victorious powers dared so much as breathe the thought that the new world order would be imperialistic. Indeed, the powers which established the League of Nations abjured imperialism as a motive in world affairs. The victorious empires were left intact, but there was to be no imperial looting; the colonial areas formerly belonging to the defeated powers were placed in trust under the League of Nations. The mandate system was to be the final solution of the problems inherent in the old system of colonial rivalry. At the close of the second World War the last vestiges of the liberal idealism of 1919 appeared to be giving way to the vaunted realism that the world would have to be run by sheer force.

There can be no solution to history's great dilemma until those who profess to regard imperialism and war as the greatest of all evils do more than fight these fires with more fire. The lesson is

[37] See above, p. 157.

there—that peace is not the end of war, but the opposite of war. It cannot be maintained by the methods of war, but only by the methods of peace. Like any virtue it must be self-sufficient—it cannot be enforced. A peace that must be enforced is merely an armistice between wars. The world has become so accustomed to war that it regards peace as the outcome of conflict and war as the outcome of what happens in peace. Actually both the war and the peace which enter into this way of thinking are the same things, not opposites. They form a vicious circle in which the seekers for a solution go round and round, from economics to politics and from politics to economics, trying to find a way out. Obviously there is no way out at this level.

All the schemes for world organization are doomed to failure unless shorn of the remaining vestiges of authority based on naked power, which is the product of hate and fear. There can be no "brave new world" on this kind of basis. There is no solution to the power problem in terms of power itself. We know that the vast majority of mankind desire to solve this problem, but it is also evident from their reactions that they regard as ridiculously naïve any scheme of order based on any other principle than force. Yet the very political principle they reject as unrealistic and naïve is implicit in the kind of economic system which socialists and liberals alike have always professed to want.

Most people profess to want freedom—economic and political freedom, as well as freedom from war; yet they continue to nurture, protect, defend, and endure, if not to admire, the system of naked power, because it is associated with nationalism and patriotism, which in turn are so bound up with historic and romantic memories that the whole complex has become a religion. The cult of freedom and liberalism takes on the appearance of a little heretical group in a great mass of orthodox believers. To ask, therefore, that people give up the system of naked power is to ask them to give up their religion. Nominally, a large part of the world—including all that had laid claim to the acceptance of Christianity—has foresworn the religion of naked power; actually, it still worships at the old shrine.

However much the liberal mind may be captivated by the idea that all that is necessary for the prevention of imperialism and war is the suppression of the barriers which create and perpetuate political and "economic" nationalism, this point of view fails to impress those who are convinced that the only remedy is a world-wide conversion to socialism. Likewise, it makes no impression on that not inconsiderable group who are frankly nationalists and imperialists. Akin to this group are the cynics, the indifferent, and those who take a pessimistic view of all endeavors for human enlightenment.

Finally, the idealists are convinced that nothing short of a considerable improvement in human morality and a willingness to practice the irenic virtues will solve the world's political and economic problems. From this point of view, nationalism is as hard to eradicate from human behavior patterns as are the imperialism and militarism and mercantilism which are supposed by the liberals to disappear automatically with the suppression of economic and military nationalism. Convinced that all these *isms* are of the same pattern, the idealist can only work towards raising the solution to the higher level of morality. Not that most idealists are opposed to any program of international organization now attainable which promises simultaneously to preserve peace and remove the immediate causes of conflict; but their own particular kind of realism convinces them that more than likely such mechanical schemes, without a high and unified and universal moral purpose behind them, can promise little more than another uneasy period of jockeying by nationalists, imperialists, mercantilists and militarists for another contest of power.

## FITTING THE MEANS TO THE END

Short of a moral revolution which would endow all men with the virtues necessary to produce harmony, but which means waiting for the millennium, is there any way out of the world's dilemma more nearly within our grasp, more practical and hardheaded than waiting for the advent of human perfection, on the one hand, and more hopeful of success than schemes which, on the other hand, propose to go to the opposite extreme of solving the problem of force in terms of force? It is not a matter of agreeing upon ends, but of finding means to a given end, or at least of finding and using good means in the hope that the end product can be relied upon to take care of itself. It is a matter, in other words, of finding and using means consistent with peace, and from this point of view it can be questioned whether the grandiose schemes of world organization are consistent with either peace, democracy, or any of the freedoms associated with peace and democracy.

When students of the problem of world chaos cast about for alternatives to this condition, they naturally try to formulate an answer in terms of the symbols of power with which they are already familiar. These symbols stand out in all schemes of world organization. Starting with the common view that an alternative must be found to the bad system of competing nationalism and the arrogant exercise of sovereign rights based on force and that the alternative must preserve all the essentials of freedom associated with democracy, the advocates of world organization soon disagree concerning whether the nations should be bound into a loose federation to preserve the peace or coalesced into a system of collective sovereignty. Disillusionment sets in when it is realized that democracy may have to be surrendered along with nationalism, that an essential freedom may disappear with sovereignty, and that, in any likely solution on these terms, a few Great Powers will undertake the actual ordering and forbidding and will exercise a police power which is not very different from that ancient power over life and death associated with imperialism. This is the dilemma of the peacemakers.

While this solution may appear to be an alternative to chaos, it is more accurately to be regarded as an alternative to old-fashioned, imperialistic conquest of the whole world by a single Great Power. In reality, the world state as usually visualized represents a proposal for nations to do collectively—actually for a few strong nations to do collectively, the rest being forced to accept their solution—what the most powerful and aggressive appears likely to do of its own accord. Between these two possibilities there is not in reality much room for choice so far as freedom and democracy are concerned. The main appeal in favor of collective action is the hope that world unity might thus be attained without the devastating war which seems inevitably associated with world conquest by a single Power.

The only real alternative to either of these kindred prospects must evidently be couched in symbols which are the opposite both of imperialism and of so-called collective sovereignty. It must be an alternative which invites instead of repels reconciliation, which aims to cleanse sovereignty and nationalism of their power complex and democracy of its hypocritical reliance on armaments, and which replaces the weapon of violence with nonviolence in its approach to the problem of creating a peaceful world system. Hard as it is for modern, sophisticated men to recognize this sort of program as an alternative to anything, least of all to take it seriously, it is as old as the Christian religion itself and as modern as Mohandas Gandhi's movement in India.

Indeed, the ideal of democracy in the modern world is an affirmation of the fact that men can live peaceably together without recourse to violence and that every day they resolve their differences by the technique of nonviolence. The rule of the majority, within the framework of law which protects the rights of the minority as well as those of the majority, is a revolutionary concept—and a great missionary ideal—which originated in a world that had experienced no moral revolution more radical than acceptance of the principle that only free men are capable of running a free society. In an age when men were determined to be free from autocratic rule and exploitation and infused nationalism with the spirit of democracy, they were reacting from the very symbols which today characterize the schemes of world organization. The failure or weakness of their ideal of democracy was not internal, within the nation-state, for here men established their constitutional liberties. They failed in retaining the ideology of power, from which they had revolted, in the field of international relations, and this ideology has remained to poison national democracy itself. The realization of democratic principles involves not only discarding autocratic rule at home, but also a constant seeking to be free of such old attributes of autocracy as militarism and power politics in the conduct of foreign relations. These symbols corrupt the political ideal of freedom and create distrust, fear, hate, and conflict.

Democracy depends for its strength and survival on a technique of tolerance and mutuality. Without this technique democracy could not exist, and democracy is weakest where the principle of nonviolence in the conduct of human affairs is weakest. The use of police power for maintenance of law is also most evident where the attributes of democracy are weakest. To say, as is sometimes maintained with a great show of wisdom, that "in the final analysis society is based upon force," is to reverse the logic of what really happens in a democracy. It is true to say that the use of force, in the sense of police power, is the last resort of a democratic society. Only of a society which lacks the attributes of democracy can it be said that in the final analysis, or basically, does society depend upon force.

There is, then, no problem within a truly democratic state which calls for a solution of the kind set forth by the advocates of a world state, or a system of collective sovereignty. Democracy requires a democratic constitution and an alert and intelligent electorate, but these are not what the advocates of a world state propose to supply. They propose to supply only that element of force, or police power, which is the last resort of a democratic society, not its first line of security. Thus they reverse the process, and in so doing make no contribution to the world's need for a technique of reconciliation.

The only political movement which offers some hope of reconciliation is that of Gandhi, but even this movement appears unrealistic to the Western mind and to much of the Indian mind as well. But unless a solution can be found in this direction, the only alternative is, indeed, the present one which places power above democracy, armament above disarmament, ordering and forbidding above freedom, ordered enterprise above free enterprise, and distrust above tolerance, mutuality, and reconciliation. But so hardened are we to thinking in terms of a technique which associates freedom with a victory of arms and the maintenance of armaments that the very thought of Gandhi and his technique of nonviolent resistance arouses within us a mixture of amused respect and incredulity and an uneasy feeling that it might work, combined with a feeling that, after all, this is no way to carry on a struggle for independence.

Gandhi's political technique of nonviolent resistance—of organized mass disobedience to imperial authority and power—is by no means to be confused with the sort of nonresistance which characterizes certain pacifist ideology, as those who have had to deal with it well know. It must be understood as a political movement with a positive, not a negative, charge. To Gandhi, the essential character of his movement is a concern, not with ends, but with means, since means can be relied upon to have ends consistent with them.[38] Nevertheless, the method of resisting the authority of violence, not with counterviolence, but with nonviolence is consistent with the end of achieving a pacific order, and it is consistent with the professions of democracy. While the resistance of violence with violence creates the sort of vicious circle which is epitomized in the statement that "the principal cause of war is war itself," the resistance of violence with nonviolence offers an escape from this self-perpetuating cycle of violence. It lifts pacifism from the metaphysical to the political level, which is the domain of practical men and far-from-perfect human nature, and it replaces the hopelessness of thinking that the end of war must await some sort of moral revolution with the practical outlook that here is a technique which works with human nature as it is, once a great teacher and leader demonstrates the way.

Gandhi has at least tried to break the vicious circle which begins with violence and always ends in violence, which is more than can be said of the more familiar type of political movement. His movement has succeeded, so far as it has succeeded at all, by its hardheaded appeal to a potential following which consists of men who are no closer to the millennium of human perfection than other men, and in fact who have been much less favored by the preachments of brotherhood and the virtues of reconciliation than men of the Western World. In a country which is already disarmed, or at most weakly armed, it is undoubtedly easier to gain adherents to a technique of resistance based on nonviolence than in countries where armaments are strong, but even in India the movement of nonviolence has depended upon bold and dynamic leadership. It has not sprung spontaneously from the masses, as it could do only if the masses were already impregnated with the idealism usually associated with the millennium. Its lesson for the rest of the world is not that nations should surrender their sovereignty in one great emotional outburst of resignation to the beauties of collective

[38] Sibley, in *The Political Theories of Modern Pacifism,* presents an excellent survey of pacifist political philosophy and clarifies the positive nature of Gandhi's movement.

sovereignty or join hands in a world organization to preserve the peace by force of arms. Rather, the movement is motivated by a desire to attain independence and sovereignty, and its lesson is that this desirable state can be fought for without violence and without compromising the principles of democracy. It differs from other struggles for independence and statehood only in the nature of its technique. It rejects military power as the symbol of freedom and thus seeks to avoid the pitfalls which have entrapped every nation which has found that the very retention of military power is a standing invitation to surrender, sooner or later, its independence.

Just as Gandhi's technique indicates that the way to secure independence and democracy is to fight for them without arms, it also shows that "the way to disarm is to disarm" and that both these movements call for dynamic leadership. It recognizes that disarmament by common agreement is difficult, if not impossible, to attain. International conferences for this purpose are unavoidably conducted in an atmosphere of mutual suspicion and jealousy and end in quibbles over what constitutes armament and disarmament. They fail to remove the suspicion with which they begin, that each party to the discussions is hiding or holding back information about what it really intends to do. Yet the fact that disarmament is generally regarded as basic to the maintenance of peace and that a world police force is essential for the maintenance of disarmament indicates with complete clarity the need of making force subordinate to, and the last resort of, the democratic system. It may appear as politically unrealistic to expect any nation to disarm unilaterally as for all nations to disarm by concerted action or for nations to surrender their sovereignty. Yet unilateral action is inherent in the nature of sovereignty, and the reduction of armaments is a proposition around which it is possible to rally much popular support, not all of which, by any means, is due to idealism, much being ascribable to its appeal to the interests of taxpayers. Such action is no less idealistic than democracy itself, and it is more consistent with the professions of democracy to take a bold and challenging step of this nature than forever to act on the basis of suspicion, fear, and frustration. Confidence that other nations will follow if one influential nation takes the lead is inherent in the action itself.

It is inherent in the nature of things that like begets like. This is what was meant by those who long ago warned of the "conquest of the United States by Spain" and in more recent years of the conquest of the United States by the methods of Hitler. Violence begets more violence. It is just as true that sincere gestures of pacific intentions invite reciprocal action, but the two methods cannot successfully be mixed. The mailed fist enclosed in a silk glove fools no one very long, and gestures which vacillate between belligerent talk and the honeyed words of diplomacy inspire confidence in no one. Men know from experience that where these ingredients are mixed the dominant one is the show of power. It is the old behavior pattern still dominant over the new, but the fact that the new can exist at all gives promise that in time it may itself become dominant. Men have already learned to behave themselves and to obey their laws, and it is this consent, not the threat of punishment and the presence of police power, which makes government possible. Gandhi, by reversing the Jeffersonian logic that government depends upon the consent of the governed, has succeeded in elevating into a powerful political weapon the doctrine of nonviolent resistance to government which is not wanted and to methods of government which are not consistent with the pacific nature of consent.[39] In doing this he has simply substituted new means for old without in the least trying to revolutionize the basis of government or to change the ends which man as a political creature regards as sacred.

The concern with means which characterizes Gandhi's ideology does not differ from the concern with means which characterizes militant or imperialist ideology, but whereas Gandhi refuses to become involved in any statement of ultimate ends, the ideologists of violence just as characteristically profess to seek the end of peace by the methods they employ. The first approach disarms the antagonist; the second arms him. The first holds that the means justifies the end; the second, that the end justifies the means. The very statement that the end justifies the means implies a choice of means as well as an ability to know the end, and it implies that there are appropriate and inappropriate means of obtaining the end. But to those who believe that means have their own abiding end there is never any problem of first knowing the end before the means can be chosen. Thus they seek to avoid the danger that the statement

39 Sibley, *op. cit.*, pp. 5–6.

of ends tends to create means which themselves become identified as ends. For when men envision some particular form of political organization or state as the end, it becomes institutionalized and the shortest possible cut to its attainment seems justified. This invariably means a resort to power.[40] When it is thought that the end has been achieved, other ends arise to take its place, but the means which have become identified with attainment of the first objective also become identified with the second and are not abandoned. Means become the perpetual slaves of stated ends, and all hope of breaking this vicious circle by a new choice of means remains doomed.

The discussion of nonviolent resistance to outside forces always raises the question of how this sort of policy can be used to maintain internal order and prevent civil war. The answer starts with the reminder that the policy of nonviolent resistance is not a synonym for anarchy. It is not a substitute for government or for the sanctions of law and order within the state. It is an arm of government in external relations, but at the same time a substitute for violence in the conduct of those relations. It is a substitute for violence in those areas of conflict where sovereignty and law and order end, namely, in the no-man's land between national sovereignties. The exercise of police power within a nation is a collective business of organized society to curb violators of the law and order of that society. War, on the other hand, is the opposite of collective activity among nations. It is the result of anarchy in a situation which contains no element of reconciliation. The victory of one nation over another, or of one part of a nation over another part, or the establishment of a world supergovernment, can eliminate this anarchy, but it cannot provide the basis for reconciliation. The technique of nonviolent resistance, in addition to being a substitute for violent resistance in international affairs, provides a basis for international reconciliation and thus works against the need for armaments and likewise against the need for a supergovernment, which the use of naked power makes inevitable.

The greatest danger is that a country, having won its independence by nonviolent methods, will be tempted to resort to civil war to maintain its former unity. This indicates, of course, that the

40 Cf. *ibid.*, pp. 7–8.

country is not yet ready for unity and may, indeed, reflect the fact
that the former appearance of unity was merely the result of an
artificial unification imposed from the outside. The only alternative, from the point of view of nonviolent resistance, is to let the
country fall apart into separate communities. This does not pre·
clude the power behind the principle of nonviolence from working
towards reconciliation. In fact, it gives it fertile soil in which to
work, whereas the maintenance of unity by force is to surrender
hope of reconciliation.

To reply that human nature still demands methods of violence
by which to attain its ends is to say that the great masses of men do
not really want such institutions as democracy and freedom, but
are willing to go on accepting the leadership of those who believe
that the only practical solution of the world's trouble is the kind of
authority represented by imperialism and militarism, or of those
who believe that this same kind of authority can be transmuted
into some sort of league to enforce peace. This kind of leadership
certainly exists in great abundance, and the only alternative which
now commends itself to the advocates of world government is the
replacement of national sovereignty with collective sovereignty.
The main difficulty in realizing this ideal is that it depends on intellectual leadership, which is of necessity identified with the problem of leading people towards the millennium of moral regenera-
tion on a world-wide scale. This is politically unrealistic. Such a
movement must have its roots in political leadership; yet it is inconceivable that leaders will be found in any country who would
be able to rally a following sufficiently large to get control of
the government on a platform of surrendering sovereignty. If the
realization of this end depends on the action of a world organization like the United Nations, which is dominated by Powers still
functioning—even though collectively—on the basis of the old
power system and ideology, the prospects are dim indeed.

Political leadership must originate in a political environment,
and the issues on which leadership is based must be positive. The
collective meeting of representatives of sovereign states is not,
despite its outward appearance, a political environment at all, but
essentially a power environment. Certainly the surrender of sovereignty is not a positive issue around which political action can be

built; it is an entirely negative issue. To struggle for the freedom of one's own country, to resist the sovereignty of another, is still the same powerful force it was when modern nationalism was in its youth. Gandhi's long campaign, the most pacific of political movements, could never have been started had his fight for freedom from British sovereignty included the negative and countervailing idea of surrendering India's new-won sovereignty to a world state. Nation-states simply do not fight to join or to lose their sovereignty in other states, much less superstates. The idea of surrendering sovereignty is as negative as the idea of nonresistance—in fact, it is a species of nonresistance.

Gandhi never made the mistake of trying to rally followers around the banner of a negative idea like this. The success of his movement lies in the fact that nonviolent resistance is positive, and therefore amenable to political technique. Compared with the negative and artificial attack on sovereignty, it is an exceedingly realistic and hardheaded approach to the political dilemma created by man's failure to treat freedom and sovereignty as the children of democracy. It is a reaffirmation that democracy itself is a technique of nonviolence and that reliance on force blights both democracy and sovereignty. Gandhi's movement requires, not a moral revolution or a perfect race of men, but a thoroughly practical and worldly wisdom which knows good means from bad in the international field as in the humbler walks of life. Life without good means is irrational and intolerable, and the deplorable state of world politics attests to this truth more dramatically than it has ever before been attested. Practical men know that this is true, but are ashamed to express faith in means which sound as unmanly as does "nonviolent resistance," which they associate with a humble little man wrapped in a sheet. That his worldly wisdom can be greater than theirs seems somehow utterly ridiculous to men famed for their "know-how" in making everything from baby carriages to atomic bombs. Use of inappropriate means to make these things would end in failure, but no more certainly than attempts to produce peace by means of violence.

As a positive movement, centering on means which are pacific, the policy of resistance by nonviolent means must compete with that other positive movement in the field of political action which

adheres to means which are nonpacific. It is not a question, therefore, of what people want—they want peace, which is, not the
termination of war, but the opposite of war. The only question is
whether they want pacific or nonpacific means of attaining this
end. And just as much as they want peace, peoples want sovereignty. If this seems like the opposite of wanting peace, it is not because sovereignty and nationalism are in themselves warlike, but
because warlike means have so long been used to secure them. The
fact that nation-states have won and maintained their independence
by war instead of by organized nonviolent resistance has stamped
sovereignty and nationalism with the mark of violence instead of
the mark of peace. World politics is as much in need of a type of control consistent with democracy as capitalism is in need of a type of
control consistent with free enterprise.

It has been implied at various points in this book that the world's
basic trouble arises from the fact that people generally behave as if
they want such things as imperialism, militarism, totalitarianism,
and even war and that they do not want democracy, freedom, free
enterprise, and peace. When one deals with these matters at close
range, it does indeed appear that people get what they want, even
what they deserve, bad as it is. Only when a more detached view
enables us to see that the fault lies principally in their choice of
means rather than in their choice of ends does the whole question
take on a different aspect. It is true that there are imperialists who
want empires and militarists who want armies and navies and that
they regard these things as ends in themselves, worth keeping for
their own sakes. For such minds there is no question of discarding
these institutions when they have accomplished their purpose, because they have no purpose outside themselves.

On the other hand, there are vast numbers of people who do not
worship these institutions as ends, yet at the same time regard any
manifestation of power as the means to some such end as national
independence. These are the "practical" people of the world, interested more in means than in ends—the busy people who are always working with and manipulating economic and political
machinery. They want wealth, and they want peace and freedom.
They have learned that the way to acquire wealth is through work,
which is one of the great irenic virtues; but they have not learned

that the ways to peace and freedom are equally pacific. On this issue they accept the methods of the imperialist and the militarist, and in accepting their methods they inevitably accept their values. Politically, they want nationalism and sovereignty, and then they proceed to ruin these values by seeking or following methods of securing them which only burden them with the weight of imperialistic and militaristic machinery. Then the machinery flies back and hits them in the face, but instead of placing the blame where it belongs, their capacity for self-deception is such that they blame the economic system or, equally bad, if they blame the political system, they single out some value such as sovereignty instead of military force by means of which they try to maintain it. This is infantile behavior in a situation which calls for maturity.

The people of the world have been much quicker to reach economic maturity than political maturity. In the one field they act rationally; they know what they want and how to get it. Even more realistically, they have become so preoccupied with intelligent methods of production and distribution that it is truer to say that they know how to get and that they accept the end-products as a matter of course. This concentration on good means to the point of forgetfulness about ends is itself a sign of maturity. But in the realm of politics the peoples of the world have yet a long way to go in reaching this high level.

It is one of the old hopes of political economy that the lessons of economic life will in time penetrate into the political sphere and teach people to use intelligent means of producing good political results. The danger is that the methods of politics will so penetrate the economic field as to turn its methods into something just as irrational and immature as those of politics. Indeed, this process has gone so far already as to raise all the problems with which we have been dealing in an attempt to understand the nature of imperialism and war.

# BIBLIOGRAPHY

Allin, Cephas Daniel, Australasian Preferential Tariffs and Imperial Free Trade. Minneapolis, University of Minnesota Press, 1929.

Anderson, James, The Interest of Great-Britain with Regard to Her American Colonies, Considered. London, T. Cadell, 1782.

Angell, James W., Financial Foreign Policy of the United States. New York, The Council on Foreign Relations, 1933.

Bacon, Francis, The Works of Francis Bacon; with a life of the author, by Basil Montagu. 3 vols. Philadelphia, Parry & McMillan, 1857.

Barnes, Harry Elmer, World Politics in Modern Civilization; the contributions of nationalism, capitalism, imperialism and militarism to human culture and international anarchy. New York, Knopf, 1930.

Bauer, Otto, "Die Akkumulation des Kapitals," Die Neue Zeit, XXXI [1] (1913), 831–38, 862–74.

—— Die Nationalitätenfrage und die Sozialdemokratie. Vienna, Verlag der Wiener Volksbuchhandlung, Marx-Studien, 1907. 2d edition, 1924.

Bentham, Jeremy, The Works of Jeremy Bentham; ed. by John Bowring. 11 vols. Edinburgh, Tait, 1843.

Bernard, L. L., War and Its Causes. New York, Holt, 1944.

Bernstein, Edward, Evolutionary Socialism; tr. by Edith C. Harvey. London, Independent Labour Party, 1909.

—— "Die Kolonialfrage und der Klassenkampf," Sozialistische Monatshefte, XIII (December, 1907), 988–96.

Blaisdell, Donald C., European Financial Control in the Ottoman Empire; a study of the establishment, activities, and significance of the administration of the Ottoman Public Debt. New York, Columbia University Press, 1929.

Blakeslee, George H. [Review of Thomas Parker Moon, Imperialism and World Politics], American Historical Review, XXXII (April, 1927), 597–99.

Bogart, Ernest Ludlow, Economic History of the American People, New York, Longmans, 1930.

Bonn, M. J., The Crumbling of Empire; the disintegration of world economy. London, Allen and Unwin, 1938.

Boulding, K. E., "In Defense of Monopoly," Quarterly Journal of Economics, LIX (August, 1945), 524–42.

Brailsford, Henry Noel, The War of Steel and Gold. London, Bell, 1914.

Brougham, Henry, An Inquiry into the Colonial Policy of the European Powers. 2 vols. Edinburgh, Printed by D. Willison for E. Balfour, Manners, and Miller, 1803.

Buckle, Henry Thomas, History of Civilization in England. 3 vols. London, Longmans, 1868.

Bukharin, Nikolai I., Historical Materialism; a system of sociology. New York, International Publishers, 1925.

—— Imperialism and World Economy. New York, International Publishers, 1929.

—— Der Imperialismus und die Akkumulation des Kapitals. Vienna-Berlin, Verlag für Literatur und Politik, 1926.

Bukharin, Nikolai I., and others, Marxism and Modern Thought. New York, Harcourt, Brace, 1935.

Burns, Emile, A Handbook of Marxism. New York, International Publishers, 1935.

Byron, George Gordon Byron, 6th baron, Letters and Journals; with notices of his life, by Thomas Moore. 2 vols. London, Murray, 1830.

Calwer, Richard, "Kolonialpolitik und Sozialdemokratie," Sozialistische Monatshefte, XIII (March, 1907), 192–200.

Carr, Edward Hallett, The Twenty Years' Crisis, 1919–1939. London, Macmillan, 1939.

Cassel, Gustav, From Protectionism through Planned Economy to Dictatorship. Cobden Memorial Lecture, London, 1934. Reprinted in International Conciliation, No. 303 (October, 1934), pp. 307–25.

Clark, Grover, The Balance Sheets of Imperialism. New York, Columbia University Press, 1936.

—— A Place in the Sun. New York, Macmillan, 1936.

Clark, Walter Ernest, Josiah Tucker, Economist. New York, Columbia University Press, 1903.

Clough, Shepard Bancroft, and Charles Woolsey Cole, Economic History of Europe. Boston, Heath, 1941.

Conant, Charles A., The United States in the Orient. Boston and New York, Houghton, Mifflin, 1900.

Cowper, William, "The Winter Morning Walk," in The Task. New York, Leavitt & Allen, 1859, Book V.

Cramb, J. A., The Origins and Destiny of Imperial Britain. New York, Dutton, 1915.

Culbertson, William Smith, International Economic Policies. New York and London, Appleton, 1925.

—— "Raw Materials and Foodstuffs in the Commercial Policies of Nations," Annals of the American Academy of Political and Social Science, CXII (March, 1924), 1–145.

Cunow, Heinrich, "Handelsvertrags- und imperialistische Expansionspolitik," Die Neue Zeit, XVIII² (1900), 207–15, 234–42.

—— "Was ist Imperialismus?", Die Neue Zeit, XXXIII (1915), 199–200.

Curtis, Lionel, The Commonwealth of Nations. London, Macmillan, 1918.

Dickinson, H. D., Economics of Socialism. London, Oxford University Press, 1939.

—— "Price Formation in a Socialist Community," *Economic Journal*, XLIII (June, 1933), 237–50.

Diffie, Bailey W., and Justine Whitfield Diffie, Porto Rico, a Broken Pledge; ed. by Harry Elmer Barnes. New York, Vanguard Press, 1931.

Duret, J., Le Marxisme et les crises. Paris, Gallimard, 1933.

Eckert, Christian, Alter und neuer Imperialismus. Jena, Fischer, 1932.

Edwards, George W., The Evolution of Finance Capitalism. New York, Longmans, 1938.

Egerton, Hugh Edward, British Colonial Policy in the XXth Century. London, Methuen, 1922.

Emery, Sarah E. V., Imperialism in America; its rise and progress. Lansing, Mich. [Reynolds], 1892.

Engelbrecht, H. C., Johann Gottlieb Fichte; a study of his political writings with special reference to his nationalism. New York, Columbia University Press, 1933.

Faulkner, Harold Underwood, American Economic History; rev. ed. New York, Harper, 1931.

Fay, C. R., Great Britain from Adam Smith to the Present Day. New York and London, Longmans, 1928.

Fay, Sidney Bradshaw, The Origins of the World War. 2 vols. New York, Macmillan, 1928.

Ferguson, William Scott, Greek Imperialism. Boston and New York, Houghton, Mifflin, 1913.

Fisher, Irving, 100% Money. New York, Adelphi, 1935; rev. ed., 1937.

Flügel, Felix, and Harold U. Faulkner, Readings in the Economic and Social History of the United States. New York, Harper, 1929.

Foerster, F. W., Europe and the German Question. New York, Sheed and Ward, 1940.

Fowler, W. Warde, The City-State of the Greeks and Romans. London, Macmillan, 1931.

Frank, Tenney, Roman Imperialism. New York, Macmillan, 1914.

Fraser, Herbert F., Foreign Trade and World Politics. New York and London, Knopf, 1926.

Glover, T. R., Democracy in the Ancient World. London, Cambridge University Press, 1927.

Gooch, G. P., History of Modern Europe, 1878–1919. New York, Holt; London, Cassell, 1923.

—— "Imperialism," in The Heart of the Empire, 2d ed., London, Unwin, 1907.

Gourvitch, Alexander, Survey of Economic Theory on Technological Change and Employment. Washington, D.C., Works Projects Administration, National Research Project, 1940.

Grossmann, Henryk, Das Akkumulations- und Zusammenbruchsgesetz des kapitalistischen Systems. Leipzig, Hirschfeld, 1929.

—— "Eine neue Theorie über Imperialismus und die soziale Revolution," *Archiv für die Geschichte des Sozialismus und der Arbeiterbewegung*, XIII (1928), 141–92.

Grundy, G. B., History of the Greek and Roman World. London, Methuen, 1926.

Hall, R. L., The Economic System in a Socialist State. London, Macmillan, 1937.

Hansen, Alvin H., Fiscal Policy and Business Cycles. New York, Norton, 1941.

Harrington, James, Oceana. Morley's Universal Library edition.

Harris, Seymour E. [Review of Quincy Wright, ed., *A Study of War*], *American Economic Review*, XXXIII (June, 1943), 417–21.

Hashagen, J., "Marxismus und Imperialismus," *Jahrbücher für Nationalökonomie und Statistik*, CXIII (July, 1919), 193–216.

Hawtrey, R. G., Economic Aspects of Sovereignty. New York and London, Longmans, 1930.

Hayek, F. A. von, ed., Collectivist Economic Planning; critical studies on the possibilities of socialism by N. G. Pierson, Ludwig von Mises, Georg Halm, and Enrico Barone; ed. with an introduction and a concluding essay by F. A. von Hayek. London, Routledge, 1935.

Hearnshaw, F. J. C., Germany the Aggressor throughout the Ages. London, Chambers, 1940.

Heaton, Herbert, "The Economic Impact on History," in Joseph R. Strayer, ed., The Interpretation of History (Princeton, Princeton University Press, 1943), pp. 85–117.

Heitland, W. E., The Roman Republic. 3 vols. London, Cambridge University Press, 1909.

Hilferding, Rudolph, Das Finanzkapital; eine Studie über die jüngste Entwicklung des Kapitalismus. Vienna, Brand, 1910.

Hobbes, Thomas, Leviathan. Everyman's Library. London & Toronto, Dent; New York, Dutton [1940].

Hobson, John A., Confessions of an Economic Heretic. 3d rev. ed. London, Allen and Unwin, 1938.

—— An Economic Interpretation of Investment. London, *The Financial Review of Reviews*, 1911.

—— The Economics of Distribution. New York, Macmillan, 1900.

—— The Evolution of Modern Capitalism. London, Scott, 1894.

—— Imperialism; a study. New York, Pott, 1902.

—— The Industrial System. London, Longmans, 1909.

—— The Psychology of Jingoism. London, Richards, 1901.

—— Rationalisation and Unemployment. London, Allen and Unwin, 1930.

—— Towards International Government. New York, Macmillan, 1915.

—— Veblen. London, Chapman, 1936.

—— The War in South Africa. London, Nisbet, 1900.

Hook, Sidney, Towards the Understanding of Karl Marx; a revolutionary interpretation. New York, John Day, 1933.

Hovde, Brynjolf J., "Socialistic Theories of Imperialism Prior to the Great War," *Journal of Political Economy*, XXXVI (October, 1928), 569–91.

Humphrey, Edward Frank, An Economic History of the United States. New York, Century, 1931.

Huszar, George B. de, ed., New Perspectives on Peace. Chicago, University of Chicago Press, 1944.

Innis, H. A., "The Penetrative Powers of the Price System," *The Canadian Journal of Economics and Political Science*, IV (August, 1938), 299–319.

Jenks, Leland Hamilton, Our Cuban Colony; ed. by Harry Elmer Barnes. New York, Vanguard Press, 1928.

Kat Angelino, A. D. A. de, Colonial Policy; abridged tr. from the Dutch by G. J. Renier, in collaboration with the author. 2 vols. Chicago, University of Chicago Press, 1931.

Kautsky, Karl, "Aeltere und neuere Kolonialpolitik," *Die Neue Zeit*, XVI (1897–1898), 769–81, 801–16.

—— Bernstein und das Sozialdemokratische Programm. Stuttgart, Dietz, 1899.

—— The Class Struggle (Erfurt Program), 8th ed., 1907; tr. by William E. Bohn. Chicago, Kerr, 1910.

—— "Finanzkapital und Krisen," *Die Neue Zeit*, XXIX$^1$ (1911), 764–72; 797–804; 838–46; 874–83.

—— "Der Imperialismus," *Die Neue Zeit*, XXXII$^2$ (1914), 908–22.

—— "Krisentheorien," *Die Neue Zeit*, XX$^2$ (1901–1902), 37–47; 76–81; 110–18; 133–43.

—— Nationalstaat, imperialistischer Staat und Staatenbund. Nuremberg, Fränkischen Verlagsanstalt & Buchdruckeri G. m. b. H, 1915.

—— The Road to Power; tr. by A. M. Simons. Chicago, Black, 1909.

—— Terrorism and Communism; tr. by W. H. Kerridge. London, Allen and Unwin, 1920.

—— "Zwei Schriften zum Umlernen," *Die Neue Zeit*, XXXIII$^2$ (1915), 33–42; 71–81; 107–16; 138–46.

Kepner, Jr., Charles David, and Jay Henry Soothill, The Banana Empire; ed. by Harry Elmer Barnes. New York, Vanguard Press, 1935.

Keynes, John Maynard, Essays in Biography. New York, Harcourt, 1933.

—— The General Theory of Employment Interest and Money. New York, Harcourt, 1936.

Kirkland, Edward C., A History of American Economic Life. New York, Crofts, 1932.

Knight, Frank H., "Bertrand Russell on Power," *Ethics*, XLIX (April, 1939), 253–85.

—— "Ethics and the Economic Interpretation," *Quarterly Journal of Economics*, XXXVI (May, 1922), 454–81.

—— "The Place of Marginal Economics in a Collectivist System," *American Economic Review*, Supplement, XVI (March, 1936), 255–66.

—— "Two Economists on Socialism," *Journal of Political Economy*, XLVI (April, 1938), 241–50.

Knight, Melvin M., The Americans in Santo Domingo; ed. by Harry Elmer Barnes. New York, Vanguard Press, 1928.

—— Morocco as a French Economic Venture; a study in open door imperialism. New York, Appleton-Century, 1938.

—— "Water and the Course of Empire in North Africa," *Quarterly Journal of Economics*, XLIII (November, 1928), 44–93.

Knight, Melvin M., Harry Elmer Barnes, and Felix Flügel, Economic History of Europe. Boston, Houghton, 1928.

Knorr, Klaus E., British Colonial Theories, 1570–1850. Toronto, University of Toronto Press, 1944.

Knowles, L. C. A., The Economic Development of the British Overseas Empire. London, Routledge, 1924.

Kohn, Hans, The Idea of Nationalism; a study in its origins and background. New York, Macmillan, 1944.

Lange, Oskar, "On the Economic Theory of Socialism," *Review of Economic Studies*, Vol. IV: October, 1936, pp. 53–71; February, 1937, pp. 123–42.

Langer, William L., "A Critique of Imperialism," *Foreign Affairs*, XIV (October, 1935), 102–19.

—— The Diplomacy of Imperialism, 1890–1902. 2 vols. New York, Knopf, 1935.

Laurat, Lucien, L'Accumulation du capital d'après Rosa Luxembourg, suivi d'un aperçu sur la discussion du problème depuis la mort de Rosa Luxembourg. Paris, Libraire des Sciences Politiques et Sociales, 1930.

Lecky, W. E. H., History of the Rise and Influence of the Spirit of Rationalism in Europe. 2 vols. London, Longmans, 1865.

—— Democracy and Liberty; new ed. 2 vols. London, Longmans, 1899.

Lenin, V. I., Imperialism, the Highest Stage of Capitalism. New York, International Publishers, 1933.

Liefmann, Robert, Beteiligungs- und Finanzierungs-Gesellschaften; eine Studie über den modernen Kapitalismus und das Effektenwesen. Jena, Fischer, 1909.

Lippincott, Benjamin E., ed., On the Economic Theory of Socialism, Minneapolis, University of Minnesota Press, 1938.

List, Friedrich, The National System of Political Economy; tr. by Sampson S. Lloyd; new edition, with an introduction by J. Shield Nicholson. New York, Longmans, 1904.

Luxemburg, Rosa, Die Akkumulation des Kapitals; ein Beitrag zur ökonomischen Erklärung des Imperialismus. Berlin, Vereinigung Internationaler Verlags-Anstalten, 1921.

—— Die Akkumulation des Kapitals oder was die Epigonen aus der Marxschen Theorie gemacht haben. Eine Antikritik. Leipzig, Frankes Verlag, 1921.

—— Letters to Karl and Luise Kautsky, from 1896 to 1918; ed. by Luise Kautsky, and tr. from the German by Louis P. Lochner. New York, McBride, 1925.

Machiavelli, Niccolò, Discourses on the First Decade of Titus Livius; tr. from the Italian by Ninian Hill Thomson. London, K. Paul, Trench and Company, 1883.

Malthus, T. R., Principles of Political Economy. London, Pickering, 1836.

Marsh, Margaret Alexander, The Bankers in Bolivia; ed. by Harry Elmer Barnes. New York, Vanguard Press, 1928.

Marshall, Alfred, Industry and Trade. London, Macmillan, 1919.

Marx, Karl, Der Bürgerkrieg in Frankreich. Leipzig, Genossenschaftsbuchdruckerei, 1876.

—— Capital; tr. by Ernest Untermann. 3 vols. Chicago, Kerr, 1906, 1909.

—— Capital, the Communist Manifesto, and Other Writings; ed., with an introduction, by Max Eastman, with an unpublished essay on Marxism by Lenin. New York, The Modern Library, 1932.

—— The Paris Commune, New York, New York Labor News Company, 1934.

—— Selected Works; ed. by Adoratsky. New York, International Publishers, 1936.

Marx, Karl, and Friedrich Engels, Correspondence. London, Lawrence, 1934.

—— Manifesto of the Communist Party; authorized English translation; ed. and annotated by Frederick Engels. Chicago, Kerr, 1912.

Merivale, Herman, Lectures on Colonization and Colonies; delivered before the University of Oxford in 1839, 1840, and 1841, and reprinted in 1861. London, Oxford University Press, 1928.

Mill, James, Elements of Political Economy. 3d ed. London, Baldwin, Craddock, and Joy, 1826.

—— Essays. London, Innes, n.d. Reprinted from the Supplement to the Encyclopaedia Britannica.

Mill, John Stuart, Principles of Political Economy; ed., with an introduction, by W. J. Ashley. 2 vols. London and New York, Longmans, 1909.

Miller, Harry E., "Earlier Theories of Crises and Cycles in the United States," *Quarterly Journal of Economics,* XXXVIII (February, 1924), 294–329.

Mises, Ludvig von, Socialism; an economic and sociological analysis; tr. from the German by J. Kahane. London, Jonathan Cape, 1936.

Montesquieu, Baron de, The Spirit of the Laws; tr. by Thomas Nugent, rev. by J. V. Prichard. 2 vols. New York, Appleton, 1900.

Moon, Thomas Parker, Imperialism and World Politics, New York, Macmillan, 1926.

Muir, Ramsay, The Expansion of Europe; the culmination of modern history. Boston and New York, Houghton, 1923.

Mullett, Charles F., "English Imperial Thinking, 1764–1783," *Political Science Quarterly,* XLV (December, 1930), 548–79.

Mummery, A. F., and J. A. Hobson, The Physiology of Industry; being an exposure of certain fallacies in existing theories of economics. London, Murray, 1889.

Mun, Thomas, Discourse of Trade. 1621.

—— England's Treasure by Foreign Trade. 1664.

Nearing, Scott, The Twilight of Empire; an economic interpretation of imperialist cycles. New York, Vanguard Press, 1930.

Nearing, Scott, and Joseph Freeman, Dollar Diplomacy; a study in American imperialism. New York, Huebsch and the Viking Press, 1925.

Nicholls, John, Recollections and Reflections, Personal and Political; as connected with public affairs during the reign of George the Third. 2 vols. London, Longman, Hurst, 1822.

Nugent, Rolf, Consumer Credit and Economic Stability. New York, Russell Sage Foundation, 1939.

O'Leary, James J., "Malthus and Keynes," *Journal of Political Economy,* L (December, 1942), 901–19.

Parkes, Henry Bamford, Marxism, an Autopsy. Boston, Houghton, Mifflin, 1939.

Pavlovitch, Michel (Mikhail Lazarevich Weltmann), The Foundations of Imperialist Policy. London, The Labour Publishing Company, 1922.

Peffer, Nathaniel, "Peace or War," in Joseph Barnes, ed., *Empire in the East* (Garden City, N.Y., Doubleday, 1934), pp. 295–318.

Penn, William, The Peace of Europe; the Fruits of Solitude and Other Writings. Everyman's Library, New York, Dutton; London, Dent, n.d.

Pigou, A. C., Industrial Fluctuations. London, Macmillan, 1927.

—— The Political Economy of War. New York, Macmillan, 1941.

—— Socialism versus Capitalism. London, Macmillan Company, 1937.

Plato, The Dialogues; ed. by B. Jowett. 3d ed., 5 vols. London, Oxford

University Press, Humphrey Milford, 1892. Impression of 1931. Vol. III contains *The Republic.*

Postlethwayt, Malachy, Britain's Commercial Interest Explained and Improved. 2 vols. London, Browne, 1757.

Priestley, Herbert Ingram, France Overseas; a study of modern imperialism. New York and London, Appleton-Century, 1938.

Primus (*pseud*), L'Impérialisme et la décadence capitaliste. Paris, Librairie du Travail, 1928.

Renner, Karl, Marxismus, Krieg und Internationale. Stuttgart, Dietz, 1918.

Reves, Emery, The Anatomy of Peace. New York and London, Harper, 1945.

Ricardo, David, Principles of Political Economy and Taxation; ed., with an introductory essay, notes, and appendices, by E. C. K. Gonner. London, Bell, 1891.

Rippy, J. Fred, The Capitalists and Colombia; ed. by Harry Elmer Barnes. New York, Vanguard Press, 1931.

Robbins, Lionel, The Economic Causes of War. London, Jonathan Cape, 1939.

Robinson, Edward Van Dyke, "War and Economics in History and in Theory," *Political Science Quarterly,* XV (December, 1900), 581–628.

Robinson, Howard, The Development of the British Empire. Boston, Houghton, Mifflin, 1922.

Robinson, Joan, An Essay on Marxian Economics. London, Macmillan, 1942.

—— "Marx on Unemployment," *The Economic Journal,* LI (June–September, 1941), 234–48.

Rodbertus, Karl, Die Handelskrisen und die Hypothekennot der Grundbesitzer. Berlin, Schneider, 1858.

—— Overproduction and Crises; tr. by Julia Franklin, with an introduction by John B. Clark. London, Sonnenschein, 1898.

Romains, Jules, Verdun. New York, Knopf, 1939.

Rose, J. Holland, The Development of the European Nations, 1870–1921. New York and London, Putnam's, 1922.

Rossetti, Christina Georgina, "Advent," from *The Poetical Works of Christina Georgina Rossetti,* p. 202.

Royal Institute of International Affairs, The Colonial Problem. London, Oxford University Press, 1937.

Russell, Bertrand, Power; a new social analysis. New York, Norton, 1938.

Salz, Arthur, "Die Zukunft des Imperialismus." *Weltwirtschaftliches Archiv,* XXXII (October, 1930), 317–48.

Say, Jean-Baptiste, A Treatise on Political Economy. Princep's edition. 2 vols. London, Longman, 1821; Boston, Wells and Lilly, 1821.

Sayre, Francis Bowes, America Must Act. New York, World Peace Foundation, 1936. World Affairs Pamphlets No. 13.

Schippel, Max, "Kolonialpolitik," *Sozialistische Monatshefte*, XIV (January 9, 1908), 3–10.

Schmitt, Bernadotte E., The Coming of the War, 1914. 2 vols. New York and London, Scribner, 1930.

Schumpeter, Joseph A., Business Cycles; a theoretical, historical, and statistical analysis of the capitalist process. 2 vols. New York, McGraw-Hill, 1939.

—— "Zur Soziologie der Imperialismen," *Archiv für Sozialwissenschaft und Sozialpolitik*, Vol. XLVI: December, 1918, pp. 1–39; June, 1919, pp. 275–310.

Schuyler, R. L., "The Climax of Anti-Imperialism in England," *Political Science Quarterly*, XXXVI (December, 1921), 537–60.

—— "The Rise of Anti-Imperialism in England," *Political Science Quarterly*, XXXVII (September, 1922), 440–71.

Seeley, J. R., The Expansion of England. London, Macmillan, 1883.

Seillière, Ernest, Introduction à la philosophie de l'impérialisme. Paris, Alcan, 1911.

—— La Philosophie de l'impérialisme. 4 vols. Paris, Plon-Nourrit, 1903–8.

Seligman, Edwin R. A., The Economic Interpretation of History. New York, Columbia University Press, 1902.

Sibley, Mulford Q., The Political Theories of Modern Pacifism; an analysis and criticism. Philadelphia, Pacifist Research Bureau, 1944.

Silberner, Edmund, The Problem of War in Nineteenth Century Economic Thought; tr. by Alexander H. Krappe. Princeton, Princeton University Press, 1946.

Simonde de Sismondi, J.-C.-L., Nouveaux Principes d'economic politique. 2 vols. Paris, Delaunay, 1827.

Simons, Henry C., "Hansen on Fiscal Policy," *Journal of Political Economy*, L (April, 1942), 161–96.

—— A Positive Program for Laissez-Faire. Chicago, University of Chicago Press, 1934. Public Policy Pamphlet No. 15.

—— "Rules versus Authorities in Monetary Policy," *Journal of Political Economy*, XLIV (February, 1936), 1–30.

Smith, Adam, An Inquiry into the Nature and Causes of the Wealth of Nations; ed., with an introduction, notes, marginal summary and an enlarged index, by Edwin Cannan. 2 vols. London, Methuen, 1930.

Southworth, Constant, The French Colonial Venture. London, King, 1931.

Spring, Gerald M., The Vitalism of Count de Gobineau. New York, Institute of French Studies, Inc., 1932.

Staley, Eugene, "The Economic Side of Stable Peace," *Annals of the*

*American Academy of Political and Social Science,* CCXL (July, 1945), 27–36.
—— War and the Private Investor; a study in the relations of international politics and international private investment. New York, Doubleday, 1935.
—— World Economy in Transition. New York, Council on Foreign Relations 1939. Prepared for submission to the Twelfth International Studies Conference, Bergen, August 27–September 2, 1939.
Stalin, Joseph, Leninism; Vol. II, tr. from the Russian by Eden and Cedar Paul. New York, International Publishers, 1933.
Sternberg, Fritz, Der Imperialismus. Berlin, Malik-Verlag, 1926.
Strauss, William L., Joseph Chamberlain and the Theory of Imperialism. Washington, D.C., American Council on Public Affairs, 1942.
Strayer, Joseph R., ed., The Interpretation of History. Princeton, Princeton University Press, 1943.
Sumner, William Graham, The Conquest of the United States by Spain. Boston, Estes, 1899.
Sweezy, Paul M., The Theory of Capitalist Development; principles of Marxian political economy. New York, Oxford University Press, 1942.
Taylor, Fred M., "The Guidance of Production in a Socialist State," *American Economic Review,* XIX (March, 1929), 1–8.
Thompson, A. H., "British Imperialism and the Autonomous Rights of Races," *Kansas City Review of Science and Industry,* III (1879), 229–34.
Trevelyan, George Macaulay, British History in the Nineteenth Century, 1782–1901. New York, Longmans, 1922.
Trotsky, Leon, Dictatorship vs. Democracy; a reply to Karl Kautsky. New York, Workers Party of America, 1922. This book was issued in 1921 under the title The Defence of Terrorism.
Tugan-Baranowsky, Michael, Les Crises industrielles en Angleterre. Paris, Giard and Brière, 1913.
—— Studien zur Theorie und Geschichte der Handelskrisen in England. Jena, Fischer, 1901.
—— Theoretische Grundlagen des Marxismus. Leipzig, Duncker and Humboldt, 1905.
Turner, Edward Raymond, Europe since 1789. New York, Doubleday, 1924.
Vagts, Alfred, A History of Militarism. New York, Norton, 1937.
Villard, Oswald Garrison, Fighting Years; memoirs of a liberal editor. New York, Harcourt, 1939.
Viner, Jacob, "International Finance and Balance of Power Diplomacy, 1880–1914," *The Southwestern Political and Social Science Quarterly,* IX (March, 1929), 407–51.
—— "Peace as an Economic Problem," in George B. de Huszar, ed.,

New Perspectives on Peace (Chicago, University of Chicago Press, 1944), pp. 85–114.

—— [Review of Donald C. Blaisdell, *European Financial Control in the Ottoman Empire*], *Journal of Political Economy*, XXXVII (December, 1929), 745–47.

Virgil, The Aeneid, in The Poetical Works of John Dryden, Cambridge ed. Boston and New York, Houghton Mifflin, 1908.

Wagner, Donald O., "British Economists and the Empire," *Political Science Quarterly*, XLVI (June, 1931), 248–76, and XLVII (March, 1932), 57–74.

Wagner, Valentin F., Geschichte der Kredittheorien. Vienna, Springer, 1937.

Weltmann, Mikhail Lazarevich (*pseud.*, Michel Pavlovitch), The Foundations of Imperialist Policy. London, The Labour Publishing Company, 1922.

Winslow, Erving, The Anti-Imperialist League; apologia pro vita sua. Boston, published by the Anti-Imperialist League [1898].

Woolf, Leonard, Economic Imperialism. London, The Swarthmore Press, Ltd., 1920; New York, Harcourt, 1920.

—— International Government. New York, Brentano's, 1916.

Wright, Quincy, ed., A Study of War. 2 vols. Chicago, University of Chicago Press, 1942.

Young, Allyn A., Economic Problems New and Old. Boston, Houghton and Mifflin, 1927.

—— "Economics and War," *American Economic Review*, XVI (March, 1926), 1–13.

Young, Arthur, Tour in Ireland. Dublin, printed by G. Bonham, 1780. London, printed for T. Cadell, 1780.

# INDEX